ONE NATION

A Vision for the United Kingdom Outside the EU

By

NICK YEOMANS

*Former Independent Parliamentary
candidate for Brighton Pavilion*

authorHOUSE®

AuthorHouse™ UK
1663 Liberty Drive
Bloomington, IN 47403 USA
www.authorhouse.co.uk
Phone: 0800.197.4150

Published by AuthorHouse 04/13/2016

ISBN: 978-1-5246-3203-8 (sc)
ISBN: 978-1-5246-3202-1 (e)

Print information available on the last page.

Any people depicted in stock imagery provided by Thinkstock are models,
and such images are being used for illustrative purposes only.
Certain stock imagery © Thinkstock.

This book is printed on acid-free paper.

This book is dedicated to my late mother,
Antoinette Bridget Yeomans, my greatest political advisor.

Lines from Longfellow, given to Churchill by President
Roosevelt, and read by him in an inspiring wireless
broadcast to the British people on 27th April, 1941

"For while the tired waves, vainly breaking,
Seem here no painful inch to gain,
Far back, through creeks and inlets making,
Comes silent, flooding in, the main.
And not by eastern windows only,
When daylight comes, comes in the light;
In front the sun climbs slow, how slowly,
But westward, look, the land is bright."

CONTENTS

INTRODUCTION

This book is a memoir of an election, a resume of my political influences, and a personal manifesto, espousing mv vision of an independent United Kingdom, united at home and confident overseas.

The purpose of this book is to formulate a strategy (both at home and overseas) for the United Kingdom outside the EU, should the British people vote to leave in the forthcoming referendum. What strategy should the UK adopt once liberated from the straitjacket of the EU? There is a danger that the UK leaves the EU without a coherent plan to capitalise upon the gains of independence. Such uncertainty is a valid concern of the undecided voter sympathetic to Brexit, and could make the difference between remaining in the EU or leaving. A clear and united Brexit strategy must be made public long before the referendum. The party system was smashed in the Euro elections of 2014, and a clear Brexit strategy (forged in the heat of the battle to get Britain out in the EU referendum) would forge an alliance of MPs from all mainstream parties – any one party is too small, and has too narrow an appeal, to form a representative government.

In May 2014, after the Euro elections shattered the party system, I wrote to MPs of all mainstream parties, calling for them to join me to form an alliance to contest the 2015 general election. The overriding goals of such an Alliance were to rebuild the defences of the UK to curb Russian and IS aggression, to secure Brexit, and to forge economic growth in One Nation, through investment in transport, housing, and energy supply. Such a coalition would have been formed BEFORE the election, rather than in smoke filled rooms AFTER the election. To my appeal, answer came there none! Even before a second identical appeal in November 2014 led to nought, I had already resolved to stand as an Independent candidate, to kick start this process. In the event of a hung Parliament, I made it clear in my manifesto that I would attempt to form a government, whether or not I ended up leading it. Regardless of whether there was a hung Parliament, or a majority government, whether I was Prime Minister, Minister or backbencher, I would have advocated these policies with equal vigour. Did I want to be Prime Minister? Yes, but not at any price.

My vision is not for the United Kingdom to retreat from Fortress Europe only to hide behind the barricades of Fortress Britain. A key reason for withdrawal from the EU should be to enhance the world role of the UK. Outside the EU, the UK would have its own seat at the WTO, and be free to forge free trade areas with the growing economies of the world. Food imports would be substantially cheaper, helping the poor in the UK and overseas. In return, the UK would win new export markets for our goods, creating a virtuous circle of prosperity. By utilising the UK's unique global trade connections, we could forge and lead a massive free trade area, which (combined with weaknesses in China's economy) could prevent China from becoming the world's most powerful economy and leading military superpower, and therefore restore the Atlantic alliance as the leading military and moral force in the world.

The developing nations would escape poverty by growing their export markets, thus rendering redundant much overseas aid, which has been used to subsidise poverty. Brexit could tackle poverty at home and abroad.

Outside the EU, the UK could control immigration, to give the space to accept refugees in times of crisis, to ease pressure on housing, health, and infrastructure, and to prevent the continual downward spiral of wages that the bonanza of low skilled jobs has created. Outside the EU, the UK would also spend the £10 billion net contribution per year currently spent on health and social care, and tax cuts for low paid, small businesses, and apprenticeships, to create high skilled jobs for the British people.

The UK must play a key role in NATO, and lead by example. Aggression can only be defeated by a military presence to deter and remove the aggressor. In addition to pledging 2% of GDP on defence expenditure, the UK must have 2 aircraft capability (with aircraft), recruit 30,000 full time troops, renew Trident without delay, and establish a submarine based missile defence system. The UK is right to take the fight against IS to Syria as well as Iraq, to ensure our security. The UK must utterly condemn and reverse Russia's annexation of Crimea and the Donbas in Ukraine; Russia's unchallenged aggression here has emboldened them to attack Syrian rebels under the pretence of joining the Western coalition to defeat IS. While they "withdrew" in March, 2016, some forces remain, and Russia has announced it will re-enter Syria at any time. His strategy is clear; to defeat the Syrian rebels and present an unpalatable choice to the West: to rely on Russia to attack IS, or risk the wrath of Russia by attacking Assad and his forces. The UK and allies must be equally clear in our strategy; to spare no time in building a coalition (which Russia must not be a part of) with the rebels to defeat IS and Assad. We cannot trust Putin as an ally against IS. If the UK fails to resist Russian aggression, then Russia will be emboldened to invade NATO countries, resulting in the UK having to declare war (under Article of the NATO Treaty).

The UK must strengthen its defences not to engage in war, but to safeguard the peace.

It is staggering that in this age of retrenchment how skewed the nation's priorities are in allocating an ever dwindling size of the cake to its people. In addition to a minimum spend on overseas aid (much of which goes to middle and high income countries, often antagonistic to the UK, with abominable human rights abuses perpetrated against women and minorities). Many of the disputes are more effectively resolved by a military presence, also essential to protect humanitarian convoys. Imagine spending this money on re-equipping our armed forces, and building our own equipment, how this would enhance our national security, and utilise the skills of our population into the bargain? Some of the savings would also be used also used to cut NI for the low paid. The Barnett Formula (whereby Scotland receives more public spending per head than the rest of the UK) is a recipe for English nationalism and fragmentation of the Union. It should be abolished, and Scotland given tax raising powers to raise the revenue, and the money spent on NHS & social care across the UK.

At home, the union must be maintained. The aim must be a United Kingdom, independent from the EU. While recognizing the call for greater devolution to Scotland, we must remember that a majority of Scots voted to remain in the Union in 2014, and voted for unionist parties in the 2015 general election. Greater devolution means greater responsibility (by granting tax raising powers), and greater independence (resulting in less economic dependence upon the UK taxpayer).

There must be a clear strategy of wealth creation for a purpose; to create the wealth which creates jobs, to pay our way in the world, and most importantly, to support those unable to help themselves. We must create what Harold Macmillan called "A Middle Way" for the 21st century, between Corbynist economics, which deters investment, and perpetuates poverty, and the Casino economy created by Conservatives, based upon speculative property finance, cancellation of infrastructure projects, cheap labour, and the cutting of social care grants (under the guise of "devolution"), which ultimately harms the vulnerable, with the NHS bearing much of the extra strain.

Wealth creation is the only method to provide jobs for those who can work, and fund the care of those who cannot work. Punitive taxation and regulation, deficit financing, and price controls push entrepreneurs abroad, and with it, the revenue upon which a civilised society depends. Competition is the life blood of economic progress.

Tax cuts must be focussed on the low paid and small businesses, and funded not by borrowing, nor by increasing tax on wealthy individuals and businesses, but by cutting government expenditure.

While all taxpayers have rightly benefitted from the raising of tax thresholds, another group of workers has been ignored. People earning as low an income as £8000 per year have to pay national insurance; in reality, income tax by another name. At the last election, I pledged to raise the threshold from just over £8000 to just under £9000, so that the low paid would benefit by £19 per week.

A strong deficit reduction programme, combined with two bouts of deflation (the first since 1960), grants the UK an historic opportunity for massive investment in transport (the One North project), social housing (to build 200,000 units by 2020), and investment in energy.

This would provide housing for all, stabilise the property market, spread economic growth across the UK, enhance transport links across the UK, make the UK self sufficient in energy, and create high skilled jobs, to boot.

Fuel poverty cannot be eliminated by government fiat. An energy freeze would only hike the prices before the freeze, hitting the poorest hardest. Nationalization is unsustainable; compensating the shareowners (which despite left wing claims to the contrary, would have to occur) would cost billions; not compensating shareholders would drive investment overseas, to the detriment of innovation in new technology. Exposing the Big Six to the harsh winds of competition, investing in home grown energy, will reduce prices.

We must care for our vulnerable, and ensure those that can work, do work. There must be a national plan to eradicate homelessness, by providing halfway houses, where people can rehabilitated to reduce their dependency upon drugs and alcohol, be trained in seeking employment, and to live in a home of their own. Controlling immigration outside the EU and from within the EU, will stop the downward spiral of wages, which, combined with apprenticeships and infrastructure projects across the UK, will break the cycle of dependency once and for all.

Integrating social care within the NHS will deliver better outcomes for patients, by preventing hospital admission, and speeding up hospital discharge. The philosophy must be to enable NHS patients to use private healthcare, not the other way around. NHS capacity must be expanded through private and voluntary providers (and private and voluntary hospitals), to complement in house services, free at the point of use. In order to be commissioned, these providers must pay their staff the living wage and zero hours contracts must be the exception and not the rule. There must be a cap on the cost of recruiting agency staff. This would be far more effective than a profit cap, which would simply deter investment. Patients should not be allowed to purchase NHS facilities privately; treatment must be given based upon clinical priority, not on ability to pay. NHS patients could use a voucher to purchase NHS treatment, or to opt for medical insurance. Patients wanting private medicine must purchase from private hospitals and doctors; this frees up NHS capacity, and they still pay towards the NHS through taxation. Abolishing GP catchment areas will enhance patient care, by enabling patients to choose their GP, not the other way around.

The priority for new housing must be social housing. Planning new housing must coincide with planning of transport links, to bring homes closer to the workforce, to enhance labour mobility. The priority must be to convert empty buildings into social housing units, before new homes are built. This will be achieved through QE, and cutting VAT on renovating buildings to 10%. The Right to Buy for tenants of social and council housing must be used not only to help tenants become homeowners, but to invest the sale proceeds into renovating existing/building new housing stock, to create a virtuous circle of housing stock replenishment. By controlling immigration, demand is reduced, preventing building in already congested areas, and in areas of outstanding natural beauty.

Welfare must be redistributive, and targeted to those who need it most. The philosophy must be: welfare for those unable to support themselves through no fault of their own. At the last election, I pledged to maintain disabled and carers' benefits, pensions, and tax credits for the low paid (people who are in need of financial support through no fault of their own), but to stop child benefit and child tax credits for the third child born after 2016 (people who make a conscious decision to bring a child into the world). The second policy was essential to ensure the outcome of the first. Imagine if the government had adopted my policy, there would have been no need to try and cut tax credits and disability benefits in the first place. In addition, child benefits should be in voucher form (for food, clothing, and heating), and this would be for all recipients of child benefit, to engender responsibility, and to ensure the money gets to the child. This will drastically reduce child poverty. The folly of paying Housing benefits directly to the tenant has been proved; many recipients of Housing benefit have mental health concerns, and struggle with finances. It has led to the eviction of vulnerable people, and the landlord losing money. I pledged to pay HB directly to the landlord. The Coalition introduced sudden cuts to welfare recipients before an investigation had been held. Many recipients have mental health impairments, and need assistance with contacting benefit agencies. A yellow card system must be introduced so that benefits are withdrawn only once it is proven that they are no longer required; these measures would prevent dependence upon food banks.

In education, selection by intelligence is infinitely preferable to selection by mortgage. The inherent irony of socialism dictates that only the wealthy can send their children to a good school by paying privately, while parents on average and lower incomes cannot afford to buy a house within the catchment area of good schools. Free schools empower parents to set up a school, but structural change is needed. Grammar schools should be allowed to expand, but new ones must be set up across the UK, to make social mobility a reality. Private schools must open up their places to scholarships, so that parents cannot buy education regardless of the educational aptitude of the child, to ensure meritocracy. There must be central government co – ordination to allocate existing school places more fairly, as there are surplus places in some areas, and huge shortages in other areas. Schools should be allowed to expand beyond their catchment areas, to where the demand originates. The money must follow the pupil, not the school.

By reducing tuition fees on engineering, science and technology courses (by raising fees on humanities courses) the UK could lead a massive recruitment drive for the best engineers, and scientists from our own population.

In short, this is a vision which combines a vigorous, dynamic and competitive market economy, with social responsibility, a rigorous control of public spending while protecting those who cannot help themselves, a strong defence to vigorously pursue peace and human rights, and strict immigration control combined with a safe haven for those fleeing persecution. The election of a far left Labour leader leaves an immense gap for such a vision to take root, flourish, and to attract supporters from across the whole UK, from all backgrounds, from all political parties and none, to generate a popular movement for change.

As the political battles are waged, and the nation's resolve at home and overseas is tested, I will continue to be an Independent candidate, provide rigorous opposition, continue to propose my plans for the UK, and campaign for the UK to leave the EU in the forthcoming referendum. I will stand again at the next general election, funding my own campaign, and free from party restraint. Follow me on Twitter #IndependentforBrightonPavilion.

CHAPTER 1

My Political Influences

- 1992:- Labour defeat, Black Wednesday, Maastricht and the miners.
- The New Labour dictatorship
- The Coalition

My first political memory is of campaigning for the SDP/Liberal Alliance in a mock election at our prep school, at the time of the 1987 general election, at the age of 10. I had no real knowledge of politics at this time; the Alliance was, like the son of an aspiring middle class Essex family in a prep school, the outsider, and this was my way of demonstrating against the established order; caning had only been abolished in 1986! I was always on the Owenite SDP wing of the Alliance; social patriotism is the red, white and blue thread that has been constant throughout my political life. Needless to say, our brave band of heroic reformers was buried in the Thatcher landslide, but I felt pity for the sole Communist, a fellow Catholic!

1992:- LABOUR DEFEAT, BLACK WEDNESDAY, MAASTRICHT AND THE MINERS.

1992 was an historic year for many reasons. Like in May, 2015, the Conservatives won a majority against all the odds. Months later, the UK was ejected from the ERM, leading to a long overdue debate about the UK's membership in the EU. A month later, the government closed 20 coal mines, which destroyed communities, and the businesses which depended upon the mines, and made the UK more dependent upon imported energy, and caused outrage across the political divide.

23 years later, the situation is ominously similar: A Conservative government, elected with a majority against all the poll predictions, facing an EU referendum within 2 years. Furthermore, 4 coal fired power stations and 2 coal mines have now closed.

The 1992 election was the first election that I followed closely. Aged 15, I remember being passionately keen for Neil Kinnock to win, and bitterly disappointed that I was too young to vote.

I always found Neil Kinnock's oratory poignant; even today, his speeches make the hairs stand up on the back of my neck.

I remember waking up bitterly disappointed at John Major's victory.

I stood as a candidate for the schools council in the autumn of 1992. My manifesto made Arthur Scargill look like a moderate; nationalising the mere, adjacent to Framlingham Castle, and stopping prefects from chucking juniors out of chairs.

I treated this like the presidential campaign that was then in full swing between Clinton and George Bush senior. I came a distant last – I also lost heavily in 1993, but lost by only 1 vote in 1994! However, I had caught the most virulent strain of the politics bug, which was immune to the most potent of serums.

My first election coincided with seismic shifts in the economic and political landscape in the UK.

In September, 1992, the UK was ejected from the ERM, and the folly of fixed exchange rates was proven. I concluded that if the political establishment of the three main parties, the CBI, TUC, and most newspapers were in favour of a policy, then this policy must be wrong. It is also ironic that 15 years of uninterrupted economic growth commenced when this key economic plank of the Major government was rejected.

Then the government closed 20 coal mines, with the loss of 20,000 jobs. These were the coal mines Lady Thatcher had pledged to keep open in gratitude to the members of the breakaway Union of Democratic Mineworkers who opposed Scargill, and returned to work. It was this that made me a bitter anti Tory radical. No principle was sacred for this government. Even at this time, I thought Lady Thatcher had a sense of fairness! It wasn't because she ran out of time that Lady Thatcher didn't privatise the railways or the coal mines; she was a patriot first and foremost, and where national sovereignty conflicted with free markets, then national sovereignty would prevail.

I remember 5th November, 1992, as if it were yesterday, when the Major government lost a vote on Maastricht. Smuggled into my dormitory was a small FM radio, and I would listen to Today in Parliament, hearing the speeches of such colossi as Tony Benn, Sir Edward Heath, Bryan Gould, and Dennis Skinner.

At this time (and even today), I was an old fashioned British social democrat. Inspired by Harold Wilson building nearly a million homes, and standing up to central bankers, and Tony Benn campaigning for public ownership, and withdrawal from the EU. I was going to set up my own party. My manifesto at this stage consisted of withdrawal from the EU, multilateral nuclear disarmament, and public ownership of the energy companies (with industrial democracy).

In July, 1993, I realised that I needed to join a major political party if I was ever going to be influence the course of events; I joined the Labour Party. I was a huge admirer of the late John Smith, the leader at the time. It is all too easy to forget that Labour's huge opinion poll leads started under Smith's leadership (not Blair's), and it was Smith who made Labour electable. Smith was the last social democratic leader of the Labour Party, the inheritor of the mantle of Tony Crosland. For me, Smith's most impressive moment was when, at the 1993 conference, he pledged to use all the economic levers to achieve full employment. Smith, unlike Blair, would have ruled out the euro, and would have trod very carefully before handing over yet more powers to Brussels, which would have undermined social democracy in One Nation. I was devastated when Smith died in 1994. I voted for Prescott as leader, and Beckett as deputy.

I proposed a motion to renationalise the steel industry; needless to say, that was rejected. In 1995 – 96, I campaigned to convert the Labour Party to withdrawal from the EU. I joined the Labour EU Safeguards Campaign, and met giants like Tony Benn, Peter Shore, and Denzil Davies. I tried to present the motion to the 1996 "Labour's Coming Home" conference, but this was buried in the pre-electoral (and utterly misguided) Blair euphoria. In my local party, I was in a minority of 1!

By 1996, I was thoroughly disillusioned with Blair's New Labour, and with John Major's clapped out Tories. I wrote articles condemning the appeasement of Serbia by Major and Hurd.

In the autumn of 1996, I joined UKIP, the only party committed to withdrawal from the EU. At this time, UKIP was led by Alan Sked, a principled Liberal historian. Under Sked's leadership, UKIP was a progressive party.

THE NEW LABOUR DICTATORSHIP 1997 - 2010

I didn't share the euphoria of the Blair landslide of 1997; I voted UKIP. I campaigned against devolution, and against the Good Friday agreement.

In 1999, UKIP won its first MEPs, and I worked as a Researcher for Jeffrey Titford, UKIP MEP, in my home town of Chelmsford. I used my position as editor of a newsletter as an opportunity to pursue my social democratic cause within UKIP, campaigning against PFI.

It was at this time that UKIP's true colours emerged, with anti Catholic sentiment expressed by a colleague, knowing that another colleague and myself were Catholics; using Brexit to scrap all safeguards for employees.

Throughout these years, I proposed motions for an industrial policy, and all schools being free of LEA control. These were defeated. I spoke at a conference in favour of public ownership of the railways; next year, I proposed a motion calling for public ownership of the railways. It was thanks to the shambles of EU imposed rail privatisation that I missed the conference all together!

My motion calling for a missile defence was crushed at the UKIP conference of 2005; opponents within UKIP misrepresented my policy, thinking that I was calling for unilateral nuclear disarmament.

UKIP seemed determined to withdraw from Fortress Europe and retreat into Fortress Britain. I left UKIP at the end of 2005.

I was very keen for David Davis to be the Tory leader in 2005, and was disappointed when he was not elected.

I joined the Conservative Party in 2007. I applied twice to get onto the Tory candidate list (in 2008 and 2009) but was twice rejected, obviously due to my UKIP past.

THE COALITION

I voted Conservative in 2010, as I lived in a marginal seat (Hove), and a UKIP vote would have let Labour in, and a Conservative government was essential to defeat Labour and save the UK from economic ruin. In addition, UKIP were unsound on defence. Who would have thought at the time that a Conservative led Coalition would have slashed defence spending?

After one final (and unsuccessful) attempt to become a Tory parliamentary candidate in 2013 (and letting my Conservative membership lapse accordingly), I decided in December 2013 to stand as an Independent parliamentary candidate at the forthcoming general election; but for which seat?

I considered Brighton Kemptown, where most of my clients lived, but this would have generated a conflict of interest. Furthermore, I ruled out Brighton Kemptown and Hove because my intervention may have split the centre right vote and let Labour in. While hardly a Tory stooge, the more Tory MPs elected the better, as the EU referendum would have been more likely.

In the end, I decided to stand in Brighton Pavilion. As the Tories came third in 2010, there was no danger that my intervention would prevent a Tory win. I also genuinely believed that the people of Pavilion deserved a sensible alternative to the Greens, that was pro – enterprise, strong defence, and law and order, but with a strong social conscience. I believed (and I still do, after the general election), that I am uniquely qualified to fulfil that role.

As the election neared, I signed a declaration of interest form, which stipulated that I would not visit clients in the Pavilion constituency, that I would not discuss the council's work with the press or media, and most importantly, that if elected MP, I would leave my job in adult social care.

CHAPTER 2

None of the Above:- Memoir of an Election – April 2014 – May 2015

Appeasement of Russia and the 2014 Euro elections – The failure of the main parties

My appeal for an Independence Coalition – May to November 2014

Manifestos, media and meeting the people – September 2014 to May 2015.

PRESS RELEASES and PUBLICITY

THE HUSTINGS

MEETING THE PEOPLE

CORRESPONDENCE WITH CONSTITUENTS

CORRESPONDENCE WITH CAMPAIGN GROUPS

THE GENERAL ELECTION

My election strategy

POST ELECTION MANOUEVRES

My strategy for forming a Coalition government after the election

THE ELECTION CAMPAIGN DAY BY DAY

7th MAY 2015: POLLING DAY

POSTCRIPT:- AFTERMATH OF THE ELECTION

APPEASEMENT OF RUSSIA AND THE 2014 EURO ELECTIONS – THE FAILURE OF THE MAIN PARTIES

An event in a far away country, involving people of whom we knew very little, galvanised my cause to become an MP and attempt to change the course of events.

In early 2014, Russian annexed Crimea, and invaded large swathes of Ukrainian territory.

Russia held a corrupt referendum, in which Crimea was intimidated into voting for annexation. Putin forewent the courtesy of consulting the people of Donetsk and Luhansk (in the Ukraine) before seizing their territory.

In early 2014, the Ukraine crisis had distilled two competing visions of UK foreign policy. A policy of deliberate appeasement (some admired Putin's "leadership" and hostility to the EU), and a policy of appeasement through inertia, forced upon the government by the swingeing cuts to UK defences, resulting in acceptance that the seized territories were now Russian, and sanctions the sole weapon in this new struggle, as espoused by the established three parties. In short, a 21st century Munich had emerged upon the doorstep of Europe.

In part, this latter policy of inertia is attributable to the inevitable Russian veto of any UN resolution condemning their aggression, as they are members of the UN Security Council. It also occurred due to Ukraine's pledge to renounce nuclear weapons, and Obama's astoundingly short sighted decision to remove missile defence from Poland. Some cited Putin's opposition to Ukraine joining the EU almost as an excuse to support Putin's imperialist ambitions. All those committed to Brexit must renounce Russian aggression.

I was determined to advocate a moral and humanitarian foreign policy, based upon peace through strength. The lessons of Munich must be heeded. The rebuilding of defences, and placing defence forces in strategic positions, actually makes peace more likely. A strong defence today prevents war tomorrow. No other party advocated such a policy in 2014, nor at the 2015 election – at the time of writing, this is still the case.

My policy of strengthened defences consisted of the following measures:-

- Ensure two aircraft carrier capability in 2015 by renting a USS Nimitz aircraft carrier with a full complement of combat aircraft, half of which would be transferred to the HMS Queen Elizabeth, which would be operational in 2015. One carrier would be sent to within striking distance of ISIL in Syria and Iraq, and the other sent to within striking distance of Russia. This would be pending introduction of HMS Prince Charles in 2020. The JSF would be cancelled, and both carriers would be equipped with a full complement of UK built combat aircraft by 2020.

- Recruit 30,000 full time troops (for RAF, Navy and Army), which would facilitate the expansion of the UK carrier fleet.

- Renew Trident immediately after the election in 2015, with 4 submarines, to ensure continuous at sea deterrence. Build all missiles in the UK, to ensure a truly independent nuclear deterrent.

- Establish a submarine based missile defence system, designed to intercept incoming missiles (nuclear and conventional) anywhere in the world.

- Manufacture all major aircraft, maritime, and weapons delivery systems in the UK, to ensure an independent defence policy, and to protect the UK high skill industrial base.

I wrote twice to the Foreign Secretary (William Hague in May 2014, and then Philip Hammond in October, 2014), urging a build up of defences in order to curb Russian aggression, and to demand the full restoration of territorial integrity to Ukraine and Crimea through internationally monitored referenda.

On 25th November, 2014, I received a letter of response from the Foreign & Commonwealth Office. It was immensely defeatist in tone. (All letters regarding defence can be perused in Appendices III & IV at the end of this book).

Firstly, the FCO ruled out a military response. History proves that ruling out a military response invites aggression. I had never advocated a first strike; I proposed sending an aircraft carrier (with a full complement of combat aircraft) along with allies, within striking distance of Russia as a signal that the UK and allies are serious about curbing Russian aggression. This would be in concert with fresh referenda to determine the destiny of Ukraine and Crimea.

Secondly, the FCO advised that NATO is not seeking to expand. It is the prerogative of putative member to states to apply to join NATO, and Ukraine's parliament voted overwhelmingly to join NATO in the late autumn of 2014. This also raises the question that many have asked:-

What is the rationale for the UK to intervene to protect a non NATO nation such as Ukraine?

The answer is clear. If Russia succeeds in illegally seizing Ukrainian territory and annexing Crimea, then Russia is emboldened to invade neighbouring nations, who are NATO members, and beyond. If this occurred, then the UK (as a NATO member) is legally bound to intervene under Article 5. In September, 2015, Russia's intentions were brazenly revealed when they launched air strikes in Syria, not against IS or Assad supporters, but to the rebel fighters. A withdrawal has been swiftly followed by an announcement of re-engagement in the Syrian conflict. Had the UK sanctioned airstrikes against IS targets in Iraq AND Syria (thereby defending the Free Syrian Army) in October 2014, this would have sent a signal to Russia not to bomb the Free Syrian Army. In the event, the Russians beat the UK to intervene in Syria by three months.

Thirdly, the FCO advised that NATO Russia Founding Act prohibits NATO members to permanently station substantial combat forces. The NRFA (designed in the aftermath of the Cold War, when Russia was being sought as an ally) has already been violated by Russia, and the UK and Nato allies can hardly stand idly by while Russia extends its forces. This, combined with the UKs defence cuts, is why such a paltry number of combat aircraft have been sent to the Baltic states.

On 26 September, 2014, in response to an appeal from the Iraqi government, Parliament voted to join these allies in air strikes against ISIL in Iraq. Cameron did not even attempt to secure a vote for UK participation in air strikes against Syria, due to the opposition of Labour under Ed Miliband – he had vetoed action against Assad's regime in August, 2013, which, combined with isolationist Tory MPs, prevented parliament from supporting such action. The consequences of confining airstrikes to Iraq in 2014 were to drive the insurgents into Syria.

Public opinion shifted, with more Tory MPs calling for stronger action, and committing the UK to spend 2% of GDP on defence. These factors (combined with much of the Labour front bench supporting action against IS) should herald a long overdue return to a bipartisan foreign policy. For the UK to be strong overseas, the UK must be united at home. Thankfully, Parliament came to its senses (inspired by Hilary Benn's great speech) and supported air strikes against IS targets in Syria. Sadly, the Russians had beaten the UK to Syria, only for them to bomb rebel fighters.

The government closed Trident facilities in Portsmouth and guaranteed them is Scotland, as a blatant act of bribery to persuade Scotland to stay in the Union. This was a highly dangerous act, as had Scotland voted for Independence, then the UK as then constituted would have lacked a nuclear deterrent.

The Euro elections (which UKIP won, and secured representation in England, Wales and Scotland) smashed the major party system. Now, aided by the EU referendum, political parties would split, and form new alliances made up of MPs from all parties, one of which would be an Independence Coalition.

MY APPEAL FOR AN INDEPENDENCE COALITION – MAY TO NOVEMBER 2014

On 28th May, 2014, in the aftermath of the shattering of the party system in the Euro elections, I emailed 32 MPs, asking them to form an Independence Alliance, to contest the 2015 general election. MPs included David Davis, Liam Fox, Kate Hoey, and Frank Field. As I felt very strongly that the Independence Alliance should represent all four corners of the United Kingdom, I included the entire parliamentary contingent of the DUP for good measure.

By definition, any MP committed to standing for the Independence Coalition would need to have relinquished their party affiliation, a huge demand for some. This would not have been the case if the coalition was not even to be considered until after the election.

At the time, it was thought that no single party was likely to form a government on its own after 2015 general election, as no single party represents a broad section of the British people. There is more unity between parties than within parties.

Hung Parliaments lead to fundamentally anti – democratic government. In 2010, nobody voted for a Conservative - Liberal Democrat coalition. A small third party holds disproportionate influence, and is able to determine the composition of the next government. It can also veto a coalition, leading to a minority government, which would lead to economic chaos.

With the likelihood of a hung Parliament, I felt particularly strongly that any coalition should be put before the British people BEFORE the election, and not cobbled together in smoke filled rooms afterwards. Horse trading occurs between politicians behind closed doors, and policies voted for by the public days before are rescinded without any democratic consultation.

The Coalition would consist of a Leader (this could not be myself, as I was not an MP in 2014, but I would have commanded strategy from Brighton), and a shadow cabinet of spokesmen.

The UK had entered the era of four party politics, with unstable coalitions causing dangerous uncertainty, with a new crisis set to emerge in the eurozone.

This would be a coalition government in waiting, united behind a clear manifesto committed to bring forward the EU In/Out referendum to October 2015, and to campaign for the UK to leave the EU.

Sadly, my appeal to MPs to put country before party, and to form an Independence Coalition (sent to MPs on 28th May and again on 11th October, 2014 [after Scotland voted to remain in the UK, and after the party conference season]), fell on deaf ears. Answer came there none.

This was undoubtedly a setback, as it was now too late to form an Independence Coalition, and the machinery of publicity that this would bring, but I decided to plough ahead, and stand for Parliament for Brighton Pavilion, with the aim of helping to form a government if no other party could do so after the election.

MANIFESTOS, MEDIA AND MEETING THE PEOPLE – SEPTEMBER 2014 TO MAY 2015.

Once Scotland had voted to remain in the Union, on 18th September, 2014, which confirmed that general election would be UK wide (thus including Scotland), the path was clear for me to stand as the Unionist candidate, unencumbered as I was by irresponsible pledges to maintain the Barnett formula in the last weeks of the referendum. The people who voted no included those who wanted some form of home rule, and those who wanted to maintain the status quo. As devo max was never on the ballot paper, there was never a mandate for "The Vow."

As I now knew the constitutional make up of the UK I sought to represent and defend, I was ready to launch a twitter account, my website, and publish a rolling manifesto.

I launched my on line campaign at the height of the party conference season, in late September, 2014. My pledge to boost NHS/social care spending by £2.5 billion per annum preceded Labour's pledge to raise exactly the same amount by a matter of hours. To me, this was too much of a coincidence, owing to the instantaneous dissemination of information engendered by the internet. My plan was financed by scrapping the Barnett formula (but giving Scotland equivalent tax raising powers), and redistributing that money to the rest of the UK, while Labour's plan involved soaking the occupants of "mansions", many of whom were asset rich, but cash poor. All that happens is that people would downsize, and a Labour government would never raise the necessary £2.5 billion.

Two of my most notable Twitter followers were Sir David Campbell Bannerman MEP (great grandson of the Liberal Prime Minister who introduced free school meals), and Al Murray, the Pub landlord, who stood against Nigel Farage in South Thanet! After the election, Andy Burnham (the defeated Labour leadership candidate, now Shadow Home Secretary) followed me, and I reciprocated in kind!

The vast majority of my followers are small businesses, and many based in the USA and Australia. I tweeted many of my pledges on the politics home twitter page.

Many politicians, actors and other celebrities have been victims of on line hacking. I was fortunate (due in no small part to my relatively low profile) in that I was never exposed to such abuses – with one exception.

In early 2015, I had tweeted that the UK and NATO countries must restore territorial integrity to the Ukraine and Crimea – for the simple moral reason of deterring aggression, but that if Putin succeeded in stealing these territories, then he would be fortified in seizing NATO territory, which would inevitably mean war. Standing up to Putin today would prevent a war tomorrow. This tweet prompted a heated exchange between myself and a Russian tweeter. The thrust of his argument was that the Donbas would never be restored to the Ukraine; at first, I thought this was a pessimistic member of the Foreign Office, but my worst fears were confirmed when I noticed the Russian flag on his Twitter post!

An essential communication tool for any Independent candidate is "My Next MP". This enables various campaign groups (environmental, social affairs, animal welfare etc) to contact the candidate, invite them to hustings, ask questions, and ask them to fill in surveys. This is an example of where technology democratises politics, by giving equal weight to an Independent as to a candidate or MP of one of the established parties.

It was via "My Next MP" that I was invited to the Civil Liberties Hustings, which took place on Wednesday, 8th April, at the Quaker Meeting House. The panel consisted of myself, the incumbent MP Caroline Lucas, Clarence Mitchell (Conservative candidate), Purna Sen (Labour candidate), Charles Bower (Lib Dem candidate), Nigel .... (UKIP candidate), and Howard Pilott (SPGB candidate).

PRESS RELEASES AND PUBLICITY

My advice to any Independent candidate whose budget prevents them from employ a press secretary to deal with the press, is to employ the next best thing: sheer bloody mindedness.

I sent 2 press releases to The Argus, both of which were published.

I sent my press release announcing my candidacy to The Argus on 28th March, requesting that it be published on Monday 30th March, the date when the election was announced, to maximise impact. In the event, it was published on Tuesday, 31st March.

On 29th April, I sent an eve of poll press release to be published by 6th May at the latest, to enable a last minute appeal to undecided voters in Brighton Pavilion.

This was to state that if I was elected Independent MP for Brighton Pavilion, I would present bills to Parliament to integrate health + social care (an extra £2.5 billion, protect central grant for social care, to prevent hospital admission), a social housing programme funded by QE, an emergency budget to raise NI threshold for low paid, cut small business rates, rebuild defences: 2 aircraft carriers, 30,000 troops, renew Trident. Also, a bill to introduce minimum sentencing, and hold EU referendum in October 2015.

In each case, the press releases were published 3 days after I sent the email; the first press release was published the day after I requested it, and second 4 days before I requested it. Ideally, the eve of poll press release would have had more impact if it had been published on 6th May, eve of poll.

The full page and half page ads available to the larger parties are not an option for independent candidates on a tight budget; the cost is in the region of £600.

An alternative is an MPU. This is a link on the website of a newspaper (in my case, the Brighton Argus), which redirects to the website of the candidate.

The MPU was set for 10,000 impressions, meaning that it was available for 10,000 people to view it, from 9 am to 5 pm, 7 days a week from Thursday 23rd April to Thursday 7th May (polling day) inclusive.

In the event, the MPU lasted for only 4 days.

NICK YEOMANS
YOUR INDEPENDENT CANDIDATE FOR
BRIGHTON PAVILION
FOR FULL MANIFESTO to CONTACT NICK
PLEASE CLICK HERE

THE HUSTINGS

As the election campaign started, The Argus advertised their hustings for Tuesday, 7th April. This was for parliamentary candidates of the 5 main parties, each of whom had a 5 minute opening address. I asked Neil Vowles (Political Editor of The Argus) for a seat on the podium, and because I was an Independent candidate, I was prepared to accept a shorter opening statement of 1 to 2 minutes. Despite 2 attempts to persuade Neil of this, I was unsuccessful. He advised that the Independent and micro party candidates would be brought into the debate.

In the event, this did not happen. I had my hand up all throughout the evening, for every question, and the chairman refused to allow me to ask a question. Howard Pilott, the Socialist Party of Great Britain candidate, posed as a member of the audience. At the end, the chair said that he needed to prioritise for members of the public. I cannot help thinking that the red white and blue rosette upset the delicate equilibrium of the more sensitive members of the metropolitan liberal elite. At the end of the hustings, many members of the public sympathised with me, so being sent to political Coventry probably gave me more publicity!

The Civil Liberties hustings the following day was far more successful. This time, all seven candidates for Brighton Pavilion (including myself) were on the hustings, and we were all given equal time for the opening statement (1 ½ minutes), and equal time to answer the questions.

I was the last candidate to do his opening statement. This gave me an advantage of commenting on other candidates' opinions.

I pulled no punches in my speech. Polemical in tone, I paid tribute to Cromwell and his Levellers, the Great Reform Act of 1832, and the suffragettes. I spoke about the steady but continuous erosion of our civil liberties since the 1990s, the weakening of trial by jury, and the detention without trial being permissible for up to 90 days. I reiterated my strong view that if intercept evidence were allowed in court, then very few suspects would need to be detained for up to 90 days, as it would speed up the process.

I mentioned that the civil liberties of the victim were also undermined by measures such as early release, a point that no other candidate made, not even the UKIP candidate, who I suspect was wary of making such a powerful point in front of an essential liberal (although highly intelligent and principled) audience.

In the question about the Snoopers Charter, the government's proposal to allow security services to access electronic communication of everyone in the UK, I argued was disproportionate, and prevents effective targeting of likely terrorist activity. It is also a propaganda victory for the terrorists, as our liberty would have been drastically reduced, and one of their goals would have been achieved.

The most effective policy is to focus the resources of our security services targeting the electronic communication of groups and individuals likely to perpetrate and support terrorism.

Officials should only be able to see the content of the messages with a warrant, and the suspect will be entitled to an appeal if the warrant powers are abused.

Enhance encryption of emails for individuals and companies.

I went on to say that Article 8, the right to a family life, was used to prevent the deportation of foreign criminals. Critics of the ECHR (including me) are always rounded on when this is mentioned; I for one would always enshrine the right to family life in any human rights legislation, but that this right, along with the right to vote, is conditional upon people NOT breaking the law.

I proposed a British Bill of Rights which would enshrine the right to a family life, the right to vote, and the right to free speech, but that these rights were conditional upon citizens not breaking the law. For example, the right to vote would be removed from prisoners; a serious offender would be deported, whether they had a family life or not. The devil is in the wording of such a Bill, but the wording must be specific enough so that judges cannot misinterpret the law.

I mentioned the most powerful example of how Article 8 was misinterpreted in answer to the question as to whether the ECHR was protecting or threatening the rights of citizens, by talking about the heinous murder of the head teacher, Stephen Lawrence.

Learco Chindamo, who killed Stephen Lawrence in 1995, in 2007, won an appeal against deportation in 2007. This was due to immigration rules that stipulated that, as an EU national who had lived in the UK for 19 years (even excluding his 10 years in jail) he was a natural resident, and could not be deported except on grounds of public security." Surely murder would constitute a huge threat to public security. Even without the EU immigration rules, Article 8 of the human rights act would have prevented his deportation, as he had lived in the UK since the age of 6. In 2014, he was released.

In short, the right to family life protect the rights of the criminal, at the expense of the rights of the victim.

In response to the question as to what was presently the biggest threat to freedom of speech in Britain, I mentioned two pieces of legislation which are so broadly defined that they can undermine legitimate expression. Sections 4A and 5 of the Public Order Act (1986) make it an offence for a person to use threatening words that could cause distress. This could cause a protestor to be prosecuted.

Section 127 of the Communications Act 2003 makes an offence to send "a grossly offensive, indecent, obscene or menacing" message. This can criminalise people who send jovial, albeit silly, messages. Section 127 was used to prosecute a young man who tweeted his frustration at not being able to see his girlfriend due to airport closure. Anyone in such circumstances would have been frustrated, and vented it on social media. If this law was implemented to the letter, the vast majority of Britons (including my humble self) would be prosecuted.

In my opinion, I performed best amongst all the candidates at the Civil Liberties hustings. The chair admonished the rest of the candidates to be as succinct and timely in their responses as myself, and at the election count, the Conservative candidate, Clarence Mitchell, said I spoke very well, despite me slating him and his party for capitulating to the Lib Dems by not scrapping the ECHR and replacing it with a British Bill of Rights!

I found out on 31st March that Living Rent were holding a hustings regarding the housing crisis that very night. I immediately emailed them, but was advised that as there were already 4 main party candidates, any more would be unwieldy. I was invited to ask questions from the floor, but this defeats the object of the exercise (to wit, publicity for the candidate), and reduces the profile of the candidates' policies.

MEETING THE PEOPLE

Due to working full time (a fortnight's leave notwithstanding) I realistically was only able to canvass on Saturday, and weekday evenings and/or daytimes.

In the event, my Mum became seriously ill in mid April, and the 2 weeks dedicated to an intense canvass were spent visiting Mum in hospital.

I started canvassing on Saturday, 10th April. Due to my limited time (and due to the fact that I had no helpers – students at Brighton and Sussex universities had not responded to my email asking for help with canvassing) I decided to canvass the broadest section of Brighton Pavilion that I could in the time available.

I started with Withdean, a very prosperous and beautiful part of Brighton, north of Preston Park, and south of Patcham.

2 of the 3 councillors were Conservative, with 1 Green. Fortunately, a trio of Conservative councillors were returned at the local elections. I suspect that this was in no small part due to the fact that parts of Withdean have no parking restrictions (which saved considerably on my campaign expenses), a situation which the Greens would have undoubtedly reversed had they controlled the town hall – and indeed, the new Labour council are set to introduce these restrictions. Ken and Ann Norman have held 2 of the seats in that ward for many years.

I met with a very positive response in Withdean.

Many people mentioned the lack of bus shelter in the locality, something about which I cod not directly resolve as an MP, but that I would certainly use my power as an MP to try and influence.

An older population, many were concerned about the lack of affordable housing for their children.

After speaking in depth to about 20 people, I had 2 definites, 4 Nos, and 14 floaters. Interestingly, on election night, I saw exactly 2 votes for me in the Withdean count!

One of the most interesting exchanges was with a former Green voter, who was concerned that the Greens would abolish Trident. I reassured her that I would renew Trident with 4 nuclear submarines without delay, and this seemed to reassure her. She was one of my probables.

A young mother mentioned the lack of school places. I advised that I would use the power of central government to reallocate school places from areas that had surpluses (some rural areas) to those with shortages, such as Brighton & Hove. Extra spending for schools will not yield results unless school places are allocated more fairly. I also mentioned that I would allow schools to open branches in the areas from where the demand is originating, to reduce congestion on the school run. This is a policy so devastatingly simple (and fiscally neutral), that many people (including this voter) were surprised that no one had thought of it before.

I made a *faux pas* when a voter asked what my policies were, and I said that I would hold an EU referendum, and advocate withdrawal. He said that, although I was undoubtedly "a thoroughly nice chap", this meant that it would be impossible for him to vote for me! I learnt from this *faux pas*, and never use a naturally divisive topic such as withdrawal from the EU as an opening gambit when canvassing a voter (the NHS was always a winner in this regard) although my commitment to an independent UK remains undiminished.

On Saturday, 25th April, I canvassed Hollingdean and Stanmer. Out of 5 voters, I had 1 definite, and 4 floaters. A voter was disillusioned with the lack of representation concerning the Hollingdean depot, so I agreed that (if elected) I would meet up with him and council representatives.

A voter who previously lived in Cyprus castigated previous UK government for taking away his house. I offered to talk to the Foreign office if elected.

A voter mentioned that 2 dustmen watched as an elderly woman tried to move her bin back, and advised that the Hollingdean depot was in hoc to the GMB. I suspect her neighbour might have been a GMB member and might have heard our exchange, as when I asked him who was voting for, he replied, "Not you, mate!"

I canvassed Patcham on Tuesday 5th May and Wednesday 6th May, and one voter advised she was torn between me and the Conservatives. I advised I would push for an EU referendum in October, and vote to leave EU (a trigger point for many Conservative inclined voters considering voting for UKIP), and that I would not be in hoc to any political parties. The lady concerned asked for a leaflet to assist her in her decision.

I then canvassed the definite and floaters I had met during the campaign in Withdean, Hollingdean and Patcham. Only the lady in Patcham who was torn between the Conservatives and me I managed to contact, via her husband, who advised that she was already at the polling station, and was not sure who she was voting for! All the other definites/probables were out, so I left a leaflet, reminding them to vote for me today.

CORRESPONDENCE WITH CONSTITUENTS

I was pleasantly surprised by the number of constituents who contacted me during the campaign.

In response to a maths teacher who asked for my views on education, bin strikes, and who to vote for nationally and locally, I advised that I would push central government to reallocate school places to where there are shortages, and allow them to expand to where the demand is originating, I'd push for reform of the strike law, so that 50% of people entitled to vote should do so before a strike takes place; I advised him to vote for me nationally, and Conservative locally, due to their competence in local government.

In response to a voter of a strong Christian faith, I advised that I did not support married couple's tax allowance, as love (not tax cuts) encourages people to marry, and that with a large deficit, tax cuts should be focussed on the low paid and small businesses, favoured sex education in primary schools, my proposed Bill of Rights which would enshrine freedom of religious expression, both in civic society and in schools, that I'd vote against abortion (except where life of mother/child was in serious jeopardy), and for euthanasia.

One of the most amusing emails actually occurred after the election.

This was in response to my policy to limit child benefit to the first 2 children, born after 2016.

I had patiently explained that the policy would apply to the third child born after April 2016, so would not affect existing claimants, and that triplets, quadruplets etc would retain the benefit. This writer – and many commentators – fell into the trap of concluding that the 2 child limit would lead to child poverty – it would not do so. It would instil responsibility, by making people think of the cost of having more children. Most importantly, it would save £12 billion over the course of a Parliament, and would obviate the need to cut carers and disability benefit. The British voter has rightly become healthily cynical, and this was exacerbated by the Tories proposing £12 billion of welfare cuts, without specifying who would be affected, causing severe anxiety for millions of people in receipt of benefits.

I received three personal manifestos concerning the environment; the first advocated sustainable felling of timber, carbon capture as well as renewables to reduce CO_2 emissions; QE investment in energy infrastructure, including insulation and renewable plant, to ensure energy self sufficiency and national security; I agreed with her proposal for water metres, to preserve water, and using our scientific expertise to clean up the rivers; and I proposed a new super ministry Environment, Energy, Housing & Transport to co-ordinate these measures.

One of the most poignant of the letters from constituents was from the spouse of a Mexican husband, who would only be able to obtain a visa if his wife earned in excess of £18,500, which is not possible as a supply teacher. The wife herself was a UK citizen, and her husband previously worked in the UK.

I responded by firstly stating that it is completely unfair than an EU citizen can settle in the UK freely, but a non EU citizen is subject to these thresholds. It is a classic example of Euro jingoism.

I also mentioned that there are no loopholes relating to previous employment and contribution to UK tax revenues. However, the fact that the husband previously worked and paid taxes in the UK should at least be taken into account. In addition, if the husband settled in the UK, their joint income would be contributing much to the UK economy. I said to his wife that I couldn't reverse this law. However, if elected MP, I asked his wife for her consent for me to write to the Home Secretary to see if an exemption could be applied to the husband.

By far the single most important issue in the election (as far as my putative constituents were concerned) was the NHS.

Many constituents emailed me with the following message:-

"Last week, the head of the British Medical Association warned that after the election patients could be charged for basic NHS services."

The petition asked if I was committed to keeping the NHS free at the point of use?

I used a standard response, advocating my proposals.

I advised that I believe that the NHS must remain free at the point of use for medical treatment. I opposed charges for people missing an appointment due to work or childcare commitments, and pledged that I will vote against charges if elected MP.

I advocated charges for purely cosmetic treatment, and charges for binge drinkers (or their guardians) for treatment when they clog up A&E.

I also proposed scrapping the Barnett Formula (whereby Scotland gets higher funding per head), and redistribute £2.5 billion for health and social care across rest of the UK.

I advised that I would use my 12 years experience of working in adult social care for 12 years to propose a Bill to integrate health and social care budgets, so patients get homecare to prevent hospital admission, to free up A&E.

The range of responses showed how divided people were on this subject.

A lecturer in social and cultural history praised my views on binge drinking cosmetic surgery, and homecare to prevent admission to A&E. She wished me luck in my campaign.

A nurse who worked in A&E again praised my views, and pledged her support to me. This was the most gratifying endorsement of the campaign.

By complete contrast, a voter criticised me for calling of the scrapping of the Barnett formula. I have always wondered whether he was registered to vote in Brighton Pavilion, or Glasgow Govan! This was a disturbing phenomenon displayed by "progressive" voters; the urge of voters (neither resident in Scotland, nor with any Scottish connections) to vote for a party (to wit, the SNP) which was not even contesting elections in England.

CORRESPONDENCE WITH CAMPAIGN GROUPS

By far the most active campaign group with whom I had correspondence was 38 degrees. Their actions did actually persuade the government not to cancel the social fund.

There were three main campaigns they conducted during the election. I had emails from several hundreds of voters in Brighton Pavilion, asking for my position on key issues.

Firstly, TTIP (The Transatlantic Trade and Investment Partnership) on further privatisation of our NHS and public services, and which would allow corporations to sue the government, and that the NHS was not exempt from the TTIP deal.

I responded stating I oppose TTIP as it undermines the democratic will of the British people, and undermines the NHS, and that if elected MP, I would vote against TTIP in its entirety at every opportunity.

Secondly, tax evasion. In late March, a petition was launched to ask candidates I am to propose a vote on an amendment to the Finance Bill which could shut the Mayfair tax loophole, which gives special treatment to private equity bosses, who currently dodge up to £700m of tax a year. The petition's argument continued by highlighting that this is money which should be going to our NHS, education and public services.

I responded by stating that I would vote to close this loophole if I was an MP. Although an instinctive tax cutter across the board, there are a lot of inconsistencies in taxation amongst high earners and high levels of income, which distort incentives.

However, the highlight of the election as far as campaigns were concerned was the 38 degrees campaign inviting all candidates to hand in an NHS Petition on Saturday, 25th April. This involved being photographed receiving the petition, and giving a short statement.

I was the first candidate to attend, and spoke to an American lady who agreed with withdrawal from the EU, as the USA had fought for independence in the 1770s.

I held the petition, and I was asked how would I protect funding for the NHS. I advised that I would scrap the Barnett formula (and give Scotland equivalent tax raising powers), and redistribute the £2.5 billion to health and social care, and integrate health and social care, to prevent people going into hospital.

When asked for my position on TTIP, I advised that this leads to US corporations suing the democratically elected government, and that it undermined UK sovereignty, and I would oppose it at every opportunity.

My comments were the briefest, but by no doubt the clearest. I have learnt in political addresses (especially responses to questions) that less is more, and my comments contrasted with the Lib Dem candidate, who rambled interminably, and wanted to "see the details" of TTIP.

Interestingly, no Conservative or UKIP candidates turned up, and I was the only centre right candidate to turn up. 38 Degrees had photographs of candidates who failed to turn up. This is undoubtedly a surefire way to gain publicity for the NHS, and to hold candidates to account. The absence of Conservative and UKIP candidates only highlights the view that parties of the centre right do not support the NHS, and by not signing the petition, are hell bent on privatising it. This I believe not to be true. However, the centre right politician is in a bind; if he fails to turn up, then he is pilloried. If he does turn up, then he is pilloried for not signing up to each and every policy position of 38 degrees. If nothing else, my presence and comments gave an alternative pro NHS argument based on integration, increasing capacity through private provision, and reallocating existing public funds rather than punitive taxation or borrowing. This I believe provides an education to the Left on the need for responsible use of public funds, and to the Right on the need for collective national direction of health and social care.

Afterwards, I discussed funding with a 38 degrees member. She challenged my views on health and social care integration, saying that it could be used as a covert way of reducing funding. I responded that I would pledge an extra £2.5 billion per year to health and social care. She advocated higher taxes; I countered by responding that higher taxes merely drive people and businesses overseas, and there is less revenue for the NHS. She said she was surprised at me for falling for such an argument, but I reiterated that it is regressive to disincentive entrepreneurship, upon which all public services depend.

As polling day approached, all candidates received a petition to Save Our NHS from We The People. They proposed a NHS Reinstatement Bill, banning private companies from bidding on contracts in the NHS.

This led to one of the most difficult decisions that an Independent candidate faces; to oppose a seemingly popular and just cause.

I responded by saying that I could not support their Bill.

I argued that my main concern with the Bill's proposals is that by stopping private firms being commissioned by the NHS to provide treatment, this will reduce capacity. I stated that I would always support treatment being free at the point of use, regardless of who provides the service.

I advocated my own HealthCare Bill, and mentioned that having worked in adult social care for 12 years, I have witnessed carers leaving in their droves, as they are often paid below the minimum wage, as travel time is not included. Zero hours contracts make caring an uneconomic profession for many people. The patient is the loser, as continuity of care breaks down. Any homecare agency contracted by the NHS or social services must pay its carers the living wage, and abolish zero hours contracts (except for reserve staff, who would need to cover emergencies). This would be UK wide, and cost between £300 - £400 million, and would be financed by cutting overseas aid. This would be a preferable alternative to Miliband's damaging 5% profit limit, which would simply reduce investment.

I argued for a single budget for health and social care. GPs, physios, nurses, and OTs would work under the same roof with the same budget, so that patients receive the treatment they need, when and where they need it. This would prevent people being admitted to hospital, and speed up discharge from hospital, and would free up A&E.

I also called for investing £2.5 billion per year from 2015 in a preventative healthcare fund, focusing on home care, physiotherapy, and treatment. This would be funded by scrapping the Barnett Formula, giving Scotland equivalent tax raising powers, and redistributing the money to the rest of the UK.

I also called for tough decisions to ensure existing resources are spent on people who are genuinely ill, through no fault of their own. I called for binge drinkers who clog up A&E put patients who are genuinely ill at severe risk, should be charged for their treatment. It would make people think twice about the consequences of their actions. The revenue from those who continue to binge drink would be used to pay NHS staff more for the extra work carried out.

I pointed out to We the People, that I appreciated that there was a difference of opinion between us about the role of private firms in the NHS, but candidates should be honest about their policies. I advised that my proposed Healthcare Bill was ambitious, realistic, and fully costed.

This may very well have cost me votes, especially in the crucial final days of the campaign, but – as with 38 degrees – I believed that people need to be educated about socialist dogma within the NHS; surely, any NHS reforms must be about expanding capacity, and delivering quality healthcare?

On 30th April, I responded to Bridget Warr, Chief Executive, of the UK Home Care Association (UKHCA), whose aim is to keep people in their own homes.

I responded by advocating my integrated health and social care policy.

1). Integrate health and social care budgets, so that patients get the care they need, when and where they need it. GPs, nurses, OTs, and physios need to work under the same roof, with the same budget. For example, care could be set up to prevent hospital admission in the first place. This would free up hospital beds.

2). Instil fairness into our NHS. I would call for binge drinkers to be charged for clogging up A&E, when genuinely Ill people wait hours for treatment. Even if this does not deter them, the savings would be ploughed back into the NHS. The NHS pays for far more treatment of overseas visitors, than overseas visitors pay our NHS. The UK needs to leave EU so we can control access to the NHS. In the meantime, NHS needs to recoup money spent on treating overseas visitors. Overseas visitors must take out medical insurance before they visit the UK, just as UK citizens must before visiting overseas. This would protect NHS funding, and would ensure that more money is available for healthcare and homecare for the indigenous population. Obviously, asylum seekers fleeing atrocities would be entitled to NHS treatment free at the point of use.

3). Under the Barnett Formula, Scotland receives much more money per head than the rest of the UK, and home care is free at the point of use, unlike in the rest of the UK. I'd scrap the Barnett formula (give Scotland equivalent tax raising powers), and redistribute £2.5 billion to the rest of the UK, in the form of a healthcare priority fund, for homecare and life saving treatment.

4). It is not surprising that when homecarers are paid less than the minimum wage (as they don't get paid for travel time in between care calls), and work zero hours contracts, that there is a huge problem of recruitment and retention. The result is poor care for the patient. For a homecare agency to be approved by social services/NHS, the agency must pay its carers the living wage and abolish zero hours contracts. This would be UK wide, including Scotland. This would cost approximately £400 million, and would be paid for by cutting overseas aid.

I made clear that, due to a lack of available resources, homecare would need to continue to be means tested, but I believe that my proposals (especially integration of health and social care) would ensure that patients receive a quality service, whether in hospital, care home or in their own home.

Fourthly, housing. I received an email from Shelter, calling for an end to the housing crisis, by building more affordable housing units. I sent a near identical response to SQUASH on 25th April 2015.

I proposed using the £600 million saved by reducing tax free threshold for pensioners from £1.25 to £1 million to invest in a national scheme of halfway houses, where homeless people come off the street, and are given treatment for alcohol and substance misuse, chronic illness, and are trained for work, so that they can then live independently. This will use organisations such as Centre Point, Shelter, Salvation Army, and social services.

I argued that VAT on new build is zero rated, but not for renovating empty buildings. Reduce VAT from 20% to 10% on converting empty buildings into social homes. This will encourage small firms and councils to convert empty buildings into homes. This would be funded by privatising BBC, so there will be no need to subsidise TV licenses for the over 75s, as the license fee will be abolished.

I called for £12 billion of QE investment into building/converting 200,000 social housing units by 2020, and mentioned that Shelter's own proposals called for £12 billion of investment. I mentioned that this proposed QE investment is 1/30th of the QE invested in the banks. I argued that the UK had a historic opportunity to do this, due to record low interest rates, and my deficit reduction programme. It would also drive a stake into the heart of deflation, and create high skilled, and high paid jobs, which will boost economic growth.

On right to buy, I called for expansion to allow this for council and housing association tenants, but ensure proceeds are reinvested in building/converting new stock. This will create a virtuous circle of renewal of social housing stock.

I mentioned that lack of supply was also compounded by unprecedented demand, and that immigration must be strictly controlled. Social housing must be prioritised for the indigenous population. I proposed that all migrants (EU and non EU) would not be eligible for social housing for 6 months, pending an EU referendum in October 2015.

Finally, on fracking. 38 degrees emailed candidates to ask if we opposed fracking.

Unlike the other emails about other topics, candidates were not asked fro their views, but to click the link if we agreed with the following statements.

"If my constituency is at risk of fracking, I will oppose it. If my constituency is not at risk, I will oppose fracking nationwide."

Yes - I'd like to sign the Frack Free Promise: http://bit.ly/1FWY8NV

There was no option to say that I support fracking, nor an opportunity for a response to explain one's views.

In the event, as there was only an option to respond if one opposed fracking, I did not click the link. I support fracking, and believe that (as in the USA) the potential problems re: drinking water can be resolved. I support it as the UK needs to use all its indigenous resources to keep the lights on, and prevent dependence upon unstable regimes.

My decision not to sign the frack free promise I believe cost me the most votes.

On the 9th April, I received an email from the Aldersgate Group, a unique alliance of members who believe high environmental standards are good for business, the economy and society.

Their priorities were climate change, energy, resources and protecting our natural environment.

I responded by saying that I agreed with many of their manifesto proposals, and assured them that I am committed to a sustainable economic policy.

As I said to the people who sent their personal manifestos regarding the environment, I advised that my priority is energy independence, to enhance national security.

Regarding greenhouse gas emissions, I proposed rewarding companies for adopting new green technology. I argued that carbon capture will ensure clean coal, and therefore the 4 coal fired power stations and 2 deep coal mines must be kept open. The UK could be a world leader in carbon capture, fracking, renewables and nuclear power, and work globally to cut greenhouse gases.

With regards to housing, new build is zero VAT rated, while 20% is levied on renovating empty buildings. I would reduce the VAT on converting empty building into homes by 10%, reduce immigration by requesting immigrants wait for 6 months before they can claim and housing, pending an In/Out EU referendum in October, 2015. Social housing must be prioritised for the indigenous population. This will preserve the Green Belt.

I mentioned that I am opposed to membership of the EU. I believe the UK should work with nations across the globe to forge agreements about climate change, which does not respect the boundaries of individual nations, nor the EU.

I also advocated £3 billion of QE to invest in renewable, carbon capture, tackling pollution, and insulation.

With regards to skills, I called for a massive recruitment drive of engineers and scientists, reduce tuition fees for graduates who study science, technology, and medicine, and finance this by raising fees on humanities degrees, so it would be fiscally neutral.

I also advocated my proposed super ministry of Environment, Energy, Housing & Transport precisely to co-ordinate sustainability, and that the House of Commons Environment select committee would hold the Ministry to account.

I also pledged that, if elected, I would certainly attend the Aldersgate group breakfast meetings.

Further on the environment, on 2nd may I also pledged that I would sign up to the Marine Charter, in response to an email from Marine Charter organization.

Also on 2nd May, I responded to the Sussex Wildlife trust, who had emailed me the following questions.

1). Q). Do you personally support our call for a Nature and Wellbeing Act, and will you work to persuade your Party to support and promote this initiative?

1). A). Living in the thriving metropolis of Brighton Pavilion, I have come to appreciate the green spaces, and will seek to protect them if elected Independent MP for Brighton Pavilion, so I support the Nature and Wellbeing Act, and would vote for it as an MP. I would do all I can as MP to prevent Preston Park from being converted into a car park. I would also fight to protect Wild Park, and the ancient woodland.

2). Q). Have you signed the 'Marine Charter', and if not when will you do so?

2). A). Yes, I have signed the Marine Charter, and would vote for it if elected MP.

3). Q). Do you agree that there are environmental limits to development and will you commit to take action to ensure local resources are sufficient to support truly sustainable development in Sussex?

3). A). I am deeply concerned about excessive new build housing in the South East, and in Brighton Pavilion. Currently, new build is zero VAT rated, while conversion of buildings is liable for 20% VAT. I would reduce VAT on building renovations to 10%, to meet the need for affordable housing, while protecting the Green Belt. I also believe that UK should leave the EU, so demand is reduced by controlling immigration.

I was also contacted by Firearms UK. This is always a difficult subject, balancing freedom for responsible gun ownership for sport etc, against protecting people.

1. Do you believe in a total ban on private firearms ownership?
2. Do you believe that private firearms ownership should face greater restrictions?
3. Do you believe the current system is balanced/there is no need for change?
4. Do you support all forms of currently legal shooting in the UK? (if there are exceptions please state)
5. Would you oppose any moves to further restrict private firearms ownership/use in the UK?

6. Do you believe that our firearms laws are in need of reformation and sensible relaxation?
7. If you support UK citizen's rights to participate in shooting sports do you also support changing the law to permit .22 rimfire pistols to be used for competitive shooting thus allowing ordinary UK citizens to properly train to enable them to compete in international events such as the Olympic and Commonwealth games?

My answers are below:-

1) No, I don't support a total ban on private firearms ownership. 2) Yes. 3) Specifically, greater checks on previous mental health, and 3 GPs to verify that someone is fit to use firearms. 4) Yes 5) See 2+3. 6) See 2+3 7).

I received an email from Hindu Matters in Britain. This was particularly important, as I sought to represent an area which constitutes a significant number of people from the Hindu community. I read their manifesto, and requested that my message below be posted on their website.

I responded as I did to all representatives of different ethnic groups by stating that as an Independent Parliamentary Candidate for Brighton Pavilion, I would represent all constituents interests equally regardless of ethnic origin or religious belief. I went on to say that I am a firm believer in integration of all communities, and that the United Kingdom has a proud tradition of integration. I mentioned that I was particularly concerned that Hindu war veterans are accorded the same rights as all war veterans, and that Hindus have proper cremation facilities.

I also responded to the Jewish Board of Deputies' manifesto, by supporting the Ten Commitments, namely that I would defend the Jewish way of life, customs etc, oppose all hate crime, promote good relations between all the UK communities, to remember and understand the Holocaust and prevent future genocide, a genuine 2 state solution (Israel and Palestine), peace projects that unite communities, importance of faith schools, religiously and culturally sensitive youth and care services, tackle poverty, human rights abuses and climate change across the UK, and celebrate Jewish heritage.

Concerns over the power of the media took a key place in the election campaign as never before.

The phone hacking scandal proved the importance of holding media owners to account, and of not letting individuals like Rupert Murdoch abuse their power. Do you support tighter rules on media ownership? And do you support the full implementation of the Leveson report?

I responded with my own considered and proportionate proposals for media reform

"I do not support the full blown Leveson recommendations, as I would be gravely concerned about the state regulating the media. I believe the Royal Charter is an effective measure, as action was desperately needed after the horrendous treatment of many people by the media. The Charter is well balanced, as it consists of a regulatory board free from politicians and media bosses, and means there is no charge for an individual raising a complaint about the media, unlike previously. However, at present, media organisations can choose to be bound or not by the regulations of the Charter. I'd push for membership to be mandatory for all media organisations. This would ensure that all media organisations are bound by the same rules. It is also the responsibility of newspaper readers to switch allegiance from newspapers that treat innocent people badly."

Despite my historical lack of participation in contact sports, I received an email regarding football governance.

"As a Manchester United fan and a voter in the Brighton, Pavilion constituency, before I vote on May 7th I would like to know whether you will support legislation to reform football governance? We believe legislative changes are necessary as outlined here:http://www. votefootball.org/proposal Your response to the question below may impact decisively on my voting intentions: Will you personally, and your party generally, support new legislation as outlined in the above link?"

Despite my lack of participation in, and lack of knowledge of, contact sports, I responded by stating that I would campaign for these proposals if elected MP, as I believe that in all organisations (political parties and football clubs), the grassroots member must call the shots.

I have long been committed to animal welfare, so it was gratifying to articulate my views to the Vegan Society.

In response to her questions, I advised her that, if elected MP, I'd push for a British Bill of Rights, which would enshrine the right of vegans to have their dietary needs met in hospitals and care homes.

That I would support improved labelling of vegan foods, dedicated vegan sections in shops and supermarkets. Education in schools.

That I proposed UK withdrawal from the EU, so we withdraw from the CAP, with its gospel of intensive farming. The deficiency payments scheme would be used to encourage farmers to diversify into sustainable crop farming, including energy production, and to encourage UK self sufficiency in food production. There will always be foodstuffs the UK cannot produce, and would have to import. By withdrawing from CAP + CET, UK would access imported food at cheaper prices, and give developing nations the opportunity to grow their economies through food exports. This will help the poor in the UK and overseas.

I opposed the means testing school meals and milk stigmatises low paid.

I stated that I fully support animal free techniques for medical research, and opposed using animals for entertainment.

I agreed with the Vegan Society's that scientific expertise must be used to find substitutes to pesticides.

I also supported their approval of a ban on animal testing. Science has advanced so much that such brutal techniques are no longer necessary.

The Vegan Society responded positively.

"Your commitments to improved vegan food labelling, vegan education in schools, payments to encourage sustainable crop farming, animal-free medical research, ending the use of animals in entertainment, and banning neonicotinoids will all be welcome to our supporters."

The engagement of young voters was a key issue in the election. I have always called for the voting age to be reduced to 16, as people aged 16 can work, get married, and serve their country in battle.

"As a representative of Bite The Ballot - the non-partisan, not-for-profit democracy movement that works to empower young people - I'm writing to ask for your support in the upcoming election, and beyond.

With so many young people turning away from 'politics', we believe that that every single UK Parliament candidate has a role to play in inspiring future generations to take a stake in society.

At Bite The Ballot, we've already inspired hundreds of thousands of people to register to vote through National Voter Registration Day. With your backing, we're now aiming to inspire as many of them to turnout to the polls and make their votes count on Thursday.

Your support will go a long way towards us reaching our goal of empowering a record-number of young people take an active role in UK democracy. We hope that, if elected, you would then continue to support the movement as a Member of Parliament, working with us to ensure young people's concerns are heard and acted upon."

On 5th May, I tweeted my support by saying:-

I'm making #ThePledge + support @BiteThe Ballot as young voters' views must be respected.

On 10th April, Trans Info asked if I would pledge my support to non binary people of Brighton. On 11th April, I was the first candidate in Brighton Pavilion to do so. Again, I reproduce the correspondence in full.

I was also the first Brighton Pavilion candidate to sign the pledge for trans members of the community.

In addition to this array of direct contact with various organisations, I was also proactive in contacting organisations, and to arrange meetings to listen to their concerns, and advocate my policies.

In response to the Chancellor's Autumn Statement on 3rd December, 2014, I tweeted like a thing possessed to the financial Times, Business for Britain, The Economist, CBI, Evan Davis and Newsnight calling for permanent rate relief, financed by part of the savings accrued by scrapping the Barnett formula. This prompted an organisation We Start Business to follow me on Twitter. I tweeted them to thank them for their support, and I asked them for their ideas. I reproduce our correspondence below:-

"It is liberating to formulate policies from first principles, liberated from any political party yoke. I have learnt a great deal about the challenges facing businesses, in addition to my experience selling parts for classic cars.

Rest assured that these proposals are already in the manifesto.

If elected as MP, I will work with MPs of all parties to implement these policies.

I wish you the very best of luck with your inspiring work to create an enterprise culture."

William Dodge, the founder of We Start Business, responded thus:-

"Thank you for your interest in our economic views. Your policies seem to be a very effective and have built on our recommendations very well. We wish you the very best with the up and coming elections."

The correspondence continued when I read their proposals, and asked for feedback about specific regulations that should be axed, and confirmed my support of their key proposals:-

"I'm very impressed by the scope and radicalism of your proposals, and they echo my philosophy of democratic capitalism.

1). Parliamentary oversight over competition law, rather than EU jurisdiction. For example, there should be at least 20 energy providers. I would apply this to most industries, including the car and aerospace industries. This will enable businesses to plan far ahead into the future.

2). The cost of registration fees is prohibitive for start ups. I would set up an Enterprise bank (as part of the bank of England) which would lend at a fixed interest rate (at MLR) precisely so small businesses can obtain credit to pay these fees and similar costs.

3). 60% of small firms report that complying with regulation costs more than £1000 per year, and compliance costs have increased since 2010, according to the Federation of Small Business. The policy of one regulation abolished for every new regulation introduced is not sufficient. There should be a net reduction in business regulation. EU air quality legislation will result in many coal fired power stations closing. I will allocate £3 billion of QE funds to energy independence, including carbon capture for coal. This will ensure businesses have a stable supply of energy, and encourage growth of businesses that supply these power stations – engineering companies, for example. The Common External tariff stops the UK from trading freely with the rest of the world, and increases cost of imported raw materials. I will campaign for UK to leave EU, and for the CET (and other EU red tape) to expire under "sunset clause." Paid parental leave should only apply to the first two births.

4). I'm certainly in favour of tax cuts, prioritised for small firms. 45% is too high.

All tax cuts must be funded up front, to control the deficit, and to ensure low interest rates.

Sole trader tax rises to 40% for any income over £41,865 per year and 45% for any income over £150,000 per year.

4.9 million sole traders in UK (Simply Business 12 Nov 14).

As a start, I would abolish the Class 2 national Insurance Rule. This is regressive, and unfair, as the self employed are not entitled to statutory sick pay, or holiday pay.

Half of self employed (I use this as the generic term, includes sole traders) earn less than £12,000. All self employed above NI threshold have to pay £143 fee (the NIC Class 2 contribution). This would cost £250 million – just 0.2 % of NI revenue. (leftfootforward.org/1014/03/budgettohelplowearners)

This would benefit all self employed. It would also be progressive, disproportionately benefitting the lower paid, and encourage more people to become self employed/sole traders. This would be financed by revenue accrued from tackling tax evasion – the rest of this revenue would be used to further cut the tax rates for sole traders.

I have already pledged to raise the NI threshold for employees from £7755 to £8,628.80 in my 2015 Budget, as a first step towards integrating income tax and National Insurance. This will also assist the self employed."

I also wrote to the Federation of Small Businesses on 7th February, stating that as I was not linked to party, and as I was funding my own campaign, if elected as MP, I would work with MPs of other parties to implement measures to boost economic growth.

I articulated the "gap in the business market" which I intended to fill with my strong pro-enterprise policies.

"I firmly believe that none of the other parties have a clear strategy for economic growth. The swingeing taxation and proposed by the Lib Dems and Labour, would drive businesses overseas, and strangle the growth that we so desperately need. We are all aware of the Green's anti business approach. The Conservatives proposed tax cuts are unfunded, and UKIP have no economic strategy for a UK independent of Brussels.

I firmly believe that the UK should leave the EU, so that we can trade freely with the rest of the world, and to instigate a bonfire of controls. I propose an EU referendum in October 2015 (needless to say I would campaign to leave); sunset clauses would be applied to the Common External Tarriff, and harmful regulations, so that if the UK left the EU, these regulations would expire immediately.

Please find attached my economic policies, which have been fully costed, and my two Budgets, one for May 2015, and a Budget for an Independent UK, to capitalise upon the advantages of EU withdrawal.

I would strengthen the deficit reduction programme, to maintain low interest rates. I support the Charter for Budget Responsibility, setting limits on government spending. Overall government spending should grow at 1% less than GDP, year on year, to ensure a budget surplus.

I would reduce the deficit by freezing benefits (except pensions and disability benefits) for 3 years; limit child benefit to the first 2 children from 2016; privatise RBS and Lloyds; efficiency savings from central government expenditure, by contracting out IT and HR systems.

These measures alone will almost halve the deficit from £99 billion to £43.9 billion by 2020. This does not include revenue from economic growth.

Deficit reduction, and fully funded tax cuts and spending plans, enables the government to borrow only to invest (through QE) in housing, transport and energy independence to enhance business – through reduced travel costs, and cheaper bills.

I would very much like to hear your views, in particular with regards to deregulation, and what regulations are particularly burdensome, and thus ripe for abolition."

Similarly, no response was forthcoming from the following email sent on 8th February, 2015, to ask the Police for their views.

"Dear Chief Superintendent Nev Kemp,

I am standing for Parliament as an Independent Candidate for Brighton Pavilion at the forthcoming general election.

I am not linked to any political party, and I am funding my own campaign. If elected as MP, I would work with MPs of other parties to implement measures to boost economic growth.

I am writing to you to ask for your views about the challenges faced by front line police officers, in particular, targets and bureaucracy that impedes the fight against crime.

I would like to ask your views on zero tolerance of crime, minimum sentencing, early release, counter terrorism measures, and whether or not the police should be armed (with regards to counter terrorism measures).

Please find attached my proposals on crime. I would be available to meet up to discuss your concerns."

THE GENERAL ELECTION

MY ELECTION STRATEGY

From the outset, and indeed since the post referendum surge in SNP support, the opinion polls suggested that while the Tories would win the most votes, Labour would be the largest party, but well short of a majority. However, the massive surge in SNP support would be sufficient to create a Labour/SNP pact with a sufficient overall majority. Such luxuries are denied to parties of the right (this is as true at Westminster as it is in the town halls), as most nationalist and minor parties are of the left.

Despite Ed Miliband's protestations to the contrary, he would have been forced to have done some deal with the SNP, had Labour been the largest party, but lacking a majority. In order to get a Queen's Speech and Budget through parliament, Labour would have needed SNP support to pass either measure.

It was my hunch throughout the election that Labour would be the largest single party, and would have formed some type of administration; at the time of the election, living standards had not quite reached their 2008 peak, and the number of people in part time work would have favoured Labour. In addition, the core of liberal intelligentsia also favoured Labour, and I felt that even a Tory minority government (or Tory coalition) was unlikely. I was proved wrong.

Fears that a Tory attempt to forge a government (based on the moral argument that they would invariably receive the largest number of votes, as did Ted Heath's Tories in February, 1974) would collapse, and would result in a Labour/SNP pact prompted me to plan to form an alternative government. Even the prospect of a majority Conservative government (with whom I am instinctively more sympathetic) was not sufficient to deter me from my plans to form an alternative government, mainly due to the swingeing cuts to defence carried out by the Conservative led Coalition.

POST ELECTION MANOUEVRES

My strategy for forming a Coalition government after the election

In the manifesto, I clearly stated that I sought to form a government in the event of a failure of other parties to form a stable government. I also made it clear that I would propose my bills in any event, regardless of whether there was a hung Parliament, or a majority government, whether I was Prime Minister, Minister or backbencher.

On 24th March, 2015, I wrote to the Cabinet Secretary, Sir Jeremy Heywood. The Cabinet Secretary is the head of the civil service, and ensures that the business of government continues, even during an uncertain transfer of power such as would follow an indecisive election result.

I advised Sir Jeremy that, in the event of a hung Parliament, the UK would need a strong majority government, in face of further economic crises, and the threats from IS and Russia. MPs including Gisela Stuart, Joan Walley, Jeremy Lefroy, Mark Reckless, Caroline Lucas, and George Galloway backed a motion which states that, if no party has a majority, then the Commons should be recalled on 11th May, "and the House should proceed immediately to debate and confirm any proposed arrangements for the composition and programme of the new government."

I advised Sir Jeremy that, even if this motion is not passed, consulting Parliament before a government is formed would ensure people, through their elected representatives, can choose their next government, and that the next government must not be formed in smoke filled rooms.

I asked Sir Jeremy to give due consideration to my manifesto, and I sent him a copy, so that the civil service could propose Bills in the run up to the Queen's Speech.

If Tories got 285+ seats, they would have been the favourites to form a government. They would have needed another 41 seats from other parties to form a government.

If, as seemed likely, Labour and SNP attempted to form a coalition, the Tories as incumbents (plus allies such as Lib Dems, DP, and UKIP) would try to form a government, and the deadline was Monday 18th May, when Tories would have known whether or not they could form a government. If so, they would have put their Queen's Speech to the Commons on Wednesday, 27th May.

If the Tories won 280 seats or less, then it would have been unlikely that the Tories could have formed a government, even with other parties.

Then Labour would have sought to form a minority government, inevitably backed up by the SNP. The SNP were forecast to get at least 50 seats, with Labour forecast to win as few as 276 seats. In this scenario, the Labour SNP pact would have obtained 326 seats a majority of 1 in the new Parliament. In all probability, Labour would have squeaked its

Queen's Speech through Parliament, as in practice Lib Dems and other nationalists are more kindly disposed to Labour.

In the aftermath of the Tories being unable to form a government (and before Labour had a chance to do so), my plan was to seek to form an alternative bloc of MPs (from Conservative, moderate Labour, UKIP, DUP and myself) to

i)   Defeat the Labour Queen's Speech
ii) If successful in defeating Labour Queen's Speech, present my own Queens speech.

If Labour were defeated in a Queen Speech I would have proposed my own Queen's Speech, which would have been presented on 10th June.

I had spent a not inconsiderable time considering the structure of the government I sought to lead, and the intellectual armoury and apparatus available to me as a Prime Minister.

In these times of fiscal restraint, I believe that central government should get its own house in order first.

The principle change I sought to effect to central government was to establish a Cabinet of 15. This is even smaller than the 19 strong Cabinet of Sir Winston Churchill's peacetime government of 1951, and would be the smallest Cabinet since universal suffrage.

It has always been a contradiction as to why policies to create jobs are administered by a different department to the creation of wealth.

I sought to follow Sir Edward Heath's example and establish 2 new "Super Ministries."

My proposed Department for Trade, Industry and Employment would forge new free trade areas once the UK leaves the EU, and embark upon a bonfire of regulations. The aim of the DTI&E will be wealth creation, and creation of high skilled jobs in the energy, aerospace and defence industries. The DTI&E would work with universities and businesses to encourage graduates into engineering and science, to rebuild the UK's shattered manufacturing base. Graduates would be incentivised to become engineers by cutting the tuition fees for science, and engineering. The Dept for Culture, Media & Sport and Dept for Science & Technology will be incorporated into the DTI&E.

My second super ministry was the Department for Environment, Energy, Housing & Transport to co-ordinate infrastructure, and strengthen communities. When new towns and cities are built, the DEEH&T would ensure that all transport and housing, sustainability, and energy needs are catered for. The DEEH&T will also be responsible for HS2, One North, and airport expansion.

Having worked in local government for 12 years, I have too often witnessed the inefficiency of duplication, and different IT systems preventing clients from receiving an efficient service.

The DDH&T would have overseen the most radical reform of local government since Sir Edward Heath's reforms of 1972, along the lines of merging district, borough and county councils into unitary authorities. The unitaries would reflect counties, or cities in areas where a city had actually been created. This would reduce bureaucracy, and (with regards to social services) would serve the same population as the local NHS Trust, essential to my plans to integrate health and social care, facilitated by a new Department of Health & Social Services.

The Department for International Development will be incorporated into the Foreign Office.

The Scottish, Welsh and Northern Ireland offices would have remained at Cabinet rank, to deal with overarching issues specific to those provinces.

The Ministry of Agriculture, Fisheries and Food would have remained at Cabinet rank, to ensure security of food supply, to ensure that the benefits of cheaper food once the UK leaves the EU are passed on to consumers, and to provide incentives to UK farmers to conserve the land.

THE ELECTION CAMPAIGN DAY BY DAY

Parliament was dissolved on Monday 30th March, and the election officially started.

I sent a Twitter message announcing the following: "Today, I confirm that I'm standing for Parliament as an Independent Candidate for Brighton Pavilion. If elected, I'll work with MPs to create an enterprise economy, rebuild defences, integrate health and social care, and bring forward EU referendum to October."

The EU referendum was a key issue from the start of the campaign. On the same day I slated Labour for denying the people a choice on EU membership, and called for Brexit, stating that the UK would not lose jobs or businesses if we withdrew, as the EU sells more to the UK than the UK sells to the EU, and therefore the EU would not impose retaliatory trade barriers.

The following day labour announced their cut in rates. Labour's cut was a self defeating object, dependent as it was upon higher taxes on larger corporations, which, I argued, would drive them overseas, and reduce growth and revenues.

On 2nd April, Labour condemned NHS "privatisation." I announced that private firms providing care free at the point of use is NOT privatisation. It drives up standards.

On the same day, Clegg and Miliband proposed tax hikes on the rich. I argued that this would drive entrepreneurs abroad, and reduce the revenue the NHS so desperately needs.

Three days later, Labour continued their "soak the rich theme", and called for the top rate of tax to be raised back to 50%. I argued that this would drive entrepreneurs abroad, stunt economic growth, and reduce the very revenue that the public services need.

Health tourism became a topic, thanks mainly to the UKIP leader Nigel Farage. I argued that NHS should charge overseas visitors for treatment, insist that future visitors take out health insurance prior to visiting the UK (just as UK citizens are required to do when visiting overseas). The exception would be those seeking asylum from atrocities, who should still be treated on the NHS as an emergency case.

Later that day, the Welsh Nationalists echoed their Scottish counterparts by announcing that if the UK as a whole voted to leave the EU, but Wales voted to remain, then Wales would veto Brexit. This Celtic lock failed to recognise that in the referendum of September,

2014, the Scots voted decisively to remain in the UK, and as such, the UK wide decision would apply to all parts of the United Kingdom.

On 3rd April, the subject of school place shortages came up (particularly a problem in Brighton & Hove), and I argued for central co-ordination, so that surplus places could be reallocated to areas with shortages, combined with limiting benefits to immigrants for 6 months, pending result of EU referendum, which if I were in a position of power after the election would be held in October, 2015.

On the same day, UKIP's economic spokesman, Patrick O'Flynn MEP, announced that UKIP will be "voices of fiscal responsibility" in the next Parliament, and "categorically ruled out a Tory coalition."

This prompted me to tweet to Paul O'Flynn and politics home that, as the Labour/SNP were regrouping to form a "progressive" alliance, then "an alliance of Tory, patriotic Labour, UKIP and DUP is the only way to defeat Labour/SNP alliance, and maintain defences."

Also on 5th April, the Lib Dems announced that "further and faster" rises were to be a "massive priority" for post election coalition talks. The next day, I tweeted that people earning as little as just over £8000 pay NI, and called for raising the threshold to £8900 across the UK; this would be financed by scrapping the Barnett Formula.

On 8th April, the Labour Shadow Treasury Minister announced: "This is not a tweak, Labour are abolishing the non-dom rule." I announced that Labour's abolition of non dom status will drive entrepreneurs abroad, reduce revenue for NHS etc.

Later the same day (this was the day after the disastrous Argus hustings), I tweeted on The Argus web page asking readers to fire at questions at me, the Independent candidate for Brighton Pavilion, to make up for the previous night's debacle.

Later that day, just after my highly successful performance at the Civil Liberties hustings, I made the case for a British Bill of Rights, ensuring criminals are deported, and prisoners cannot vote. I also said that if elected MP, I'd call for a British Bill of Rights.

On 9th April, I announced my defence policy on politics home. I advised that Tories will renew Trident, but not reverse troop cuts, Lab reduced Trident to appease SNP, while UKIP + Lib Dems would downgrade Trident. In addition, the Greens would abolish Trident. I announced that as Independent for Brighton Pavilion, I'd cut aid and have 2 aircraft carriers plus aircraft now, recruit 30,000 troops, and build all combat aircraft in the UK.

On 9th April, 2015, my nomination as Independent Candidate was confirmed, and I placed a link to my website, where people could read my manifesto. I also reiterated my key manifesto pledges.

On 11th April (the day I started my canvassing), the Tories pledge NHS spending by £8 billion per year was called a "fantasy" by Labour – and by myself! I tweeted that the Tories had not told the people how they would boost funding by £8 billion per year – apart from vague promises of "economic growth", which from the prospective of the global slowdown of 2016 seems foolishly optimistic. I announced that Labour's mansion tax would ultimately reduce revenue. I called for scrapping Barnett Formula, and use £2.5 billion of this for NHS + social care fund, to prevent A&E admission. I also called for charging binge drinkers who use A&E – this proved immensely popular on the doorstep, and that if MP for Brighton Pavilion, I would campaign for this.

On 12th April, the Tories announced they would raise the inheritance tax threshold to £1 million (for a couple). While as a committed free marketer, I have always favoured reductions to all taxes, I did not think this was a priority, while the low paid and small businesses were faced with high NI and business rates. I tweeted that this was not a priority. With millions on low pay, the NI threshold should be raised from £8060 to £8933, funded by scrapping the Barnett Formula. I also called for carers to be paid the living wage, funded by cutting overseas aid.

On the same day, the Green party leader (Natalie Bennett) announced on the Andrew Marr show that they would introduce a 60% top rate of tax, stating that "Some people are taking too much out of society." What Green and other leftists always fail to realise is that the wealthy entrepreneurs actually give a huge amount to society, by creating the jobs, and billions in revenue for our public services. I tweeted, "This [60% top rate of tax] will cause entrepreneurs to leave UK in their droves. If MP, I'll never vote for tax rises."

On 14th April, David Cameron announced his new Right to Buy Scheme, based on a "brown field regeneration fund."

I announced my own right to buy scheme for council and housing association tenants, provided that for every house sold, another is built. This would create a virtuous circle. I proposed £12 billion of QE for 200,000 social houses by 2020. This could be done due to record low interest rates, and will create high paid jobs and increase housing supply.

On 16th April, entirely of my own volition, I tweeted my warnings about Russian aggression, and how it directly impinged upon national security. I tweeted, "National security is the silent issue in this election. A Russian warship and 2 bombers strayed close to UK territory. Russian bombers were over RAF Lossiemouth when the typhoons were scrambled. The scrapping of Nimrods without a replacement effectively places the UK without reconnaissance ability; Russians can track movements of UK forces, but not vice versa." I called for investment in UK satellite reconnaissance.

On 19th April, Vince Cable announced that "It would be difficult to work with either the Conservatives or Labour", but would do so in the "national interest."

I tweeted, "A Grand Coalition is needed, made up of Tory, UKIP, DUP, and patriotic Labour. Committed to EU referendum in October, 2015, more troops, 2 aircraft carriers and fighters, tax cuts for low paid and small businesses, and NHS and social care integration."

On the same day, the SNP revealed their true intentions when their leader Nicola Sturgeon announced on the Andrew Marr show that SNP MPs will be able to "change the direction" of the next government "without bringing that government down."

I tweeted in response that "An SNP presence/influence in the next government will endanger security of UK, as Trident would be undermined/scrapped."

And....

"A Grand Coalition of Tory, UKIP, DUP and patriotic Labour is an essential counterweight to a Labour/SNP pact."

On the 20th April, Sturgeon commenced her next battle in the SNP ground war: to wit, to offer the "hand of friendship" to voters across the

UK, as she launched her manifesto. Her rationale was that there were innumerable leftist voters in England and Wales who bemoaned an "austerity – lite" Labour Party, but their hopes would be realised even if Labour only won 275 seats or so, as the 50 SNP MPs would combine with Labour to forge an Alliance.

I tweeted in response, "The SNP has no right to offer policies to the rest of the UK, nor seek to govern a nation it wants to leave."

I highlighted the reality of a Labour SNP pact, and the danger it posed to national security: "Unless Labour scraps Trident, SNP veto budgets. If MP for Brighton Pavilion, I will do all I can to stop Lab – SNP pact."

Back on 19th April, Ed Balls (Labour's Shadow Chancellor) bemoaned the Lloyds sell off, saying we "must make sure the taxpayer does not get ripped off again" by the Lloyds share sale. What Balls & Co never realised was that taxpayers are ripped off when governments nationalise businesses, as higher taxes are required to buy the shares, and compensate shareholders. I favoured the government's share sale; indeed, I would have gone further, and privatised RBS and Lloyds in one fell swoop, a la Big Bang!

I tweeted in response, "Selling shares finally gives a taxpayer a stake in Lloyds; proceeds used to cut deficit. It is public ownership in the best sense of the word."

On 20th April, Ed Miliband announced on welfare and the "undeserving poor", that it's "not for politicians to tell parents whether they can have more children."

I tweeted to Ed Miliband and politics home that "Limiting child benefit to first 2 children (unless triplets, etc) will encourage responsibility."

On Tuesday, 21st April, the BBC's Daily Politics commenced a series of high quality debates on key election issues, with spokesmen from all 5 main parties. The debates were chaired with vigour by Andrew Neil and Jo Cockburn. As the debates commenced, I announced that I was the Independent Candidate for Brighton Pavilion, and that I was my own "party's" spokesman on the issue of the day!

The first debate was on foreign affairs. I announced that the UK must reinstate search and rescue mission. I argued that if the UK controlled our own borders, then UK would have the space to accept its fair proportion of refugees.

I argued that Labour's veto on airstrike against IS in Syria undermines UK security, and that we must have 2 aircraft carriers (with aircraft) with 1 carrier placed within striking distance of Syria.

I went on to say that the 0.7% of GNP committed to overseas aid is not value for money. £6 billion of our aid is spent "on our behalf" by EU. Cut £4.5 billion from aid, to recruit 30,000 troops, 2 aircraft carriers + aircraft. This would equate to 2% of GDP on defence.

When UK's role in the EU was discussed, I tweeted that "UK global influence would increase if we left EU, as we would have our own seat at World Trade Organisation."

When the debate was over, I tweeted that "It's shameful that Russian aggression was ignored in Foreign Affairs debate. A conspiracy of appeasement! People in disputed territories [Crimea, and the Donbas] must have a referendum, buttressed by aircraft carrier presence near Russia."

On 22nd April, the economy debate was held. I mentioned that none of the parties mentioned NI employee thresholds, which I said should be raised from £8060 to £8933; this would cost £2 billion, and would be funded by scrapping the Barnett Formula. Low earners would be up to £1000 better off.

The Tories announced the need for £12 billion of welfare cuts, but refused during the election to say where those cuts will come from. I argued that vulnerable people need to know where the Tories £12 billion of cuts will come from.

I argued that to reduce the deficit, child benefit should be limited to the first 2 children, which would save £12 billion over the course of a Parliament. The deficit would be further reduced by privatisation if Lloyds and RBS, and contracting out HR and IT. This strengthened deficit reduction programme would lend credence to a programme of QE investment in infrastructure, which would result in higher paid jobs and more revenue.

I linked the cost of living to the need to control immigration. I argued that mass immigration drives down wages, increases benefits, reduces tax revenue, and drives up housing costs. I went on to argue that outside the EU, the UK could control immigration, a points system, and encourage UK residents to take jobs.

I argued that the UK business has nothing to fear from leaving the EU. The main argument is that the EU has a massive trade surplus with the UK – this has been the case ever since we joined in 1973. The EU wouldn't impose tariffs against the UK. UK must forge free trade areas across the world, as this would result in cheaper food, and new export markets.

The UK has always lagged behind its industrial competitors (USA, Japan, and Germany) in capitalising upon technological innovations. On 26th April, I proposed a new plan to encourage graduates to take up engineering, to enhance our industrial base, essential for productivity, and preventing an excessive reliance on property and speculative finance. This plan involved reducing tuition fees for medicine, science and engineering by raising fees on humanities, arts, and media courses. Thus the policy would be fiscally neutral, the government would save money as engineering graduates would find lucrative employment, enabling them to pay off their loans.

On the same day, Ed Miliband hit out at "special interests" opposed to labour's rent cap.

I tweeted that rent controls would discourage investment, and reduce supply of rental properties. Under the laws of economics, and profit maximisation, rents would be hiked before controls occurred. I argued that rent controls would hurt tenants. I signed off my saying that I spoke not only as the Independent candidate for Brighton Pavilion, but as a private tenant. I went on to call for 200,000 social housing units, to increase supply, and stabilise rents and prices. I also argued that demand had to be reduce by immigration controls; impose a delay of 6 months before immigrants could claim benefits, pending EU referendum in October, 2015.

Later that day, my calls for a Grand Coalition to provide an alternative to a Labour/SNP pact were echoed by Sarah Wollaston (Conservative MP), when she called for a Tory-Labour grand coalition. I responded by reiterating my call for a coalition of Tory, patriotic Labour, DUP + UKIP, and that if elected MP, I would support such a Coalition.

On 27th April, the Daily Politics hosted the home affairs debate. I argued that as UK is currently unable to control EU immigration, UK people are often priced out of jobs. Open borders also prevent the UK from admitting genuine refugees fleeing atrocities in Syria.

I went on to call for merge the police forces into 7 authorities, scrap PCCs, and reinvest the savings into frontline policing.

On the Snooper's Charter, I argued for a balanced bill; target those likely to commit atrocities, but that if the entire population were monitored, this would be a propaganda victory for terrorism.

I argued for a proportionate penal system, pushing for minimum sentencing, and using rehab as an alternative to prison for first time drug users, where no other crime has been committed. Early release must be ended, and intercept evidence should be used in terror trials.

On 28th April came the debate on defence. I argued that Russia and IS demonstrated the need for stron defence at all levels. We need satellites to monitor Russian movements, renew Trident, 2 aircraft carriers and aircraft now, 30,000 troops, funded by cutting aid.

I argued that it was no coincidence that Russian and IS aggression occurred after UK defence cuts. When the UK resolve weakens, aggressors are strengthened.

I called for the reintroduction of control orders, use of intercept evidence in terror trials, to reduce 90 day detention without trial.

Under stern questioning from Andrew Neil, the Green spokesman said they would allow people to join Al Queda and IS; I tweeted this proves their total unfitness to govern, either locally or nationally.

It appeared that the Labour spokesman highlighted the Labour split. Sometimes, Labour would reduce Trident to 3 submarines; this would mean that the at sea deterrent would not be continuous as it is with 4.

Andrew Neil highlighted my point about weakening defence resulting in aggression, when he said that if Ukraine had kept nuclear weapons, Putin may not have invaded the Ukraine. I argued that if Ukraine had been a NATO member, again Putin would not have invaded. I argued that UK must help Ukraine to join NATO.

While the Tories committed to 0.7% of GNP for aid, they would not commit to 2% GDP for defence. I reiterated my call to redistribute funds from aid to defence. I called to cancel the JSF, and build our own combat aircraft. I called for the Queen Elizabeth to be launched this year, and rent a UK carrier until the Prince of Wales is ready in 2020.

My warnings about reduced defence were highlighted when a senior defence chief advised that the UK cannot deploy a single army division long term; I reiterated my call to recruit 30,000 troops.

Later that day, GDP growth was slower than forecast, causing a clash between David Cameron and Ed Balls. I tweeted that slow growth has partly been caused by highest business rates in the developed world. If elected MP, I'd call for permanent rate relief on premises with rateable value of up to £12,000, and £1000 discount for shops, restaurants and pubs. This would cost £1 billion, and would be funded by cutting overseas aid. To further boost employment and growth, NI threshold should be raised from £8060 to £8933 across UK, costing £2 billion, funded by scrapping Barnett Formula.

On 29th April, The Times published an open letter to the incoming Prime Minister, advising it would be "irresponsible folly" to abandon Trident. I tweeted that if elected Independent MP for Brighton Pavilion, I would vote for full renewal of Trident, with 4 submarines, to ensure continuous at sea deterrence. I reiterated my call for 2 aircraft carriers and aircraft, and to recruit 30,000 more troops.

On the same day, the Daily Politics hosted the health debate. I criticised the Tory and Lib Dem unfunded proposals to invest an extra £8 billion per year in the NHS. I advocated my proposal to scrap the Barnett formula, and reinvest £2.5 billion for health and social care integration.

A common misnomer during the campaign was to equate the involvement of private firms in the NHS with privatisation; using private firms to expand capacity free at the point of use is NOT privatisation. I also argued that such competition drives up standards.

Too often, the debate on the NHS is a Dutch auction, with each party trying to outbid the next in how much it pledges to spend. As with Tory and Lib Dems, their proposals were unfunded, and relied upon economic growth, which of itself cannot be guaranteed. We now know that the NHS chief's call for additional investment was reduced from £16 billion to £8 billion, to ensure acceptance by the Conservatives. Labour's proposal to raise £2.5 billion from a mansion tax was self defeating, as people would downsize, and the revenue would decrease. Extra spending is inevitable, but my proposals were realistic, and sought to create a truly One Nation NHS by scrapping the Barnett formula, and reinvesting £2.5 billion of the savings in the NHS in England and Wales.

The use of existing funds must be justified before pledges of extra spending are made. I tweeted that binge drinkers should be charged for the treatment on A&E. This would deter such behaviour and ensure staff are paid for extra work.

I argued that home care workers are paid less than the minimum wage, as travel time is not included. The current system causes carers to leave, and disrupts care. I argued that home care agencies must pay their carers the living wage and abolish zero contracts hours, and that this would be paid for by cutting aid.

On 30th April, I had a 5 minute slot on Juice FM, a local radio station in Brighton. I was asked how as an Independent Candidate I could make a difference, and whether I had a chance of winning. I explained that I was the only Independent Candidate in Brighton Pavilion (the other independent had withdrawn), I am free to advocate policies, free from party discipline. I have funded the campaign entirely from my own funds, and am thus free from vested interests. If elected MP, my freedom from party label would be an asset when piloting bills through the Commons to rebuild defences, cut taxes for small businesses and the low paid, and integrate health and social care.

I used my phrase "When UK resolve weakens, aggressors are strengthened" to justify rearmament. I argued that if people wanted a mainstream MP, who would get on with the job, then I was their man!

On 2nd May, I announced on my website and on Twitter that if elected MP for Brighton Pavilion, whether or not there was a hung Parliament, I would propose bills to integrate health and social care, cut taxes for low paid and small businesses, rebuild defences, and bring forward the EU referendum to this October. I also reiterated that I would vote against a Labour/SNP Queen Speech.

On 4th May, I added my name to several MPs and other candidates who called for the reversal of the DPP decision re: Lord Janner.

Later that same day, I commented on celebrity endorsements, a practice I don't normally follow. This was prompted by an email from Juice FM (on which I had been interviewed a few days earlier) to all parliamentary candidates, commenting upon Russell Brand's endorsement of Greens in Brighton Pavilion, and Labour nationally. My message was uncompromising, and stood up for the man in the street. Due to the popularity of Brand amongst youth, this may well have cost me votes. However, I felt it was right to condemn his actions, after calling for people not to vote, and combined with his atrocious conduct over the years.

"Hi Nick,

As part of making our coverage as fair as possible I am writing to ask if you have a response to Russell Brand backing a Labour vote in the UK and endorsing Caroline Lucas for Brighton Pavilion?

Please reply to this email with a response, if you wish."

I responded thus:-

"Dear Rose,

Many thanks for your email. While I do not criticise Russell Brand in these politically fluid times for backing one party in Brighton Pavilion, and another party nationally, (I support neither Labour nor Green), I do take issue with him endorsing parties when he has repeatedly advised people not to vote. I take it as a compliment that Russell Brand (with his behaviour and conduct over the years), has not endorsed me as the next MP for Brighton Pavilion. Celebrity endorsements do not matter at this election. What matters are the views of tens of thousands of people who work hard, play by the rules, and look after their families."

I did not receive any feedback to my comments; I suspect it cost me many votes, although how many would be impossible to say.

On 5th May, the Daily Politics held the welfare debate.

I tweeted a main concern of the election campaign; who would be affected by the Tories' undisclosed welfare cuts. I reiterated my policy of limiting child benefit to the forts 2 children (born after 2016). The cuts to benefits had made working people poorer; I proposed raising the NI threshold form just over £8000 to £8933; people earning £8000 would be £1000 a year better off.

I endorsed the Tory proposal to reduce the benefit cap to £23000 across the UK.

The subject of the living wage came up; I could not pledge a large, across the board increase. This would be a too expensive, irresponsible pledge which would raise and dash the hopes of the low paid, and impose an extra burden on business. I proposed a living wage for care workers, many are paid below the minimum wage, as they're not paid for travel time. This would be paid for by cutting overseas aid.

I argued that the Green's proposal for guaranteed income is unaffordable, and would increase welfare dependency.

The most controversial element of the Coalition's welfare reforms was the bedroom tax. I argued from the beginning that there must be clearly defined exemptions, for example, for those who need a bedroom for carers, and where special needs children cannot share a bedroom. I pointed out that there is money available for tenant who downsize, and this must be accompanied by building more single occupancy accommodation, to reduce the need for the bedroom tax in the first place.

I argued that the rise of food banks is a scar on the conscience of the nation. The food banks grew in earnest in the aftermath of the financial crash of 2008/09; they didn't suddenly emerge during the Coalition government. It was a failure of socialism; the government spent at a far higher rate than the economy grew. When the crash came, it was the most vulnerable who were affected the most by the cuts.

I was the first to support cutting benefit for those who don't need it, and punishing those who fraudulently claim it. However, the immediate cutting of benefit BEFORE a review of that person's entitlements has taken place causes abject poverty, and the necessity for food banks. Often, the person has not responded to a letter, but this is often because they have an illness or disability which may prevent them from doing so, and this is where social services and GPs have a role. The sudden cutting of benefits is a false economy; apart from the obvious human suffering this causes, extra public expenditure is spent upon rectifying the situation caused by poverty, such as medical treatment. Integration between health and social care will not only achieve the best outcome for the person, but will encourage the best value outcome for the client. I speak more of this in the chapter on health and social care. In the welfare debate, I argued for a yellow card system, so that an investigation takes place before a decisions is made about benefit sanctions.

Later that same day, I tweeted that I support "Bite the Ballot."

Also on the 5th May, I emailed several small businesses, with an eve of poll plea, claiming there were 48 hours to save small businesses, and that my policies were the most business friendly and pro – growth:-

"There are now 2 days until one of the most critical elections for decades.

The result of this election will determine whether the UK continues to prosper, or whether the economic recovery is halted dead in its tracks by a Labour/SNP government.

If the Greens are re-elected, there would be another anti business vote in a hung Parliament.

As an Independent Parliamentary Candidate for Brighton Pavilion, economic growth is a central plank of my manifesto.

Abolishing the deficit by 2020 is essential to keeping interest rates low, and cutting taxes.

Business rates are amongst the highest in the developed world. The Conservatives have only given temporary relief. Labour's rate cut is at the expense of higher corporation tax for larger firms, which would damage enterprise across the economy.

If elected MP, I would present an Enterprise Bill, to cut the deficit by limiting child benefit to the first 2 children born after 2016, privatising Lloyds and RBS, contracting out HR and IT throughout central government, and tackling tax evasion. The Bill would make permanent the rate relief for small businesses with a rateable value of up to £12,000, and make permanent the £1000 discount on shops, pubs, and restaurants. This would be funded by cutting overseas aid.

I would bring forward the In/Out EU referendum to October 2015 (to reduce uncertainty), and I would campaign for the UK to leave the EU, so businesses are free from EU regulations, and can trade freely with the growing economies outside the EU.

If elected MP, I would never support a Labour nor a Labour/SNP/Green government, as they would destroy the economy.

In Brighton Pavilion, the Conservatives are third, and will not win in Brighton Pavilion. I urge you to vote for me as your MP."

On 6th May, the day before polling, the Daily Politics held their last debate, about trust in the political system.

I called for PR for all elections, English votes for English laws, people (not fellow MPs) to recall MPs, an elected Lords, and votes at 16.

Later that same day, I sent an eve of poll tweet. I quote it here in full:-

"To all voters in Brighton Pavilion:- If elected Independent MP, I'd represent all constituents free from party restraint. I've self funded my campaign, I'm free from vested interests. I'd present bills to integrate health and social care, cut NI for low paid, cut small business rates, rebuild defences, build social housing through QE, and bring forward EU In/Out referendum to October, 2015. These commitments funded by cutting aid + scrapping Barnett formula. To patriots, a vote for me isn't a wasted vote, as Tories 3rd in Pavilion. If MP, I'd vote against Labour or Labour/SNP/Green govt."

I concluded this historic tweet by quoting my old campaign slogan.

"Voting for None of the Above? Vote for Nick Yeomans Independent tomorrow. Read manifesto @nickpavilion15.co.uk"

While my tweet was directed at voters in Pavilion, I made no bones of the fact that it was accessible to voters across the UK. This gave me the chance to influence undecided voters about the perils of a Labour minority government, which would effectively mean a LAB/SNP pact, and consequent economic ruin, and a weakening of our defences. As with my comments about Brand, this again may have cost me votes in Pavilion (due to the sizeable student population who are more sympathetic to the SNP).

Later that same day, I discovered from a more technologically aware friend, the delights of the hash tag, a phrase that has an entirely different connotation for those who grew up in the 1970s or before!

I hash tagged daily politics, and politics home, where if people clicked my hash tag, they would be directed to my manifesto.

I wish I had discovered the hash tag earlier, as my messages would have reached a wider audience.

7TH MAY 2015: POLLING DAY

Thursday, 7th May dawned bright and crisp. Just after 7 am, in a Jasper Conran single breasted anthracite grey suit, and a gentleman's long coat of the same brand (adorned with my rosette), I ventured to the polling station, a Community Hall in Compton Street, just off the Seven Dials in Brighton. I was the first of the candidates to cast my vote, and beat the other national leaders to their respective polling booths.

I renounced my usual polling day routine of listening to Beethoven and Elgar, and after canvassing the definite and the almost definite (driving my trusty Citroen BX Diesel!), I adjourned (in casual attire) to Saltdean to dine with friends.

To me, music can set the mood, and prepare the psyche for the rigours of election night. Beethoven's Fifth Symphony in C minor is the quintessential election night music. I always aim to play it just before going to the count; if one is journeying by car, and provided the journey is at least 40 minutes, then play it on one's car stereo. When I stood for school's council elections in the early 1990s, I played it on the election night; in 2001 (as UKIP candidate for Billericay) I played the Fifth on the Blaupunkt stereo of my Citroen ZX Diesel shooting brake, en route to the count.

My pre election lunch in Saltdean prevented me from listening to the Fifth – upon returning to my flat, I barely had time to dress, let alone listen to music. I managed to find an interval (at approximately 2 am) when I sneaked out of the count, and leaning against a pillar, listened to the Karajan recording of the Fifth on my smart phone!

The opening V for Victory theme of the opening movement lends dramatic urgency to the opening of the count, and the enormity of the decision, both for the UK, and the world – not for nothing was this used as the Morse code signal for victory for the Allies in World War II. The lyrical and poignant second movement (my personal favourite piece of any symphonic writing) lends serenity, and reinforces the feeling that the campaign is over, and allows time for reflection over the campaign; the struggle against Fate epitomised by the Third movement calls to mind the uncertainty of the final result, and the forces ranged against democracy; this movement leads (without a break) into the triumphant finale, where freedom thrashes the forces of tyranny. The fifth is perfect pre – election musical escapism; as with all escapism, one is dreaming about what might be (and indeed, could very well be), in contrast to the *actualite*. But that is surely the point; the actualite seeks to be changed, and musical escapism from it should be enjoyed by all humanity.

I arrived at the Brighton centre just before 10 pm; before entering the count, I sat alone reading my election victory/defeat speeches. I always prefer solitude at the commencement to the count. I was surrounded by several Labour and Green activists. We all awaited the exit poll with excitement and anticipation; I was pleasantly surprised (the Greens and Labour shocked) when the exit poll predicted the Conservatives as by the largest party (although at this stage without a majority), at least 80 seats ahead of Labour. This prompted one of the most memorable comments of election night when Lord Ashdown proclaimed that if this poll was true, then he would publicly eat his hat!

Having presented my ticket, I entered the count itself. The enormity of the building epitomised the enormity of the decision the people of Brighton Pavilion, Brighton Kemptown and Hove were to make towards the fate of the United Kingdom over the next five years.

The three parliamentary constituencies each had an allocated table (the local wards had their own tables), and the wards in those constituencies each had their own dedicated table. Initially the votes were sorted, and spoilt ballot papers were discarded. I as one of the candidates along with Purna Sen (Labour) and Clarence Mitchell (Conservative) were asked to adjudicate the validity of contested ballot papers. I recognised the irony of one ballot paper, which had a gigantic cross, followed by the words "None of the Above!" Apart from this being my election slogan, I noted that the cross was nearest to my name of the ballot paper, and the voter had drew a line down all the names, but the line had not reached my name; as the candidates were listed alphabetically, I was at the bottom of the ballot paper! As such, I jokingly said that this should be a vote for me!

Other classic examples of contested ballot papers are where the cross is between 2 candidates. Obvious invalidated papers are those where the voter has specified 2 or more candidates, where no candidates' boxes have been ticked, where the paper is completely blank, or where someone has written a comment, instead of identifying their choice.

In contrast to the count at Hove Town Hall, where one could keep one eye on the local count, and another on the national count unfolding on TV, at the Brighton Centre, one had to egress into the foyers to keep abreast of national developments, and miss the local proceedings. This was further compounded by the ban on smart phones in the count (and thus following proceedings on the internet) When it was clear that the final declaration would be hours away, I decided to watch the national proceedings.

I saw live the defeat of Ed Balls (I was personally elated, as this was a defeat for authoritarian Brownism); then of Vince Cable (who had fought honourably for his policies while in Cabinet); and then of Danny Alexander, who would undoubtedly played a key role in any Cabinet containing Lib Dems. Of all the losses, I personally regretted Danny Alexander's loss the most. He had been a brave Chief Secretary to the Treasury under George Osborne, and recognised the need for deficit reduction, but in a manner that protected the most vulnerable.

Nick Clegg held on to his seat, Mark Reckless lost Rochester & Strood for UKIP; and Nigel Farage sadly failed to win a seat in Parliament for UKIP in East Thanet.

Throughout the evening, I walked along the long tables, and gauged the feel of the count. By now, the votes were being sorted by candidate, and each candidate had a tray, so we could see the votes piling up in each ward. As dawn broke, each ward had 1 tray for each candidate. My tally in Withdean remained stubbornly low at 2 votes throughout the night; this was surprising, as this was an area I canvassed heavily, and in which I received a very positive response.

I didn't notice much of a showing in many of the other wards; Preston Park was respectable. Interestingly, I scored by far the highest tally in Hanover & Elm Grove, an area I had not canvassed, and in my mind was the most Green ward of the entire city. I attribute this to the fact that I carried out many social care reviews there within recent memory (I hadn't carried out any reviews in Withdean or Preston Park for the best part of a decade), and that people had remembered this. This can be the only reason, and it strengthens my theory that my relatively high poll (in terms of independent candidates) was attributable to a positive personal reputation.

My aim in the campaign was obviously to win, and become the Independent MP for Brighton Pavilion. I knew this was most unlikely, but I prepared assiduously for being an MP nonetheless.

If victory eluded me, my aim was to come a close second, or beat one of the main five parties. Again, this was unlikely, but perfectly possible. The abysmal showing by the Lib Dems would be exacerbated by the anger of the large student population, when the Lib Dems reneged on their tuition fee pledge. This could cause their vote to fall to such a low level, that I would beat them by default. Obviously, the vast majority of students who voted Lib Dem would vote Green (who pledged to abolish the fee outright) with Labour as a second choice (who pledged to reduce the fee from £9000 to £6000). My more realistic pledge (and after all, an honest and achievable policy would have more credence with students) to reduce fees on economically viable degree courses (such as computing, biotech and engineering) by raising fees on less essential courses such as humanities. This policy would have caused a mix reaction from students studying particular courses, but would have made a difference. Sadly, due to a low profile campaign, and my list of priority pledges not including tuition fees, this did not occur.

I also hoped to beat UKIP amongst voters who, like me, wanted the UK to leave the UK but had a broader world view, and recognised the need for intervention in humanitarian crises and the need to stand up to dictators.

The aim would have then to have come fourth, behind Green, Labour and Conservative, but beating UKIP and the Lib Dems.

In reality, my minimum aim was to avoid coming last – to avoid being beaten by the Socialist Party of Great Britain. I was fortunate in that I was the only Independent candidate to stand for Brighton Pavilion – another Independent had dropped out. This gave me a unique selling point in Pavilion. My aim was thus to score the highest among independents/microparties, the latter being represented by the SPGB. I was also keen to gain a triple figure vote – so many independents seemed to gain 60 – 70 votes.

As the count neared its conclusion, I noticed that I was consistently ahead of the SPGB in all wards, so I was fairly confident I would achieve my objective of being the highest scoring independent/microparty.

Brighton Kemptown was the first seat to declare, and I was relieved when Simon Kirby retained his seat. Hove then declared, and Labour regained the seat, after the Tories won it in 2010. I was sad that Graham Cox (a councillor and a police officer) was not elected, as he was a genuine candidate, and had worked very hard.

Finally, at about 7:30 am, the Pavilion result was declared. I was told the result moments before the public announcement. Due to the high profile of Caroline Lucas, the result was broadcast on national TV and radio. I was thus disappointed that addresses were limited to the winning candidate and the runner up – a live broadcast of my speech would have attracted publicity for my campaign and my message.

A cheer erupted from each side of the hall simultaneously as my result was announced, in true stereophonic fashion.

In the event, I obtained 116 votes, 28 ahead of Howard Pilott, the SPGB candidate. I increased the Independent vote share above the 2010 level, simply because no Independent stood in 2010. The insurgent parties (UKIP, Green and SPGB) also increased their vote share, while the main three lost votes. Pavilion was the insurgent's election, where 3 radical parties and an Independent gained votes at the expense of the main three parties.

The greens gained 10.5% of the vote. Correspondingly, the Lib Dems lost 11%, and Labour lost 1.7%. It is safe to assume that almost all of the Lib Dem vote went to the Green, and Labour and Conservative (who lost 0.9% - a total of 2.6%) contributed to the bulk of UKIP's increase of 3.2%.

As an armchair psephologist, I think that remaining 0.6% of UKIP's vote, and the votes for the SPGB candidate and myself, came from people who had never voted before – I suspect mainly from people who had not voted for years.

The election result also demonstrated the increased sophistication of the voter. While the Greens retained the parliamentary seat (and indeed increased their vote share and majority), yet they lost control over the council, and indeed came third. This meant that the maladministration by the Greens was not translated into the national result.

I emerged from the town hall at about 8:30 am, and had a full English breakfast. It was while tucking into this hearty meal, that the Tories gained an overall majority; in the event, they obtained 37% of the vote and a majority of 12 seats.

In my opinion, this was an ideal result, as it meant there was no doubt about the legitimacy of a conservative government, but the majority was sufficiently small to prevent complacency, and they would need to recognise the views of UKIP and DUP + UUP on EU, and the need for a strong defence.

That morning, sleep eluded me, due to a mixture of adrenalin, and very noisy road works outside my flat.

POSTCRIPT:- AFTERMATH OF THE ELECTION

Later on Friday 8th May, over a celebratory cigar, accompanied by vintage port with cheese and water biscuits, I tweeted my thanks to the 116 electors who had cast their votes for me. I wrote a suitably valedictory message on my web page:-

"As the only Independent Candidate in Brighton Pavilion, I'd like to thank all the people who voted for me on Thursday. I received 116 votes (0.2% of the vote). I beat the Socialist Party of Great Britain, a century old party. We faced an uphill struggle with a massive Green surge, but it is vital to fly the flag for our unique brand of democratic unionism, strong defence, and quality health and social care for all.

A Conservative majority government (with healthy pressure from the DUP, UUP & UKIP), creates a Unionist majority. As a patriot, I wish the new government well, and I urge all my supporters to join me in holding the government to account, campaigning for strong defence and national self determination.

The SNP won all but 3 seats in Scotland, but 50% of Scots (and 90% of the UK) voted for Unionist parties. There is no mandate to break up the Union, even if Scotland alone is considered. I proposed a fair constitutional settlement for the whole UK, by scrapping the Barnett formula, but in return, granting Scotland equivalent tax raising powers; proportional representation and boundary reform, so all votes count; giving people (not fellow MPs), the power to recall MPs; an elected House of Lords.

I will continue to be an Independent candidate, and campaign for the UK to leave the EU in the referendum. I will stand again at the next general election, funding my own campaign, and free from party restraint. Follow me on Twitter #IndependentforBrightonPavilion."

I decided to remain as the Prospective Independent parliamentary candidate for Brighton Pavilion. This (and the associated website) gave me a platform to call the government to account, and to propose my own policies, and as a platform for an Independent candidate to advocate UK withdrawal from the EU. In addition, I decided to maintain a rolling manifesto and budget, so that if an early general election was caused (most likely if the UK voted to leave the EU, causing such political upheaval that an election would likely occur), or a by election in Pavilion, I would be ready to stand.

After the election, I proposed my Queens Speech (virtually identical to the one published before the election) and an alternative budget (to the Conservative Budget of 8th July 2015) which I posted on my website on 23rd July. I had left my pre-election budget on the website for 2 weeks, as it maintained the priorities I had set out during the election. In addition, the crafting of an alternative post election Budget took longer than usual, due to costing credible policies that reversed the government's regressive measures.

The ditching of the electrification of the Pennines (included in my transport programme) and cutting the tax credit threshold was an immediate rejection of the One Nation principles for which this government claims to be the custodian.

The Budget maintained my main priorities (redistributing funds from overseas aid and Barnett formula to NHS + social care, rebuilding defences, a homelessness plan, cutting NI for low paid, and a living wage for carers). The Chancellor astounded friend and foe alike when he committed 2% of GDP to defence. This was morally right, but politically not very astute. Such an announcement before the election would have trumped UKIP, and prevented many staunch Tory voters from voting UKIP, or, like myself, standing as an independent on a rearmament platform!

The 2% figure was not the central aim of my defence policy; what matters is to devise the world role for the UK (standing up to IS in Iraq and Syria, deterring Russian aggression, with spare capacity to fight a Falklands scale operation), and then building the military hardware and recruiting the manpower to implement this policy. When 2 aircraft carrier capability from 2015, renewing Trident with a UK system without delay, recruiting 30,000 extra troops, and a submarine missile defence system were all taken into account, this amounted to a £4.5 billion increase in defence expenditure, which would have increased defence expenditure to 2.19% of GDP, upon immediately forming a government.

I supported the measures to limit child tax credit to first 2 children born from 2016, but I did not support reducing the threshold for tax credits from £6420 to £3850. This hurts the working poor, and harms the very people the Conservatives claim to support through their One Nation policies. This accounted for a large part of the £12 billion savings to the welfare budget that the Conservatives did not have the courage to state PRIOR to the election.

This very punitive measure would have only saved £3.3 billion over the Parliament, barely a quarter of the government's proposed welfare cuts. Again, the proposed cuts to PIP would only have saved £1 billion over the Parliament.

My proposals to limit child benefit and child tax credit to the first 2 children born from 2016 alone would have saved £12.4 billion over the Parliament (the government acknowledged that £12 billion a year is simply not achievable within the foreseeable future, and extended their deficit reduction plans to almost the end of the 2015 Parliament, and their 2 child limit does not kick in until 2017). I maintained my plans to freeze working age benefits (excluding pensions and disability benefit to 3 years, 1 year longer than that proposed by the Chancellor. This would have saved £4.5 billion over a Parliament.

The net result of these measures (savings from child benefit and tax credit combined with reversing the tax credit threshold) would have reduced the welfare bill by £13.6 billion over the Parliament, yielding £2.37 billion more welfare savings than the government's Budget. At the same time, these measures would have protected the low paid, pensioners, and the disabled, and two humiliating climb downs by the government, who are now paralysed from reforming welfare (including sensible polices such as the 2 child limit) in the future.

On 3rd August, 2015, the Chancellor announced that he would sell off Lloyds shares.

On 4th August, 2015, the Chancellor announced sell off of RBS shares, set to raise £2.1 billion, earlier in July. As stated in my manifesto, I would have privatised the entirety of RBS and Lloyds, a la the Big Bang privatisations of the 1980s, but when the banks were more commercially viable, and the price would have increased, which would prevent an inflationary surge of mass purchase. This would have yielded £20.55 billion at 2014 prices (even more in 2016, the most likely date I would have privatised the banks). This would have provided an immediate £20 billion down payment of the deficit, early on in the Parliament, to insulate the UK against external financial shocks, and give credibility for the £30 billion QE programme for energy production, social housing and integrating the transport networks of the North, a genuine One Nation programme that would make Ed Miliband choke on the phrase!

Combined, these welfare reforms and bank privatisations would have already yielded £34.15 billion, well above the £30 billion outlined in the Charter for Budget responsibility. This did not include the savings from contracting out HR and IT at central government, or the increased revenue from economic growth.

Despite the government's mantra of 100 days of action to get policies on the statute book and set the agenda for the next 5 years, two major constitutional reforms were significantly delayed. This is short sighted, as constitutional measures are cost neutral, and can facilitate faster legislation, and a slender majority of 12 can be whittled down to a minority government due to defections, resignations and deaths. This occurred to the John Major government of 1992 – 1997.

The first was the Bill of Rights, not included in the Queens Speech of July 2015. While the Lib Dems vetoed replacing the ECHR during the Coalition, this should not have prevented Conservative policy groups from preparing draft Bill of rights, enshrining the key principles, in particular, that the right to family life should not prevent a foreign criminal from being deported. These key principles could and should have been put in the Conservative manifesto, and a draft Bill included in the Queen's Speech. A controversial measure such as this needs to be implemented very quickly, while the government has public good will behind it, and while it still has a clear majority.

The second was EVEL (English Votes for English Laws). The emboldened SNP tested the new government within weeks, and it is deeply regretful that the government failed this test.

In mid July 2015, the SNP decided to vote against the weakening of the fox hunting ban, even though this ban affected England. This was a highly opportunistic manoeuvre, designed to highlight the narrowness of the Conservative majority. In many ways, the SNP's manoeuvre was unavoidable; the EVEL could only have been implemented by autumn 2015 at the earliest, due to the complexity of the issue, and to ensure proper Parliamentary scrutiny. The SNP would have exploited this vacuum in any event. But, 24 hours later, Cameron responded by capitulating, by dropping the free vote on weakening the hunting ban, and that the draft EVEL proposals would allow Scotland to veto English only legislation.

Cameron chose an issue whereby without support of other parties, the Tories would be unlikely to win a weakening of the hunting ban, as they have proposals of their own.

It would have been far better to call a vote on an issue that would unite the Tories with a large bulk of the Labour party – for example, the renewal of Trident. This would have decisively routed the SNP, and discouraged the SNP from stalling tactics to defeat laws they do not like, but which do not affect Scotland. By dropping legislation before the vote in Parliament in fear of the SNP, the government has strengthened the SNP to try and thwart the crucial Trident vote due in 2016.

A clear EVEL Bill should have been put before the Commons, whereby English vote for English laws at every stage of a Bill's passage through the Commons (combined with scrapping Barnett formula and giving Scotland equivalent tax raising powers). This would have won a massive majority of the Commons, amongst many Labour MPs as well as all Conservatives and unionist parties, and would have settled the balance of power within the Union once and for all.

As I write this in August, 2015, the fluidity of politics, and the alliance of opinion across parties rather than within them, has reached unprecedented heights.

The 2% commitment of GDP to defence was advocated by backbench Tory MPs, UKIP, Liz Kendall, the Labour leadership contender, military chiefs, and NATO and US defence spokesmen. While not claiming credit for adoption of this policy, I was ahead of the pack in calling for rearmament from early 2014, and the dissemination of my policy on Twitter, and the following from Tory MEPs and military people clearly was a decisive factor in the government adopting the policy.

At the general election, I called for the EU referendum to be held in October, 2015. Again, the fact that the Conservative MEP David Campbell Bannerman, and many other Conservatives, were following me on Twitter, this must clearly have had an influence on the government bringing forward the referendum date to 23rd June, 2016.

The idea of using QE for infrastructure (at the election no one else was proposing this) is now being advocated by Jeremy Corbyn, the favourite to become the Labour leader.

My policies appeal to the bulk of the Conservative party, the social patriots of the Labour party, the unionist parties of Northern Ireland, and millions of people who have never voted before. My campaign is the first stage on the road to the realignment of politics, the smashing of the old party system, and a new politics of conviction.

My vision for the United Kingdom is Unionist and democratic, combines a low tax, competitive economy with quality health care and welfare for those unable to help themselves, combines string defence with a moral foreign policy, standing up to dictators. It is a clear vision, a genuine One Nation vision, a radical yet sensible alternative to the hard left vision of state control, and the far right vision of isolationism and impoverishment of the working poor.

CHAPTER 3

Creating One Nation – A Fair Constitutional Settlement for the UK

AN EARLY EU REFERENDUM FOR AN INDEPENDENT UK

The Westminster Establishment talks of devolution of powers "throughout the United Kingdom", and yet ignore the greatest threat to our democracy; the UK's membership of the EU. Restoring the right to elect and remove those who make the laws we obey, and taxes we pay, would restore democracy to the whole United Kingdom, and is a cause behind which the whole country can unite.

Since 1992, when the Maastricht Treaty effectively ended the sovereignty of Parliament, I have consistently called for the UK to withdraw from the EU.

I believe that the laws we obey, and the taxes we pay must be decided by those whom we elect to and remove from office. This is a fundamental democratic principle.

Regardless of one's views on the UK's membership of the EU, the uncertainty created until the referendum is held is disadvantageous for businesses, and prevents the UK from pursuing an effective foreign policy. I will focus on the impact of EU membership on our economy, and foreign policy in the relevant chapters in this book. Here, I will focus upon the constitutional impact of EU membership, and the timetable of a referendum, and Brexit.

From the mid 1990s, when I first became involved in politics, I have consistently argued for a legally binding referendum on the UK's membership of the EU, and have consistently advocated UK withdrawal from the EU, because renegotiation would have been futile. This in turn is attributable to renegotiations being based upon compromise and horse trading; if the UK had won powers on immigration, in return, we would have transferred powers over business regulation, for example.

I welcomed David Cameron's decision, in January 2013, to hold a legally binding referendum by the end of 2017. Undoubtedly motivated by the advance of UKIP, and the disproportionate negative effect this has on Conservative votes, it was nonetheless an opportunity for those who seek a self governing nation to achieve that goal.

Cameron's credibility was undermined by his reneging on the "cast iron guarantee" to hold an EU referendum on the Lisbon Treaty – although admittedly this had been ratified before he became Prime Minister. However, the logical next step would have been to pledge an In Out EU referendum. At the 2010 election, I believe this would have prevented UKIP from splitting the votes in many seats in the West Country and the Midlands, and would have resulted in a Conservative majority, unhindered by Liberal Democrats in the implementation of the referendum. Indeed, I wrote to Cameron before the 2010 election to advise him of this. The Lib Dems effectively prevented Cameron from holding the referendum before the 2015 election; hence his pledge by the end of 2017. This in itself was dependent upon Cameron winning the next election (in 2013 this was hardly a foregone conclusion), and with an outright majority, to prevent Lib Dems forcing Conservative to renounce the referendum, as the price of Coalition support.

In the run to the election, I had repeatedly argued for the election to be held as soon as possible. I always argued for October, and this would not clash with general, local and assembly elections in May/June. I pledged that, if elected an MP, I would have called for the referendum to be held within 6 months of the election.

From the time I launched my election campaign in September, 2014, I had thus argued that the EU referendum should be held in October, 2015. Holding the referendum in May 2015 would have been too close to the general election.

My EU referendum bill would have renounced the "Celtic Lock"; both the SNP and Plaid Cymru have argued that, even if the whole UK votes to leave the EU, this should not occur if either Wales or Scotland has voted to remain within the EU. In September 2014, Scotland voted decisively to remain in the UK, and Wales has never voted for an independence referendum, and as such, they cannot prevent the UK leaving the UK if the UK (of whom Wales and Scotland are a part) votes to withdraw.

I also advocated that, should the UK people decide to leave the EU, then the powers over immigration, trade, tax, would be returned to the UK immediately. In addition, the annual transfer of funds from the UK to the EU (the net contribution) scheduled for each November, would not take place. This would have been achieved by applying sunset clauses to the budget contribution, and the UK's application of the Common external Tarriff, and to the European Communities Act 1972, which placed EU law above UK law if there was a conflict between the two.

Had I become Prime Minister, Brexit would have been the settled policy of my government, and to which all public policy would have been geared.

I believe this would have restored the trust in the political system; a government taking a clear stand, and leading public opinion. Had we formed a pre electoral alliance (as I had dearly hoped), then the voters would have been clear about our policy.

The risk of this strategy would have been the possible endorsement of EU membership in the referendum. However, had we formed a government with Brexit the central policy, this would have been unlikely.

A FAIR CONSTITUTIONAL SETTLEMENT FOR THE WHOLE UK

ENGLISH VOTES FOR ENGLISH LAWS

It is undemocratic that Scots MPs can vote on matters affecting England, while English MPs cannot vote on Scottish only matters. The Hague proposals still allowed Scottish MPs to veto an English only bill. The debacle whereby the SNP voted against the hunting law (which only affected England) was a clear statement of intent from the SNP, taking advantage of the inevitable gap before any reform re: English votes could be implemented. Cameron responded by capitulating, and watering down the bill. This has set a dangerous precedent and has all but scuppered plans for reform.

Many think that an English Parliament is the answer, as this would contain solely English MPs voting on solely English legislation. The English parliament solution has a certain constitutional tidiness to it. However, in an ear of cuts to social services, and a healthy cynicism towards professional politicians amongst the electorate, this would lack democratic legitimacy. It would create yet another tier of government; the Westminster Parliament already votes on English laws and taxes, and British wide laws, taxes and spending. By definition, the majority of the Westminster Parliament consists of MPs representing English constituencies.

English MPs should vote on English only matters, and Scottish MPs should vote on Scottish only matters, at all stages of legislation.

A FAIR FUNDING SETTLEMENT

In these times of austerity, gains and sacrifices should be shared across the whole nation. The Barnett formula grants Scots higher funding per head that the rest of the UK, which allows free social care for the elderly. Meanwhile, the rest of the UK is subject to means tested charges for social care, on a declining grant.

Although Devo max was never on the ballot paper, it is clear that Scots do want a greater deal of fiscal autonomy. This is reasonable, as Scotland has always had a different education and legal system from the rest of the UK. The Barnett Formula creates resentment in England, Wales and Northern Ireland at the generosity towards the Scots, while it creates resentment in Scotland as it acts as a deterrent against greater devolution.

Complete fiscal independence is tantamount to complete national independence; it would break the union, and prevent the harnessing of technological and entrepreneurial innovation to the growth of the whole UK. It would lead to unfair competition among the nations of the UK.

I proposed during the election a bold plan. Devo max should do what it says on the tin.

The Barnett formula should be scrapped, but in return, Scotland would be granted tax raising powers to raise the equivalent revenue currently provided by the UK taxpayer. The £4.5 billion should be redirected to extending business rate relief long term (£1.010 billion) and increasing spending (£2.5 billion) on social care and health in England and Wales.

NO TAXATION WITHOUT REPRESENTATION

AN ELECTED HOUSE OF LORDS.

The necessity of a revising chamber was clearly presented when, on Tuesday, 27th October, the Lords voted to delay the government's proposed changes to the tax credits, most notably the propose to reduce the threshold for the lowest paid.

While the Lords cannot reverse a fiscal decision of an elected government, approved by the House of Commons, it can delay it. As the House of Lords is currently unelected, it lacks the moral and democratic authority to veto fiscal legislation passed by the House of Commons, even though the government had no democratic mandate to introduce tax credit changes.

Any legislative body that can introduce, amend and veto the taxes we pay and the laws we obey must be answerable to the people. I propose that the House of Lords becomes an elected Senate, with the powers to veto tax and spending measures that are NOT in a government's manifesto.

The House of Lords is far too large. Instead of 800 peers, there should be a limit of 100 peers, 2 for each county of the United Kingdom (that is, including Northern Ireland).

The Senate should be elected every 10 years, half way through the fixed term Parliament. If the Senate were in place now, the next elections would be held in October, 2017, October 2027, and so on, every decade.

Holding Senate elections half way through a Parliament would represent the mid term opposition to a government, and increase the representation of the Opposition parties, this holding the government to account.

The elections would be held under PR.

FIXED TERM PARLIAMENTS AND VOTES OF NO CONFIDENCE

I wholeheartedly support the fixed term parliaments – this automatically removes the advantage of incumbency to choose the date of the election.

This democratic measure has been countermanded by the rule that 2/3 of Parliament must support a motion of no confidence in the government of the day, thus prompting a dissolution of Parliament. This means that even a minority government is immune to being defeated in a no confidence vote. It places excessive power in the hands of the executive to thwart the will of the people through Parliament. Had the 2/3 rule applied in March 1979, then the Callaghan Labour government would have survived! This rule must be amended so that a simple majority in Parliament can defeat a government, thus lead to a dissolution of Parliament.

LOCAL GOVERNMENT

At a time when the central government grant to local councils (which accounts for 75% of local government expenditure) is being cut, there is a huge amount of duplication of duties, and separate IT systems, which slow down service delivery, productivity, and waste of dwindling public resources. With district, town, and county councils, the local populace face no less than three separate authorities organising their local services. This does not include Whitehall and Brussels; Scottish and Welsh residents face no less than 6 layers of government with their respective Assemblies. The time has come to reduce the tiers of government to 2;

free from the shackles of the EU, the voter would hold Westminster, and their single local authority to account.

The time has come for the most radical reorganisation of local government since 1974.

Essentially, all existing councils should merge to become City or County Councils, otherwise known as unitary authorities.

These unitary authorities would enhance regional autonomy without creating additional regional assemblies, reduce duplication and bureaucracy. Critically, they will generate efficiency savings (along with a directive to contract out all IT and HR systems, a policy of one chief executive, and 1 director for each department). All of these savings should be reinvested into the front line, create the machinery to build social housing, and to integrate heath and social care. The county council would shadow the respective NHS Authority, as the first step towards integration. Prior to that, the social care element of the central government grant would be protected – a £1.25 billion increase over the previous financial year. In short, larger councils will be better equipped to tackle inequality, and with social care funding safeguarded, this will encourage councils to set their priorities.

The recent proposals by the Chancellor to devolve the raising and expenditure of business rates to local authorities will exacerbate inequality, as many of the lower income authorities cannot afford to cut rates, thus preventing many businesses locating to these areas, to create jobs, and provide revenue for essential services. Furthermore, as a result of these proposals, councils will receive less money redistributed from central government.

The 50:50 ratio (whereby councils retain 50% of the rate revenue, and redistribute 50% to central government to be redistributed) should be reintroduced. The aforementioned UK wide business rate tax cut (fully costed) will ensure that all businesses benefit from the tax cut, and will not be dependent upon the whim of local authorities.

Contract out all HR & IT systems across local government, and a policy of one chief executive per department. Reinvest these savings into the front line.

VOTING REFORM

It is well known that votes are not fairly distributed across the UK, and yet the Lib Dems reneged on the commitment to reform boundaries of parliamentary constituencies. Boundary reform would make seats in parliament more accurately reflect the democratic wishes of the people. This is a measure that doesn't require a referendum. Boundary reform must be taken out of the political arena The Electoral Commission (with its unimpeachable record of integrity) should be charged with the responsibility of redrawing parliamentary boundaries. This will ensure a fairer representation of the people's democratic choices at Westminster.

While the British people voted 2 to 1 against Alternative vote in the 2011 referendum, the result of the 2015 election clearly calls for a fresh debate about proportional representation. UKIP obtained 3.8 million votes (12.6% of the vote), yet only obtained a single seat. Had a proportional system been used, UKIP would have obtained 82 seats. The Conservatives would only have obtained 240 seats, 86 seats short of a majority, and would have been dependent upon UKIP, DUP and UUP support to form a wafer thin majority alliance. Indeed, had the Conservatives combined with UKIP, DUP + UUP, they would have had 332 seats, 1 seat more than they obtained on their own in the election result.

In Scotland, the SNP gained exactly 50% of the vote, yet obtained 56 of the 59 seats (or 94.9% of the seats). Under PR, they would have obtained 29 or 30 seats, depending upon how the votes were distributed among the seats. In any event, Scotland was evenly divided between a party that wanted Independence, as against the other parties, all unionist.

In 2015, it is indefensible that legislation (including a referendum to determine the UK's self determination) can be vetoes by peers whom we do not elect and cannot remove. There should be a fully elected second chamber, to reduce political patronage. The Senate (representing the whole UK) would be elected every 10 years, in the mid term of a Parliament.

The Senate would have power to veto legislation (including budgetary) that is not in the manifesto. The Senate would be elected by pure PR, and consist of 100 senators, 2 from each county.

THE POWER OF RECALL OF MPS

In light of the expenses scandal, the right of constituents to hold their MPs to account in between elections must be enshrined in law. The power of recall must be given to voters (who would be able to sign a petition to force a referendum on whether or not to sack their MP) and not a committee of MPs, as carried in the Queen's Speech of June, 2014.

Douglas Carswell and Mark Reckless showed great courage and integrity by submitting himself for re-election when they defected from the Conservatives to UKIP. It should be mandatory that whenever an MP changes parties, they must submit themselves to their constituents for re-election.

REDUCING THE VOTING AGE TO 16

If people can fight and die for their country, start work, and get married at the age of 16, then people must have the right to choose who represents them in Parliament.

Further to the aim of getting a much broader cross section of people engaged in politics, the boggiest obstacle is the lack of finance and of time to pursue a political career.

I speak from bitter political experience. The reaction of Conservative Party managers (both locally and nationally) to the fact that I worked full time as an employee was one of disbelief and incredulity; this demonstrates how dangerously out of touch the parties are.

If politics is ever to regain the trust and confidence of the British people, then it must represent a broad cross section of the British people, in terms of age, gender, and disability, but critically, in terms of social background.

The major political parties should set aside some of their funds for bursaries, and recruit people who are not financially independent, and be selected as candidates.

The idea of party machines ensuring each candidate abides by every dot and comma of the manifesto are long gone; open primaries would enable the public in that constituency to select their candidates.

CHAPTER 4

A World Role for the United Kingdom

- THE EUROPEAN UNION vs NATIONS STATES. UK WORLD ROLE
- DAVID CAMERON'S "DEAL" – 19th February, 2016.
- BREXIT – THE POSITIVE CASE
- CUTTING DEFENCE: A DANGEROUS GAMBLE
- THE CASE FOR REARMAMENT
- THE THREATS FROM STATES: RUSSIAN EXPANSIONISM
- THE RENEWED RUSSIAN BUILD UP
- ISLAMIC STATE and RUSSIA'S BETRAYAL
- IMMEDIATE UK ACTIONS TO CURB IS AND RUSSIAN AGGRESSION
- STRENGTHENING CONVENTIONAL AND NUCLEAR DEFENCE
- COUNTER TERRORISM MEASURES
- SANCTIONS
- CURBING RUSSIAN AGGRESSION
- CRIMEA AND UKRAINE:- RESTORATION OF TERRITORIAL INTEGRITY, FREE ELECTIONS AND NATO MEMBERSHIP
- THE REFUGEE CRISIS
- TRANSITION TO DEMOCRACY IN SYRIA

The UK has always been a world player; this has been our history, and it is our destiny, for good or ill. The UK has played a huge role in shaping world history over the centuries.

The UK has trade links with the English speaking world forged over centuries, and fought alongside the United States to defeat Nazism and Communism.

Today, the UK's economic might (we still have the broadest trade links of any nation in the world) has been weakened by the emergence of China as an economic (and military) superpower. Later in the 21st century, it is anticipated that China will be the most powerful nation on earth, both in terms of its economy, and its military.

This would be a catastrophe for the freedom of mankind. Along with Russia, China is a member of the UN Security Council, and in concert with Russia continuously votes against intervention in Syria and action against Russia. In short, China is blackmailing the world into fighting dictators and extremists, and so long as it retains this power, any action against Russian expansionism and IS extremism is doomed.

The United Kingdom must use its new found independence from the EU, to forge free trade areas with the rest of the world, and become the leader of the world's largest trade area. This is essential to the UK's economic future, to create the jobs and the revenue needed for the NHS. But it will also create an alliance of free trading nations (and nothing more) so powerful, that it will eclipse China, and dwarf the sclerotic EU. Weaknesses in China's economy will accelerate this process. This new, bold Anglosphere of like minded nations (in concert with the United States) will forge the economic might and military presence to challenge the hegemony of an emergent world policeman in the form of China.

THE EUROPEAN UNION V NATION STATES

I start with the UK membership of the EU, which is so pivotal to our world role, with regards to how the EU prevents the UK from assuming a world role.

The EU was formed by French and German statesmen determined that Europe should never take up arms ever again. The first step was the European Coal & Steel Community of 1950, designed to pool the coal and steel resources of France and Germany, so that the forces of production would not be used by one country against the other in aggression.

Winston Churchill (at this time leader of the Conservative Opposition) called for the ECSC as the first step towards a United States of Europe. There are two great myths about what Winston meant by this.

Firstly, what Winston meant by a "united states" was an alliance of free nations; he was not calling for a federal Europe. How could he have credibly done so, when he led the liberation of the occupied European *nations* [author's emphasis], rather than a fictional entity called *Europe*?

Secondly, that through his clarion call, Winston called for UK inclusion into this European initiative. Winston's words on Europe [written in 1930] speak for themselves:

"We have our own dream and our own task. We are with Europe, but not of it. We are linked but not combined. We are interested and associated but not absorbed."

In 1944, Winston said:-

"If Britain must choose between Europe and the open sea, she must always choose the open sea."

Often, these two statements are attributed to a single statement uttered by Winston in the 1950s. Regardless of this rather academic point, it is clear that Winston would, at the very least, oppose British participation in the European project, as indeed he did during his Indian Summer premiership of 1951 – 1955.

For good measure, what is beyond doubt is that in 1963, in his 89th year, whilst seated up in bed with a glass of brandy, with his budgerigar Toby perched on his head, Winston told Field Marshal Montgomery that he adamantly opposed Macmillan's application to join the Common Market.

Clement Attlee resolutely opposed UK participation in the ECSC, as indeed did Sir Anthony Eden. Eden's patriotism was further demonstrated when he declined to attend the Messina conference in 1955, which laid the foundations for the Common Market. Pro Europeans argue that this was a strategic mistake, as it prevented the UK from forging the Common market into a more open, and Atlanticist organisation. This is a common mistake of the European lobby. Had Eden attend the conference in 1955, he would have been unable to steer the putative Common Market in such a direction. The die had been cast in 1946, when the European project had been anchored around a Franco German axis; had Attlee tried to steer the Common market in an Atlanticist direction, he would have failed even at that early stage.

Ironically, it was Eden who unwittingly determined that the UK would eventually join the EEC. In 1956, Eden sent forces to recapture the Suez Canal, seized by Colonel Nasser. Eden had not consulted the Americans (it was a clandestine operation with France and Israel), and in the run up to the 1956 presidential election, President Eisenhower was most reluctant to support such a war. As the UK was heavily dependent upon US support for sterling, Eden had to withdraw. This led not only to Eden's resignation in 1957, but to Dean Acheson, the US Secretary of State proclaiming that the United Kingdom had "Lost an Empire, but not yet found a role."

The man who succeeded Eden as Prime Minister, Harold Macmillan, was the first Prime Minister to attempt to join the EEC, an objective he announced in 1961.

Macmillan, keen to restore the "Special Relationship" with the USA, combined with the failure of the UK to procure an indigenous nuclear deterrent when the V bombers were withdrawn from service as nuclear bombers later in the 1960s, purchased Polaris missiles from the USA, under the infamous Nassau Agreement. Harold Wilson was correct in the first part of his statement when he said that Polaris was "Neither independent, nor a deterrent."

Macmillan was instrumental in forging "the winds of change", granting independence to former colonies, and thereby transforming the Empire into a Commonwealth.

It was Macmillan's vision of a United Kingdom playing a key role with the USA, and the Commonwealth, that was decisive in de Gaulle's veto in 1963.

Harold Wilson became Labour Prime Minister in 1964. Arguably even more pro Commonwealth than Macmillan, and the most eurosceptic Prime Minister until Lady Thatcher, Wilson announced that he would join the Common Market in 1966. In October, 1967, de Gaulle again vetoed the UK's entry, on the grounds that the UK was heavily dependent upon US resources to maintain the value of sterling. Ironically, within a month, the UK was forced to devalue sterling, and with it, threw off the shackles of American imperialism, and could pursue an economic and foreign policy compatible with membership of the Common Market.

Edward Heath (who had led the first application to join the Common Market in 1963) became Prime Minister in 1970, and was hell bent on joining the Common Market, on abject terms, regardless of the cost.

Heath was aided by the resignation of de Gaulle as French President in 1969; his successor Pompidou was far more amenable to accepting the UK into the EEC.

After successful negotiations with Pompidou in 1971, in October of that year, Parliament voted overwhelmingly to join the EEC; the intervention of 69 Labour rebels was critical. Had Labour unanimously voted against the EEC, then Heath's application would have failed, as Conservative rebels would have negated the government's majority of 30. It is most likely that the UK would then never have joined the EEC, as the oil crisis of 1973 commenced a decade of industrial chaos.

Heath broke new ground by attempting to run a foreign policy in alliance with the EEC, as opposed to the USA.

Wilson's renegotiation in 1975 secured a fairer deal for the developing nations, and secured a crucial opt out from the euro; had Heath had his way the UK would have joined the euro by 1980; these are oft overlooked substantial gains from a much maligned renegotiation strategy.

Lady Thatcher firmly anchored the UK in alignment with US foreign policy; she had paved the way in 1979, pursuing a rigorous policy against communism. Lady Thatcher was instrumental in opposing the deepening of the EEC, and wanted to widen it, to include the former communist countries of central and Eastern Europe.

The failure of enforced integration of disparate nations was tragically demonstrated by the fragmentation of the former Yugoslavia in 1991-2. The catastrophic failure of the EC to intervene (despite it being a *European* Community) was obvious, aided by a policy of appeasement by Major and Hurd. The Dayton accords of 1995, and the intervention to stem genocide in Kosovo in 1999, clearly demonstrated that only intervention by the UK and USA, with like minded countries such as France, can avert humanitarian crises and defeat tyranny.

The experience the Balkans also clearly demonstrates that the tide of history favours the emergence of nation states, rather than a world of regional "blocs."

Within the EU itself, the victory of the Front Nationale in France, the election of a Greek government on an anti – austerity ticket, and the rise of UKIP in the UK all indicate a tide against the integration of the EU, and a strong trend towards national self determination.

The Establishment fear that outside the EU, the UK's influence would be weakened. This is wrong. On the contrary, it would be strengthened.

Currently, the UK is one of 28 nations represented by a single EU trade commissioner at WTO trade meetings. Outside the EU, the UK would have its own seat at the WTO, and would be free to forge free trade deals with the rest of the world, unencumbered by needing to obtain the permission of 27 other EU members.

The EU channels the overseas aid of member states to the donor countries. The UK has limited control over its aid budget (of 0.7% of GNP). It is argued that the UK would not be able to influence aid, without exercising power through the EU institutions. If the UK withdrew from the EU, then we would withdraw from our application of the Common External Tariff, and this would enable developing nations to export their foods to us, so they can escape poverty through growth, and so we can reduce the need for aid in the first place.

DAVID CAMERON'S "DEAL" – 19TH FEBRUARY, 2016.

The deal reasserts primacy of EU Treaties. 19 out of 22 substantive points in Cameron's EU deal either reinstate the status quo, or will not be delivered by renegotiation.

In terms of sovereignty, the UK allegedly gained a clear statement that the UK is not committed to further political integration, and that the phrase "ever closer union" cannot be used to foster UK involvement in EU integration. These protections will not be effected until a new Treaty is signed, after the referendum in June, 2016.

In September, 2015, Juncker announced a new EU Treaty, splitting the EU into 2 groups. There will be a core group of the 19 eurozone members, and an "outer core" of non eurozone members, including the UK. The White Paper will be released in early 2017. Only then can the European Parliament instigate the procedures for the new Treaty, which may not be concluded until 2025. If the UK votes to remain in the EU in the 2016/17 referendum, then this will be a mandate to remain in the UK until the terms of the new Treaty are clear.

There is no guarantee that the treaty would be ratified; even if it is, it will be long after the referendum. So there is no guarantee of the reforms being implemented even if the UK votes to remain. Therefore, it is inevitable that, if the UK voted to remain, then the UK will be further subsumed into the further political and economic integration of the EU.

Even if the reforms are enshrined in Treaty change, the threshold for national parliaments to block new EU laws are high; 14 other member states, or 55%, actually higher than the current 33%, would need to agree. So there is no national veto, and the UK can be outvoted. Furthermore, the 19 eurozone members have a permanent 65% majority under the qualified majority voting system, and regularly outvote the UK. This means that opting out of eurozone rules is incompatible with EU membership.

In any event, on 7th June, 2015, the veto over EU legislation was discarded by Foreign Secretary Philip Hammond.

The former attorney general Dominic Grieve said that EU law remains supreme in the UK, and that it would be in breach of ECJ.

Judges in the ECJ could "override whatever legislation we had passed, because that it the way in which the EU operates."

(Vote Leave 10th feb 16)

The single market is due to completed in digital products and banking, and to cut red tape.

The opt outs on economic governance and ever closer union are set to be ratified by treaty, but only after the referendum. There is a danger that if UK voted to remain on the basis of the deal, then there is no guarantee that the protections of the deal will be enshrined in the Treaty. Further to this point, Angela Merkel told fellow EU leaders that "on the question of amending the Treaties, we do not know if we will ever have a change of them." French MEP Sylvie Goulard described the deal as "legally dubious and politically dangerous." Cameron lodging the deal with the UN confers no legal status whatsoever. The ECJ trashed the Danes' cast iron guarantee (Vote Leave 22nd Feb 16). Lord Pannick QC advised that the deal "would have no binding effect in our courts or in the Court of Justice of the EU." (Vote Leave 25th Feb 2015)

The self destruct clause means that if the UK votes no, then the "set of arrangements....will cease to exist." This gives hope to my idea of a speedy Brexit, perhaps trashing the 2 year exit stipulated under Article 50 of the Lisbon Treaty.

Over a 7 year period, migrants will receive no in work benefits for the first 4 years, with the entitlements going up over the 7 year period, the gradient decided by the EU. This is a watering down of the outright ban (and even the 13 year period), but EC advises that the brake will be activated immediately after the EU referendum.

Despite the Conservative manifesto pledging that EU nationals in the UK would not send back any child benefit children not resident in the UK, this has been watered down so that children receive a reduced amount, based upon the standard of living in that country. (Telegraph, 20th February 2016).

Despite Cameron pledging that all EU migrants must have a job offer prior to arriving in the UK, this was not even part of his renegotiation.

This emergency brake may be defeated by the ECJ, or delayed possibly until April 2017, on the grounds that it constitutes illegal discrimination. As with the other safeguards, this is dependent upon treaty change, not even considered (and still less guaranteed) until after the referendum.

BREXIT – THE POSITIVE CASE

The draft deal reasserts primacy of EU Treaties. The draft deal will only have force if and when the treaty containing the proposed changes if ratified. There is no guarantee that the treaty would be ratified; even if it is, it will be long after the referendum. So there is no guarantee of the reforms being implemented even if the UK votes to remain. There is also no guarantee that, if the UK voted to remain, that the UK would not be further subsumed into the further political and economic integration of the EU.

A vote to leave must mean a vote to leave the EU, including the Single Market.

The Norwegian option in some regards constitutes an even worse deal than the status quo. The UK would be bound by Single Market rules, but have no say over the rules. Norway still has to accept free movement, and pay a budget contribution to the EU.

The UK can *access* the Single Market without being a *member* of the Single Market, governed by its rules, without accepting free movement, and without paying a budgetary contribution.

If opinion polls are to be believed, there has been a narrow majority in favour of remaining in a reformed EU. At the time of writing (January 2016), however, Brexit inclined voters are more inclined to change their mind than the "inners." In order to persuade wavering voters of Brexit, the campaign to leave the EU must focus on a positive vision for the UK outside the EU straitjacket. By focussing almost exclusively on immigration, the Out campaign runs the risk of running a narrow campaign, by ignoring the economic and democratic case for Brexit. And how the UK can spend the money currently spent on the EU budget.

My vision is not for the United Kingdom to retreat from Fortress Europe to hide behind the barricades of Fortress Britain. The whole purpose of withdrawal from the EU is to enhance the world role of the UK.

Outside the EU, the UK could control immigration, to give the space to accept refugees in times of crisis, to ease pressure on housing, health, and infrastructure, and to prevent the continual downward spiral of wages.

There are six positive reasons for Brexit, which must be reiterated day and night until the 23rd June, 2016.

1) For the UK people (through Parliament) to decide the laws we obey and the taxes we pay.

2) The freedom to control immigration to suit the needs of the UK labour market, and to ensure that public services, infrastructure, and welfare benefits are not overwhelmed. Controlled migration enables the UK to accept refugees.

3) The ability to strengthen security by operating unilaterally, and in concert with NATO allies and Five Eyes partnership, which EU threatens with EU foreign, defence and security policy. The ability to control our borders, and to deport foreign criminals and terrorist suspects.

4) The freedom for the UK to forge free trade deals across the globe, by having our own seat at the WTO. Outside the EU, the UK would access cheaper food and raw materials, in return for new export markets. The developing nations could escape poverty by accessing UK market, and reduce aid.

5) The ability to control our fishing grounds, access food at world prices, and encourage sustainable farming. Assume control over UK fishing grounds, and abolish the CAP in the UK, access food at world prices, and introduce a deficiency payments scheme, to encourage agricultural sustainability.

6) The abolition of excessive regulations through a bonfire of controls, and to ensure the competitiveness of the City of London

7) Redirect the £9.567 billion (the average annual UK's current net contribution to the EU budget from 2015/16 – 2020/21 [OBR]) to tax cuts for low paid, reducing VAT to 5% on building repairs (impossible inside the EU), NHS + social care, and apprenticeship tax cuts (replacing the apprenticeship levy). The rebate would be spent on an agricultural deficiency payments system. Automatically immune from eurozone bailouts and regulation. An independent UK will create more high skilled jobs.

There are many people who have valid reasons for wishing to remain in the EU, due to the perceived uncertainties of leaving. I will tackle these fears one by one, and attempt to reassure the undecided voter.

1). RESTORATION OF DEMOCRACY

Prior to Maastricht, foreign and defence policy, police, justice, borders, home affairs, asylum, immigration and human rights was undertaken at IGC level. The fields of EEC competence were trade, agriculture, competition, and environment. This changed with Maastricht; EU now assumes control in energy, humanitarian aid, education, health and human rights. (Boris Johnson, Sunday Telegraph, 6th March 2016).

In 1973, the UK had 17% of the vote share in the Council of Ministers – that is now down to 8%. On 72 occasions the UK has unsuccessfully attempted to block motions before the European Council.

Sir Jeremy Heywood, head of the civil service, published guidance which severely restricts access to Brexit ministers re: information, especially vital information re: welfare statistics, legal cases relating to EU law, and immigration figures.

The UK has been outvoted on ¾ of cases (or 101 since 1973, 16 under Cameron's premiership) we have taken to the ECJ, including price hikes on beer, tax hikes on energy saving materials by declaring the UK's 5% VAT rate on materials "contrary to EU law" (thus increasing energy bills by £100s extra per year), circumvention of social chapter opt out, prolonging of the worldwide export ban on British beef, and increasing the cost of house building. (Vote Leave, 2nd March 2016).

A red card veto can be issued if 55% of EU member states decide to block legislation on grounds of subsidiarity. There is no national veto. As the 19 eurozone members have a permanent 65% majority under the qualified majority voting system, and regularly outvote the UK. This means that opting out of eurozone rules is incompatible with EU membership.

UK has not blocked a single proposal placed in front of the European Council from becoming EU law. The UK has opposed 72 measures which have gone on to become law. UK has lost 101 out of 131 cases placed before the Court (Vote Leave, 10th March, 2016)

President of the European Parliament Martin Schulz declared any EU reform "would not be irreversible." Cameron's deal is worthless without Treaty change.

Since 1996, UK has never blocked a single piece of EU legislation.

Granting Westminster a veto over unwelcome legislation is due to be considered in the renegotiation. Surely, the only guarantee of Parliamentary sovereignty is to withdraw from the EU.

Remain argues that, in the event of Brexit, the UK will somehow be bound by rules that it has no say over; this is a fundamental nonsense. Post Brexit, the UK would be bound by rules that Parliament has chosen to retain, reject, or amend.

2). SECURITY

On 12th February, Cameron said that EU membership was crucial to tacking ISIS and Russia; this is nonsense, as EU judges make it well nigh impossible to deport the daughter in law of extremist cleric Abu Hamza, despite her being a convicted criminal.

Former head on Interpol says EU system is "like a hanging sign welcoming terrorists to Europe."

Powers of intelligence and police are controlled by EU Court – not us.

EU prevents us from removing criminals, such as the Rafacz case.

EU law forbids Schengen area countries from carrying out systematic checks on anyone with an EU passport from entering. How does this affect the UK? This enables terrorists fighting aboard to return to the UK, who do not need to pass through a single border from Greece to the English Channel. Other EU nations are introducing border controls; the UK must do so now, before we leave.

ECJ makes it harder for UK to strip citizenship from British nationals who have gone abroad to engage in terrorism.

Charter of Fundamental Rights stops UK from deporting foreign criminals and suspects if it would violate their "private or family life." ECJ is likely to accept case law based upon the alcoholic could not be sent back to a Muslim country. It also prevents European nations halting flow of boats across the Med which has cost so many lives.

EU is also planning to a EIA, European Intelligence Agency. US attorney general Loretta Lynch has warned that this is "seriously concerning" that EU is undermine sharing of info with key allies Canada, Australia and the USA.

EU has also caused problems re: defence procurement.

The treaty change won't be in place BEFORE the referendum, so if UK votes to remain, the substance of the deal may change after the referendum.

(Vote Leave, 15th Feb 2016)

Already, ECJ advised that it may rule that UK cannot deport criminals with children who are EU citizens.

In February, 2016, ECJ ruled against deportation of daughter-in-law of Abu Hamza. Miciej Szpunar (advocate general at ECJ) says deportation would deprive her of family life with her young son. Govt policy of deportation of foreign nationals sentenced to 12 months in prison is illegal when EU citizens are involved.

Even a British Bill of rights with a sovereignty clause would not change primacy of EU law, as it is enshrined in UK statute. So the ECHR is inextricably linked to EU membership, and therefore only Brexit can guarantee a truly British Bill of Rights.

(Sunday Telegraph, 07-02-16)

Major General Julian Thompson (who landed 3 Commando Brigade at the Falklands, and practices NATO plans for war against the Soviet Union) wrote on 29th Feb 2016 in the Telegraph the myths re: EU and security.

1). That the EU has kept the peace in Europe since 1945. It was the US Marshall Plan rebuilt the war torn European nations after WWII. NATO founded in 1949 also deterred the USSR from attacking. Not in the Basque conflict, nor Northern Ireland troubles, nor the Turkey Cyprus situation did the EU play a part in resolution of these conflicts.

   The Croation War of Independence was resolved by NATO manned UNPROFOR. The Bosnian War was resolved by Dayton Accords granting NATO authority. Albania unrest was also resolved by NATO, along with the first Kosovan War, and further unrests in Kosovo in 2008, and 2011-13.

2). That the US wants UK to remain in the EU. The US defence and security community want to retain the links with ATO, and Five Eyes Alliance (whereby UK, USA, Canada, Australia and New Zealand share intelligence), and actually believe that our EU membership undermines the UK relationship with NATO and other allies in terms of intelligence sharing.

3). That Brexit will aid Putin's Russia. The opposite is true. The euro crisis weakened southern Europe, and French criticism of NATO, thus duplicating mission, all reduce effectiveness.

4). That the EU helps UK to defeat IS terrorism through the European Arrest Warrant. State to State extradition works very well. The inability of EU to police its own borders enabled home grown Da'esh terrorists to get back into Europe to launch attacks. As members of the EU, UK is unable to stop those with EU passports entering the UK. The Five Eyes alliance is far more effective in countering terrorism. The UK can share intelligence on a case by case basis with EU member states. (Telegraph, 29th Feb 2016)

On 23rd March, 2016, Sir Richard Dearlove (former head of MI6) argued that Brexit would not endanger UK security, and would indeed enhance our security.

Sir Richard cited two main advantages of Brexit. Firstly, that the European Convention on Human Rights could be abolished, thus granting the UK the power to deport terrorist suspects. Secondly, that outside the EU, the UK could control her own borders, and thus control who enters the UK.

Sir Richard advises that intelligence co-operation is done on a bilateral basis, with nations inside the EU and outside, and that this would not change if the UK withdrew from the EU.

The Third Party rule "states that the recipient of intelligence from one nation cannot pass it on to a third without the originator's agreement."

Sir Richard also states that the "European Rapid Reaction Force has not matured into an effective expression of Europe's aggregated military power. Britain's defence interests remain firmly hitched to NATO." (Sir Richard Dearlove, Prospect Magazine, April 2016).

3). MIGRATION

EU Charter of Fundamental Rights prevents us from deporting violent criminals and gives EU court power over almost any security issue.

EU has taken our power to interpret vital 1951 UN convention on refugees.

Under EU law, UK is bound to accept the free movement of people, provisions controlled by EC and ECJ.

We have no control over who enters UK from Europe and no not control laws on hoe to remove EU passport holders from the UK.

EU law forbids UK from automatically denying EU citizens who lack travel documents entry into the UK, and from checking on a regular systematic basis whether EU citizens are lawfully resident in the UK.

In 2015, ECJ deemed that govt cannot require migrants from other EU states to have a permit issue by UK govt, even though permits form other EU nations are consistently forged, making it easier for terrorists to enter UK using forged documents.

EU law required UK to admit EU citizens with an EU passport, but we have no control over how the EU members issue that passport.

Some 440,000 jobs were created between September 2014 to September 2015, and ¾ were awarded to non UK residents.

In December, 2015, the number of foreign passport holders exceeded 5 million for the first time. In the last 4 years, the number of foreign passport holders has increased by 612,000.

There are now 2.04 million EU migrants in UK; a rise of 215,000 in 2015 alone. (Times 20th Feb 16) Net EU migration into UK was 172,000 Sept 2014 – Sept 2015. More than half the total of 323,000 total net immigration over the same period (Vote Leave 27th Feb 2016). 42% of EU migrants who arrived in UK came without a job offer (Vote Leave 25th Feb 2016)

According to HOC figures published in November, 2014, there were 252,000 working families from the EU claiming tax credits, and 48,000 single people. (BBC News, 29-01-16).

In January, 2016, the EU announced that the NHS no longer needs to check the qualifications of doctors and nurses coming to work in the UK from the EU. EU rules will give them electronic passports enabling them automatically to practice in hospitals and GP surgeries anywhere in the EU. Nurses will get these passports this year, with doctors getting passports in 2018. There will only be a 2 month deadline to check the qualifications – of this is missed, then the electronic passports will be missed. The GMC advises that these checks typically take 4 months. Also, GPs and nurses from EU will not be tested on their English language abilities – skills essential to prevent accidents occurring due to miscommunication.

This is yet again an example of the Prime Minister watering down the proposed renegotiation package.

EU leaders met in March 2016 to attempt to deal with the migrant crisis. This included "re-energised" talks to make Turkey a full EU member. The EU (thus including the UK) has agreed in principle to give 75 million Turks access to the passport free Schengen zone by June, 2016. This extends the visa free zone from the English channel to the Syrian border. In the interim, any migrant arriving in Greece from 20th March 2016 will be given a quick interview to determine whether they will be allowed to remain or be sent back to Turkey from 4th April. The returns scheme will need 4000 staff, and cost £235 million to administer. (Daily Mail, 19th March 2016)

A key concern is that the abolition of free movement works both ways; while the UK will be able to control immigration from both from the EU and outside, UK citizens will lose the right to settle, study, and work in the EU, as they currently can. While all EU mainland members are signatories of the Schengen agreement, UK citizens could still travel unfettered across the continent, subject to passport checks. However, as the UK would have abolished free movement, and because we are not Schengen signatories, the EU may well stop UK citizens travelling, studying, working or settling in the EU. As with trade barriers, the EU would be unlikely to do this, because of their dependence upon UK business and tourism. If the EU did impose reciprocal barriers to free movement, this is not the end of the world. Why should it be more difficult to apply to study, travel, work or settle in the United States than in the EU? Applying for visas would be a small price to pay for the restoration of our national independence. The concern that EU citizens in the UK would be sent to the EU, and vice versa, is unfounded, as if the UK leaves the EU, the EU would be obliged to grant permanent settlement rights to Britons living in Ireland and mainland Europe, and the UK would reciprocate this for EU nationals living in the UK. The Vienna Convention of 1969 enshrines this principle in law. (Allister Heath, Daily Telegraph, 02 Mar 2016)

The concern is the perceived unfairness of abolishing free movement to EU citizens, almost of Europhobia. This is nonsense. How can it be fair to allow free movement to EU citizens, but to deny this to non EU citizens, especially to our kith and kin in the British Commonwealth? The government's restriction on immigration by definition has to limit non EU migration, as the UK cannot control EU migration while we remain in the EU. This means that migrants enter the UK not based on talent, and what they can contribute, but simply because they are members of the EU. A policy of zero net immigration, with an annually amended cap based upon a points system, which assessed the demands for skills in the UK, should be the UK immigration policy post EU.

Integral to this must be a drive to make work pay, though cutting NI for low paid, apprenticeships. This will be aided and abetted by preventing the downward spiral of wages caused by mass immigration. A policy of ultimate zero net migration actually increases the capacity of the UK to accept refugees fleeing atrocities and natural disasters. A UK migration policy will be firm, but fair and humanitarian.

Cameron stated that if we left the EU, migrants currently in Calais could move to the UK overnight. The agreement between the UK and France regarding our borders in Calais was an agreement negotiated by UK and France in 2003, and is separate from the EU membership. In October, 2015, the French government advised that it had no intention of opening up the border, and confirmed this in response to Cameron's comments last week. Under the Locquet Treaty, France gains support form UK logistics in managing the migrant sites, and France has a commercial interest in maintaining their border controls, as SNCF has 55% stake in Eurostar. France and UK can terminate the Treaty, but there must be 2 years notice. Any cancellation of Treaty would result in UK extending carriers' liability to Channel Tunnel, ensuring passengers have leave to enter the channel tunnel and cross channel ferries. Outside the EU, UK would have more control over migration than as members of the EU. (Vote Leave 12-02-16).

Yet again, the threat of moving the border to Dover was mentioned in March, when France's economy minister claimed the UK's border controls in Calais could end if we vote Leave. In 2015, French interior minister Bernard Cazeneuve, said this was "not a responsible solution... It is a foolhardy path, and one the government will not pursue." The Locquet Treaty is separate from EU membership. Switzerland withdrew their application bid the same day.

It emerged in early March that there could be hundreds of thousands more migrants living in the UK that officials claim. While official figures state that 257,000 EU migrants arrived in the UK in 2015, over the same period, some 630,000 EU citizens registered for a National Insurance Number. In the last 5 years, 2.25 million EU nationals have registered for a NU number, but official statistics only reveal that 1 million EU citizens arrived in the UK over the same period. According to Eurostat, the number of asylum seekers coming to the UK increased by almost 20% in a year. UK received 38,370 asylum seekers, more than 15 other EU nations combined. The asylum seekers arrived to EU doubled from Syria, Iraq and Afghanistan almost double. UK powerless to deport illegal migrants as they have nowhere to go (Daily Telegraph, 4th March 2016).

UK will contribute to £500 million to new Turkey/EU deal (Leave EU 8th March, 2016).

4). TRADE

Another fear is the perceived loss of trade and jobs, due to fears that the EU will deny free access to the Single Market.

The EU preaches the gospel of free trade, but only within the EU. The EU is a customs union, imposing tariff and non tariff barriers against non EU nations. The tariffs average 1% (but this is 1% of massive value of trade, and make the difference between customers buying EU and non EU goods). The tariffs against motor vehicles are 10%, up to 20% on machine goods, whisky and textiles. The CET and CAP raise the price of goods and agriculture, subsidising production, thus making goods and foodstuffs artificially cheaper than world prices, thus stifling competition, and discriminating against non EU goods. This leads to EU members (including the UK) producing more of what we are worst at, and less of what we are best at producing. Our consumers pay excessive prices. As the UK imports far more from the EU than we export to EU at inflated prices, the profit goes into the EU companies. The loss of free trade is estimated to cost the UK 4% of GDP. (GPD 2014/15 was £1,808,712,000,000 (Statista); therefore, 4% of UK GDP = £72,348,000,000).

After Brexit, the UK would need to maintain regulations to maintain EU standards for exports to the EU, but this accounts for 10% of GDP.

Brexit is also said to threaten FDI; FDI enters UK due to return on foreign capital here. Post Brexit, FDI will continue, and increase, especially in the sectors favoured by free world trade.

(Patrick Minford, Daily Telegraph, 29th Feb 2016).

There are concerns as to whether the UK manage without an EU trade agreement. However, if the UK voted to leave, then WTO rules would be the default position, that of non discriminatory trade. This is the killer fact to forever bust the euro trade myth:- if the EU discriminated against UK exports, this would be illegal under the rules of the WTO (Time to Say No, Alternatives to EU Membership, 2011). China conducts trade under WTO, and indeed, 1/3 international trade is conducted under WTO rules.

According to IMF, EU share of world trade shrunk from 30% in 1980 to 17% in 2015. (Telegraph, 6th Jan 2016). EU share of world economy was 30.7% in 2003, only 23.7 % now, and looks set to fall below 20% by end of 2010s. (The Commentator, 15th Feb 2016).

The EU has a massive trade surplus with the rest of the EU (the EU sells us more than UK sells to the EU, the UK had a balance of payments deficit with the EU of £39 billion). In addition, the share of exports going to the EU has fallen from 54% to 46 % from 2007 to 2013. (IEA Brexit Prize: Plan to leave EU by 2020 by Daniel C. Pycock).

In 2015, UK sold £89 billion more of goods to the EU that the EU sold to us. UK exported more to the rest of the world than the EU for the second year in a row, the gap widening from £1.7 billion to £17 billion in 2015. 90% of world trade demand over next 10-15 years will originate from outside the EU. (Vote Leave 11-02-16)

3 million jobs depend not upon EU membership, but upon free EU trade. This would continue, import than export to EU. 47% of UK exports were to the EU in 2015, down from 62% in 2005 (ONS). Could fall to 40% by 2019. (The Commentator, 15th Feb 2016).

UK households are estimated to save £146 per year as soon as CET abolished (Get Britain Out, 11th March, 2016).

The EU has raised agricultural and manufacturing prices by around 10%. Goods are subsides by EU, so EU sell food at higher prices, but making them artificially cheaper than world prices.

Outside EU, UK would pay world prices for exports and imports. Prices would fall by 8%.

EU goods would be cheaper, and non EU imports would be cheaper, not subjected to Common External Tariff.

70% of current UK trade is in goods exported outside the EU and in services such as advertising, law and education, immune from EU regulation (Prof Patrick Minford, The Sun 15 Mar 16).

Aside from tariff and non tariff barriers, the EU is due to damage the UK's very ability to trade. MEPs voted on 9th March for legislation which could severely damage UK ports. It could damage the £400 million invested in UK ports each year; port productivity is 1.3 times higher than the UK average. 75% of UK's largest ports are privatised; 80% of EU ports are state owned. The EC's port services regulation poses major risks to the competitiveness of UK ports.

Since 2009, the direct value of the port sector has increased by 6.4% in real terms, (UK Trade and Investment).

Ports at Felixstowe and Southampton were expanded with 100% private funding. Rotterdam and Hamburg were constructed with 1.1 billion and 788 million euros respectively.

The PSR would affect 43 ports in the UK. Specifically, the regulation seeks to enhance competitiveness of EU state run ports; the UK is already competitive, and thus this one size fits all regulation would undermine UK port competitiveness. The EU seeks to regulate access port services, port changes, and financial transparency. THIS would harm job creation and investment.

The PSR runs counter to Cameron's supposed victory for subsidiarity when he "proposed a new mechanism to finally enforce the principle of subsidiarity."

RISKS TO PORT COMPETIVENESS

- EC proposals would impose a regulator on the UK port industry; the competitiveness of UK ports obviates the need for a regulator.
- The regulator would insist on price proportionality, and thus undermine commercial and investment confidence in UK ports. Such uncertainty will affect investment decisions; typically, ports yield a full return on investment after 25 years.

- The regulations may grant exemptions from state aid rules for some EU ports, this undermining competitiveness of UK ports.
- Regulatory creep could further undermine competitiveness, with further EC policies implemented by the ECJ.

(CPS Economic Bulletin Number 74 4th March 2016)

Therefore, it will patently not be in the EU's interest to erect barriers to the UK. Another concern is the tariffs on trade between UK and the rest of the world, tariffs that do not exist within the EU. But this is precisely because the UK is bound by the EU Common External Tariff, which imposes tariffs on non EU nations, who impose tariffs in return.

If the UK withdrew from the EU without a free trade agreement, then the value of exports from 2019 -2023 would be £25.7 billion lower than if the UK secured a free trade deal with the EU. In the former scenario, exports would also be lower than the status quo (ie the UK remaining in an essential unreformed EU). By negotiating EFTA + (with an EU "passport" for financial services), export growth would be £10.3 billion over and above a straightforward EFTA agreement over 2019 – 2023. (Lea, R. Global Vision Perspective House of Commons Library Data, April 2008. Niebohr, J. "The Four Lies about Leaving the European Union", The Bruges Group, January 2013).

Daniel Hannan (Conservative MEP South East), stated that "the IMF...nations within the eurozone will grow at an average of 2.7% over the next five years [up to and including 2017] while the Commonwealth surges ahead at 7.3%." In fact, this was grossly over optimistic, as in fact the eurozone grew at 0.3% and 0.1% for the 2 consecutive quarters in 2013. (Hannan, Daniel "Look at these graphs: any possible argument for remaining in the EU has been blown away." Daily Telegraph 7th June 2012).

Further to the burgeoning Commonwealth trade, 80 community and business leaders from the Commonwealth backgrounds have written an open letter to PM calling for UK to regain control over migration and trade policy.

(Vote Leave 17th Feb 2016)

The EU has no agreements with the technological industry leaders, USA, Japan and Singapore. These are lucrative markets (both for the UK and those countries) which could be tapped into by forging free trade agreements (under WTO rules) by the UK having its own seat at the WTO.

The abolition of trade barriers between USA and UK could increase UK GDP by £4 billion to £10 billion per annum. (IEA Brexit Prize: Plan to leave EU by 2020 by Daniel C. Pycock)

In addition, Akio Toyota (the chief executive of Toyota) confirmed that Toyota will continue to build cars in the UK in the event of a Brexit.

I propose a new global vision for the United Kingdom, liberated from the EU, forging free trade areas with the growing economies of the world. The UK would forge free trade areas that dwarf the EU, in terms of economic might and population size. The UK as the leader of the free trade areas can compete with China. Free trade helps developing nations grow, and reduces the price of food, tackling poverty at home and abroad. Immediately, sunset clauses must be applied to the Common External Tarrif and other EU regulations, so that immediately after the referendum, the UK will cease to apply these tariffs to non EU countries. Also immediately, the UK must state clearly to the EU that in the event of Brexit, the UK will not apply tariffs to the EU. This will be the starting gun to ensure very rapid negotiations (within days not months) to agree a free trade deal with the EU.

By 2030, 1 billion more people would have joined the world economy, resulting in urban construction over the next few decades could equal the entire volume of construction in world history.

Demand for energy will grow by approximately half by 2030. Technological and environmental developments require global (not EU bloc) co-operation.

Instant exchange of money and services on line does not recognise the artificial barriers imposed by the EU customs union. The forging of free trade areas (enhanced by the UK having its own seat at the WTO) will remove this obstacle. After Brexit, it is vital that the UK does not embark upon protectionism through customs unions, as the prime reason for Brexit is leaving the most protectionist customs union, the EU.

So a Brexit (combined with a free trade agreement with the EU) would be a win win situation, as the UK – EU trade would not be damaged by the CET, and the abolition of tariffs between UK and other non EU nations would lead to 1% reduction in the cost of importing items, which can be passed on the consumer. While the tariff is 1%, it is 1% of a large overall figure. As previously mentioned, the situation with cars is even more severe, with a 10% tariff. A few years ago, UK dealers would import cars from the EU, and reduce the costs due to zero tariffs. By the UK trade freely with the rest of the world (especially Asian tigers), the cost of a £10,000 car could be reduced to £9000 (if all of the 10% tariff saving was passed on to the consumer), and provide healthy competition to EU car exporters. The EU would be foolhardy to continue to 10% tariffs on cars sold to the UK. In short, Brexit will lead to the EU banging on the UK door to sell us cars and other items. 1 million German cars were sold in the UK in 2015.

As a genuine global free trader, I would not want to replace the UKs application of the CET with a UK tariff against EU trade. Genuine free trade benefits all those who participate. The EU's massive trade surplus with the UK of £39 billion would naturally deter the EU from erecting tariffs against the UK, but to ensure certainty for business, I am in favour of negotiating an EFTA + deal. To eliminate the uncertainty that many undecided voters naturally fear, a paving bill to ensure immediate Brexit would apply. In addition, the UK should state immediately to the EU that in the event of Brexit, the UK would not impose tariffs against the EU. These measures would be the starting gun for very rapid negotiations (concluded within days not months), to ensure free trade between the UK and the EU, while enabling the UK to forge free trade agreements with the rest of the world. Therefore, there would be no external tariffs, either against the EU, or the rest of the world.

Currently, the UK is a signatory to EU negotiated free trade agreements with non EU countries. In addition, in 2009, EU took power to deal with IPAs (Investment Protection Agreements) away from UK, who had negotiated 94 – since then, the EU has negotiated none. IPAs protect investors against arbitrary interference by governments, with an independent system of arbitration. (Dominic Raab MP, Daily

Telegraph 23 Feb 2016). If the UK left the EU, then the UK would need to re-negotiate bilateral/multilateral agreements to maintain access. This would be the first time since 1972, that UK trade negotiators have secured trade agreements, as since 1973 the EU has assumed responsibility for this. No UK trade negotiations, as EU does this. Will need a lot of negotiators to forge deals, but is entirely feasible.

Outside the EU, the UK would have its own seat at the WTO, and be free to forge free trade areas with the growing economies of the world. Food imports would be substantially cheaper, helping the poor in the UK and overseas. In return, the UK would win new export markets for our goods, creating a virtuous circle. By utilising the UK's unique global trade connections, we could forge and lead a massive free trade area, which (combined with weaknesses in China's economy) could prevent China from becoming the world's most powerful economy and leading military superpower, and therefore restore the Atlantic alliance as the leading military and moral force in the world. It would be wise to introduce MFN in free trade agreements – this means when host country opens up, across different sectors, and with different countries, Germany benefitted from protections. MFN status would secure free trade deals quickly.

The developing nations would escape poverty by growing their export markets, thus rendering redundant much overseas aid, which has been used to subsidise poverty. Brexit (especially with the abolition of CAP) could tackle poverty at home and abroad.

5). FARMING & FISH

The CAP is a system of farming subsidies to artificially reduce the price of inefficient EU produced food stuffs to below world prices. The CAP means a 17% tariff on food prices vis a vis world food prices for the UK consumer (approximately £400 per year to the consumer), and it denies developing nation the opportunity to export their food to nations such as the UK. (IEA – Abolish the CAP, let food prices tumble – Kristian Niemietz 18th January 2013). In 2015, the UK taxpayer paid £5.5 billion for the CAP, but received only £2.9 billion back, only just over half (Vote Leave, 23rd March 2016).

The Common Fisheries Policy was cynically cobbled together weeks prior to Edward Heath's negotiations to join the EEC commenced in June, 1970. Under the CFP, a coastal zone of 12 nautical miles was reserved for the exclusive use of the nation, 6 miles was open to nations who had "historic rights" to these national waters. If a trawler exceeds its quota, surplus fish are thrown back. The EU is estimated to throw back 1.7 million tonnes of fish, 23% of all EU fisheries catches. Although discards were banned, the quotas still apply, and so the surplus fish are made into fish meal, instead of being sold as fresh fish. It won't deter the resource grab, aided and abetted by the CFP.

UK inshore fishermen make up 77% of UK fleet but gain access to only 4% of the UK's quota.

In November, 2014, Greenpeace revealed that 43% of England's fishing quota is held by foreign fishing businesses. A single Dutch trawler holds 20% of the English quota (6% of the UK quota); 5 vessels hold 20% of the UK quota.

The UK fleet was cut by 19% in 1992, and a further 40% in 1996.

In 1970, UK landed 948,000 tonnes of fish landed from UK vessels; 417,000 tonnes by 2008, approaching the 1915 level of 405,000 tonnes when the North sea was a war zone.

UK is a net importer of fish to the tune of £2.66 billion per annum.

The CFP is estimated to cost the UK £2.81 billion per annum, including cost of unemployment to fisheries and related industries, grant aid to EU states, loss of access to home waters, and higher food prices factored into social security payments. The cist to the consumer is £186 per household per year - £3.58 per week.

Outside the EU, the UK can and must reclaim the internationally agreed 200 mile EEZ. (Stolen Seas:- How the UK suffers under the CFP. Ray Finch, UKIP MEP, 2015).

Powers over agriculture and fisheries would be returned to the UK, with appropriate variations for Scottish and Welsh assemblies. As I wrote earlier, the UK only receives half of what it contributes to the CAP. This is part of the rebate that the UK receives from its approximate £19 billion gross contribution; therefore, the UK is merely getting its own money back. This money will be retained by the UK to finance a deficient payments scheme to UK farmers. Furthermore, Parliament can amend the scheme, especially to promote sustainability, to preserve the environment. The UK must replace CAP with UK wide agricultural policy, but retain variations for the devolved governments.

6).

i) EU REGULATION

The Clinical Trials Directive, implemented in 2004, caused significant disruption to testing new medicines, as it contributed to a decline in the number of applications for clinical trials and increased costs and delays in setting them up in the UK. 12 years on, the reformed regulations have not taken effect.

EU harmonisation of regulations undermines the democratic accountability of Parliament – QMV has abolished the veto in many areas. Harmonisation also reduces the innovative faculties of regulators. (City AM 22nd Feb 2016)

EU Commission raided 2 billion euros from Horizon to pay for problems caused by euro.

UK cannot reduce VAT on sanitary products.

Car insurers cannot insure men and women differently, despite the different risks.

EU regulation costs £33.3 billion to the UK economy.

Under EU law it is very difficult to implement minimum pricing for alcohol.

Larger companies can better cope with EU regulations, due to hiring lawyers to lobby for regulations that suit them. EU regulation is estimated to be 10 times more damaging to small businesses than large ones. (Dominic Raab MP, Telegraph 23 Feb 16)

The total cost of EU regulation is estimated to be £75 billion "How much does the European Union cost Britain?", Congdon, Prof. T (September, 2012); even the net cost (taking account of benefits) is estimated to be £45 billion – or 2% - 3% of GDP. ("The Single Market:

a vision for the 21st Century", Statement by EU Commissioner for Enterprise and Industry 2006 [January, 2007])

Open Europe assessed 2500 Impact Assessments (since 1998) and found that the annual cost of EU regulations in 2009, was £19.3 billion, and the cumulative cost since 1998 was £124 billion. The BCC examined a smaller sample of regulations (but with the largest associated costs) and estimated the annual cost to be £7.6 billion per year, or a cumulative total of £60.8 billion.

The cost to business of compliance with regulations is offset by benefits to employees and consumers.

The cost benefit ratio of EU regulations is 1.02, whereas for UK regulations it is less than half, at 2.35.

The Working Time Directive (which costs the UK economy between £3.5bn and £3.9bn)

- The Large Combustion Plant Directive (Energy/Climate Change measures costs £3.4bn)
- The Temporary Agency Workers Directive (which costs £2bn per-year)
- The Alternative Investment Fund Managers Directive (which will cost £1.5bn per-year)

This gives an estimated total of between £10.4 billion and £10.9 billion per year.

Of course, simply because a regulation has been implemented by the EU does not mean that it should automatically be repealed should the UK withdraw from the EU.

For example, the working time directive is not mandatory, as employees can opt to work more than 48 hours. Personally, I would maintain the status quo – that is not forcing employees to work more than 48 hours, but allowing employees to do so. There is a cost to a company in lost production to a company that cannot employ workers to do a 50 hour week, and a cost to a company in higher wages, and to the employee in higher tax on the overtime. Therefore, my policy of essentially retaining the WTD (with employee opt out) would not make a difference to the cost of this regulation post Brexit.

The Temporary Agency Workers Directive ensures agency workers receive the same pay, leave and conditions as permanent workers undertaking the same job. Again, I would retain this policy. Having worked in adult social care, it is often only by recruiting from agencies that social workers and care workers can be recruited, so they must be paid the same to encourage recruitment and retention. The flexibility afforded the agency worker, in being able to relocate at short notice, is offset by the shorter notice period should the employer intend to terminate their employment.

The Large Combustion Plant Directive I would repeal, and replace this with a QE investment programme to incorporate carbon capture into coal mines, coal fired power stations, and factories that use carbon to manufacture goods. This would kick start the reduction in CO_2 emissions. I would complement this with a variable levy, that applies a carbon tax, but gives tax rebate (through corporation tax rebates) to companies that invest in carbon capture. With this system, companies are rewarded for innovation that reduces carbon emission, rather than merely punishing companies who cannot afford to reduce carbon emissions.

The alternative Investment Fund managers directive required AIFMS to select only brokers and counterparties that are subject to regulatory supervision. The AIFMS must also submit quarterly, semi-annual, or annual reports to their respective member stat regulator. This is clearly an extra piece of unnecessary regulation. The UK has been a world leader in regulation of the financial markets.

I would maintain the Working Time Directive (with employee opt out), and the Agency Worker Directives (and enshrine them in UK law, so that Parliament [not the EU] can amend them), but repeal the AIFM directive, and the Large Combustion Plant Directive. This is a proportionate regulatory framework, which protects employees, reducing business regulation, and allows for the individual to opt out.

Repealing the latter 2 directives alone would save businesses £4.9 billion per year.

My proposals to cut business rates and reduce VAT to 10% on building renovations would save £1.680 billion per year.

If the Common External Tariff is considered as a regulation (which the UK's application thereof clearly counts as a regulation), then the loss of free trade attributable to CET is estimated to be £72,348,000,000 in 2014 -15. This is a gross figure, assuming the uninterrupted of tariff free trade with the EU. Combined with the £4.9 billion combined cost of the AIFM directive and the Large Combustion Plant Directive, this yields a total cost of EU regulations of £77,248,000,000 per year, near enough to Professor Tim Congdon's estimate of £75 billion per year.

When the savings to business of VAT cuts to building renovations and business rates, then the savings to UK business from these reforms are £76,680,000,000 per year.

ii)   THE IMPACT UPON THE CITY OF LONDON

London is the most economically powerful city in the world, with a £600 billion economy, 5.6 million jobs, and 18 million visitors per year. London's 975,000 small and medium firms say that EU regulation makes it harder for them to hire. (Zac Golsmith MP, City AM, 21ˢᵗ Feb 2016).

The other fear is the impact upon the status of the City of London as a key financial centre. In 2015, the annual Zyen survey placed London as the number 1 global financial capital, ahead of New York and Hong Kong. The lead has widened compared with other financial capitals. It is attributable to London leading on the 5 main competitiveness categories (people, business environment, market access, infrastructure and general competitiveness).

Opponents of Brexit fear that the UK leaving the EU would undermine the financial status. Again, the Norway argument seems to hold sway here; that if UK withdrew, we'd be bound by EU regulations that we cannot control. That only applies if UK went down the EEA route; if a clean break were made, then we would not be bound by regulations anyway. In any event, the extension of QMV means that under the present arrangements, the UK has little influence over the rules.

On the whole, investors state that Brexit would enhance the status of the City of London.

It is no coincidence that the top 3 European centres (London, Zurich and Geneva) all lie outside the eurozone, while 3 Asian centres rank above the Euro's financial centre. The top ranked eurozone centre (Frankfurt) is ranked 13. Paris ranks 37th, between Amsterdam and Warsaw.

The reason why eurozone centres are well behind Asian countries and London, is due to EU regulation. Zurich and Geneva destroy the argument that the size of the internal financial market is essential to its success.

Critical factors to the success or failure of financial centres are business culture, critical mass, skilled labour availability, rule of law, economic stability, and moderate regulation.

By remaining in the EU, the UK risks being bound by the same rules that govern the eurozone, which would greatly harm the competitive edge of the City of London. Such harmful regulations include transaction taxes, banking regulation, and caps on salaries/bonuses, all of which can quite adequately be carried out by the UK.

While the UK only accounts for 1% of the global population, UK has the world 4th largest banking industry, the 3rd largest insurance sector, and second largest fund management, and legal services sectors.

The UK has 41% global share of FX trading, 49% of OCT derivatives, 17% of cross border lending, and 22% of international insurance. London also leads Europe in terms of investment and private banking, hedge funds, private equity, exchange traded derivatives, and sovereign wealth funds.

The financial sector accounts for 10% of GDP, and contributed a higher share than that (£58 billion) to the overall tax receipts of £515 billion raised in 2013/14.

The financial sector generated a trade surplus of £62 billion in 2014, the largest surplus of any economic sector in the UK.

The decision not to join the euro has been vindicated by the UK accounting for 74% of European financial services in 2014. Non EU investment assets account for 65% of total UK investment assets. (Leave. EU Media Briefing:- The City & Finance, Ewen Stewart 11-01-16).

London remains the top investment location for Middle East despite Brexit fears. 127 high net worth investors from Saud Arabia, UAE, Qatar, Bahrain, Oman and Kuwait, revealed that London was the most preferred city of 196 worldwide locations to invest in real estate.

10 out of 18 said a new relationship with EU would have a positive impact upon decisions to invest in London real estate, while 4 said it would have no impact. Half said Brexit would have a negative impact, but the other half said Brexit will have a positive or no impact.

Weakening euro and sterling will help drive further investment, as most Middle Eastern countries' currencies are pegged to the dollar.

Across all international locations, 63% said they would be investing in 2016, majority of whom prefer mainly residential (54%) ahead of commercial (22%) or a mix of both (23%).

iii) ECONOMIC GOVERNANCE FOR NON EUROZONE COUNTRIES

There are no proposals to repatriate EU social and employment law, a key 2010 manifesto pledge. There are no changes to the EU working time directive.

"Measures, the purpose of which is to further deepen the economic and monetary union, will be voluntary for member states whose currency is not the euro." Already, the UK would be consulted about, and would not be bound to pay for the financial stability of the euro.

Cameron's other aim was to reduce the "burden" of excessive regulation, and extend the Single Market.

BBC News, 02nd February, 2016

If non eurozone states opposed financial transaction taxes, they could delay measures by calling for further debate. The European Council president would then consider their objections, seek an amendment to legislation that addresses key concerns.

George Osborne wrote in City AM in September, 2015, "One of the greatest threats to the City's competitiveness comes from misguided European legislation. So a central demand in our renegotiation will be that Europe reins in costly and damaging regulation."

While the Tusk proposals protect B of E macro economic policies, and protect UK taxpayers from Euro bail outs. Without treaty change, the City is threatened by regulation. (City AM 3rd Feb 2016)

The Five Presidents Report was published in 2015. The Five are Presidents of European Commission, the Council, the European Parliament, the European Central bank, and the European Stability Mechanism. The essence of this report is to create an economic government of Europe. Part of this government is a euro wide Treasury, with a unified tax and budgetary policy. Insolvency law, company law, property rights, and social security systems would be integrated. Even though UK remains outside the eurozone, the Presidents state "Much can be already achieved through a deepening of the Single Market, which is important for all 28 EU member states." Thus single market legislation can be used to force the UK to adopt measures of further economic integration. (Boris Johnson, Sunday 6th March 2016).

Cameron's pledge to protect the UK and her financial institutions from closer integration of the eurozone countries is in jeopardy, when Tusk tentatively offered a mechanism for non eurozone member states to "raise concerns, and have them heard." However, the caveat here is "without this [mechanism] turning into a veto right."

7). COST

i) COST TO THE UK TAXPAYER

The UK has paid £150 billion gross to EU budget since 2005; this equates to £350 million a week to the EU (even considering the net contribution, the UK still pays £184 million per week). This equates to half the Scottish school budget, four times the science budget, and 60 times what is spent on the NHS cancer drugs fund. Also, UK taxpayers liable to pay for huge bill of euro crisis. UK could save £19.1 billion by not paying to EU budget.

EU controls laws on hospital building, privatisation, and procurement – the 2012 disaster over rail franchises which cost UK taxpayers £50 million.

Since 1973, the North West alone has contributed £39 billion to the EU; £1.9 billion a year (Vote Leave, 12-02-16)

In 2011, Cameron pledged that UK would not bail out the euro; and yet, in June 2015, Cameron gave £850 million to bail out Greece. Then in September, 2015, UK paid the £1.7 billion prosperity surcharge to the EU budget, where the UK is punished for high performance.

During the last parliament (2010-2015), the UK paid gross £87 billion to EU; compare this to the £36 billion cuts made to public services. Put another way, being outside the EU would have obviated the need for those cuts, and indeed, enabled extra investment. (Telegraph, 6th Jan 2016).

Undecided voters are also concerned that if we left the EU, we would lose funding. For every year since we joined in 1973 (apart from 1975), the UK has been a net contributor the EU budget.

The UK will pay £19.2 billion as a gross contribution to the EU Budget per year in 2015/16. It will be £96.5 billion over the next 5 years, (from 2016-17 to 2020-21 it will increase by £1.67 billion) or £371 million per week. (HM Treasure EU finances, 2015 Cm 9167 Dec 2015 + Vote Leave 16th March 2016). Scotland spends £1.5 billion (gross) to the EU budget every year. The annual budget contribution will be equivalent to purchase six Queen Elizabeth aircraft carriers. It is equivalent to three times the science budget; half dedicated schools' grant; The net contribution of this money subsidises the EU; the UK gets its rebate, and some money is returned to be spent not according to the democratic wishes of the British people but the EU. This mainly consists of agricultural support, and regional projects which are not decided by the British people.

Therefore, EU funding of UK projects is merely the UK getting its own money back. This money will be retained by the UK to finance a deficient payments scheme to UK farmers. Furthermore, Parliament can amend the scheme, especially to promote sustainability, to preserve the environment. Replace CAP with UK wide agricultural policy, but retain variations for the devolved governments. £2.9 billion per year.

The average net contribution to the EU budget over this Parliament will be at least £9.567 billion per year – (average annual 2015/16 – 2020/21 net contribution OBR).

This includes the £1.7 billion extra that the UK is scheduled to pay, due to the strong economic performance of the UK. This has been spread out so that this year, the UK will make a net contribution of £10.4 billion (£500 million more than the estimated £9.9 billion), and next year, will make a net contribution of £9.5 billion (£1.3 billion more than the estimated £8.2 billion). Due to this revaluation of the UK's contribution based upon economic success, similar increases are likely over the course of thus Parliament; however, I retain the £9.567 billion average as a conservative assessment when calculating how to invest this saving.

(Vote Leave, Take Control)

The net transfers the UK makes to the EU annually are equivalent to 350,000 people working full time at the average salary sending all their wages to the EU. This is a larger body than the British Army at the start of World War II, many cities, and equivalent to the population of Belgium and Malta.

Only 36 out of 100 FTSE companies urged UK to remain. Some of these companies received £94 million in grants from EU to remain in.

France and Italy are in a debt trap; that is, they cannot grow their nominal GDPS sufficient fast under any circumstances (certainly not without being governed under a common monetary policy and currency) to stop debt increasing. Most debt is owed overseas. Interest rates on their binds will soar, they will be unable to refinance, and will have to leave the euro. This could happen by 2019, and UK (although currently exempt from eurozone bailouts) will invariably be called upon to assist – along with Germany. (Jim Mellon, City AM, 23 Feb 16)

In terms of personal wealth, the New World Wealth has estimated that the average wealth per UK citizen could rise from $147,000 to $180,000 by 2020 if a Brexit occurred. Conversely, the average figure would drop to $140,000 if the UK decided to remain in the UK. This Brexit inspired boom is attributable to the power to control borders, and thus reduce mass immigration, and stop the bonanza of low skilled jobs and downward spiral of wages. (City AM 22 March 2016).

ii) THE IMPACT UPON JOBS

While the UK has between 2.5 and 4 million jobs dependent upon EU *trade* (which is different from being dependent upon EU *membership*), the EU has more than twice that number of jobs dependent upon trade with the UK. With an EU (especially the eurozone) suffering mass unemployment, the EU are hardly going to impose trade barriers with the UK, and jeopardise their balance of trade surplus with the UK. (IEA Brexit Prize: Plan to leave EU by 2020 by Daniel C. Pycock)

In short, not a single job in the UK depends upon EU membership. Indeed, the downward spiral on wages due to unfettered EU migration contributes to an increase in unskilled jobs. A controlled immigration policy enables the UK to train and employ indigenous workers in high skilled job, and the infrastructure projects that are needed to cope with the economic growth due to global free trade.

Bank of England report in 2015 advised that British builders hourly pay has dropped from £15 to £7 per hour, due to influx of migrants. (Tom Harris [former Labour MP for Glasgow South] Daily Record, 18 Mar 16)

Former Belgian Prime Minister, Yves Leterme, said that the argument that UK jobs would be in jeopardy if we left the EU is not a "convincing argument." He went to say that it is in the EU interest to have free trade with the UK as "the European economy needs the UK market, close co-operation and trade."

In 2015, HSBC announced that it may move its HQ to EU, due to uncertainty about EU membership; on 15th February, HSBC announced it would stay in the UK.

CEO of Hitachi announced they will invest in UK because of UK being one of the largest world economies on 18th Feb (Vote Leave, 19th Feb)

MAKING BREXIT A REALITY – AN INDEPENDENT UK WITHIN DAYS

A Leave vote must mean a vote to completely withdraw from the EU. There must be no truck with a Norwegian option, whereby the UK would access Single Market, but with no say over the legislation or regulations. With full Brexit, concerns abound that this would limit access to Single Market. In reality, Single Market has surplus of trade with UK, so will ensure access.

Another concern is the transitional period after the UK votes to leave. If the UK votes to leave, the government would be obliged to trigger Article 50 of the Lisbon Treaty, which is invoked when the UK government sends a letter to Pres of EU Council, stating its intention to leave EU.

Negotiations only start once the letter has been received, and UK government can decide when the 2 year notice period starts.

The UK would then negotiate a withdrawal treaty during the 2 year period (this can be extended). The Treaty would need to be approved by QMV by EU, and not ratified by EU Parliament, but would need to be passed by Westminster. There is no guarantee of this.

The second part is a framework for negotiations towards an alternative trading agreement with the EU after the UK leaves. 2 years is too long to wait until the burdens of EU protectionism cease, with businesses crying out to trade freely with the rest of the world; too long for the £8 billion net contribution to continue, while NHS and social care face a funding crisis, excessive immigration placing stress on hospitals and schools.

The process of Brexit will be a larger legislative exercise than 1972, when we joined. Each law affected by the EU would need to be examined, and how many such laws would be discarded, how many would be maintained.

Whitehall should immediately commence contingency planning for a Leave vote. Please refer to section [] for specific policies and sunset clauses. Indeed, this is possible, and was highlighted by Sir John Cunliffe (deputy Governor of the Bank of England) when he said "... it is fir whoever wants to leave to trigger the leave process." (House of Commons, 8th March, 2016). Greenland left under the ordinary revision procedure (Treaty of European Union art. 48 [2]). This allows for any amendment to primary EU law, it can be used to permit a member state to leave.

Parliament should support a paving EU Treaty Secession Bill now to override Article 50.

This Bill would enshrine the following:-

1) That EU membership ceases the day after the UK votes to leave.
2) Apply sunset clauses to the supremacy of EU law over UK law, freedom of movement, EU budget contribution, CAP, CFP, and our application of the CET.

The Bill would only be enacted if the UK voted to leave; at this point, Parliament is sovereign, and then could vote to repeal Article 50 and implement the EU Secession Act. If the UK voted to remain, then the Act would not be enacted.

In addition, Brexit campaign should proclaim that UK will not impose tariffs against the EU, in return for the EU not imposing tariffs against the UK. This will be the starting gun for negotiations for UK - EU free trade that would be concluded within days, as the EU has a clear interest in trading freely with the UK, as the EU sells more to the UK than the UK sells to the EU. This would demolish a key concern of undecided voters.

This means that if the people vote to leave, the benefits of independence can immediately accrue.

NO MEANS NO: AVOIDING A SECOND REFERENDUM

Some of those who wish for the UK to remain in the EU have a cunning trick up their sleeves. They state that if the UK voted to leave, then this would not necessarily count as the final answer. During the 2 year notice period, the UK could face pleas to remain. The 2 year notice period could use the No vote as a bargaining chip to improve terms, resulting in another referendum. No provision in article 50 for second referendum.

This is fundamentally anti-democratic, as it will be challenging the mandate of the UK people.

Article 50 is a green light for the political establishment to try and reverse a Brexit decision by the British people. For example, if the negotiation were extended to 2020 or beyond, then a Labour government could vote against the withdrawal treaty.

Hence my calls for Brexit to take place immediately after a No Vote, which would be actioned by sunset clauses. There must be a paving bill to scrap Article 50, and implement the sunset clauses.

No must mean No.

CASE STUDY – GREENLAND

Only one EU member state has withdrawn from the EU – Greenland.

Greenland entered Common Market in 1973 (at the same time as the UK) as part of the territory of Denmark kingdom (who also joined in 1973), although the majority of Greenland citizens voted no. In 1979, Greenland achieved home rule from Denmark. Then in 1982, Greenland voted emphatically to leave the EU.

A combination of distance from the EU mainland, culture, economics and finance contributed to this decision.

As a result, the EU lost 60% of its territory.

Greenland is 2000 to 3000 miles away from the European mainland. Greenland has modern housing, good internet, shopping + office complex.

Greenland's future prosperity is based upon a key natural resource – fish.

Fishing policy was previously directed by Copenhagen, then Brussels. The 2 largest Denmark fishing companies in kingdom of Denmark are Greenlandic, and constitute the top 10 fishing companies in Europe.

It took 3 years before Greenland could leave the EU, as a satisfactory fishing deal (dealt with by Danish negotiators) had to be negotiated. The delay was due to the EU trying to define its own fishing policy.

CUTTING DEFENCE: A DANGEROUS GAMBLE

"To urge preparation of defence is not to assert the imminence of war. On the contrary, if war was imminent preparations for defence would be too late."

So said Winston Churchill on 28th November, 1934, during his speech to the House of Commons, calling for an acceleration of air force expansion, to stem the threat to European stability caused by Nazi Germany.

This maxim should be heeded by all of our leaders, and all those who aspire to lead.

The first duty of any government is to defend the realm.

History tells us that when the UK resolve weakens, aggressors are strengthened. The Coalition has cut defences to the bone; this is highly dangerous, and makes war more likely.

These are dangerous times for the security of the United Kingdom. Russia bullies of Ukraine and Crimea; Syria's Assad commits genocide; Hezbollah and Hamas kill innocent people in the Middle East, all with the support of the Iranian regime, determined to acquire a nuclear arsenal. The Sunni insurgence in Iraq is also a consequence of reducing our defences. The response of the government in 2014 to re-open diplomatic ties with Iran was the wrong response.

However, the recent nuclear deal in January 2015, when the P5+1 agreed to lift sanctions against Iran (as Iran agreed to restrict its sensitive nuclear activities), ushered in a perceived improvement in relations between Iran and the West.

Under the deal, for the next 15 years, Iran will have 24 days to comply with any IAEA access request. If Iran refuses, then an 8 member Joint Commission (including Iran) will rule on the issue, and can decide (by majority vote) to reimpose sanctions. If Joint Commission cannot re

UN sanctions would be automatically reimposed for up to 10 years, with a possible 5 year extension.

Iran also agreed to UN's arms embargo for up to 5 years, which the IAEA can relax, provided that Iran's nuclear programme is peaceful.

Iran is now sending Hezbollah arms through Syria. There is now a Russia, Iran and Hezbollah military triangle in Syria. Hezbollah can put ground forces in Syria, which even Russia would shy away from doing directly. One only needs to read the menacing statement from Hezbollah, on the 30th September, 2015, the very day that Russia commenced air strikes in Syria. Moscow now "has its partners on the ground in the Syrian army and its allies, like us."

There is a joint operations room to co-ordinate military operations between Russia, the Syrian Army, Iran and Hezbollah. Russian combat aircraft provide aerial cover for Iranian and Hezbollah fighters on the ground.

This is a strategic bid by Putin to dominate Syria as a prelude to assuming leadership rile on the Middle East. (Al Monitor 02 Nov 2015).

Upon assuming office in 2010, the Conservative Lib Dem Coalition sought to drastically reduce defence spending as part of the deficit reduction programme. This resulted in both aircraft carriers being delayed, and initially being launched with no aircraft on board; cutting troops by 30,000; scrapping the Nimrod, thus leaving the UK without essential maritime reconnaissance capability; delaying a decision on Trident renewal until 2016, and allowing a review of the type of deterrent to be used – a sop to the then Lib Dem coalition partners.

While it was true that the Coalition had inherited a £38 billion budget "black hole" in the defence budget, none of these cuts were necessary. The government immediately allocated 0.7% GNP to overseas aid, which demonstrates that the 2010 level of defences could be maintained, if the willpower was present.

The government's aid pledge was essentially politically motivated, as a method of rebranding the Conservative Party as a compassionate party. The government also argued that such a large aid budget would tackle poverty, and the consequent lurch to extremism amongst the poor and the dispossessed.

This is true up to a point; carefully targeted aid can alleviate poverty, and through vaccination, and water sanitation, the worst effects of poverty can be abolished.

However, the balance between aid and military presence has tilted too far towards the former. Aid granted to countries ruled by dictators is merely abused by those dictators, and doesn't reach the people who need it. Therefore, a military presence is often needed, at the very least to protect the aid convoys, and to secure regime change where necessary.

THE CASE FOR REARMAMENT

I proposed my own defence review at the time, and the issue of strong defence became a central plank of my campaign in 2015.

If the government can pledge £4.5 billion to aid (most of which was either wasted in administration, went to despotic regimes, or went to Russia, and the Indian space programme), then it could easily transfer this money to reverse the defence cuts.

Such a policy (some mistakenly refer to this strategy as unilateral rearmament – in fact, the policy is to restore the UKs defence to pre SDSR 2010 levels) will not be easy; but there is no alternative if the UK is to preserve its own security, and to play a major role in confronting tyranny.

Critics of trident argue that it has not deterred IS, nor Russian aggression in Ukraine, Crimea, and now in Syria, and therefore does not work as a deterrent. It is true that Trident does not deter insurgencies such as IS; counter intelligence, and targeted air strikes are the methods necessary to counter such insurgencies. Russia felt emboldened to invade Ukrainian territory precisely because Ukraine renounced nuclear weapons, NATO removed missile defence from Poland in 2009, and because neither Ukraine, Crimea not Syria is under the protection of the NATO umbrella. But a further indecision has also contributed to Russian aggression; the Conservative's decision to postpone renewal of Trident to 2016, in order to appease the Lib Dem partners, who were granted a review of the UK nuclear deterrent. After the election, it was proposed that the decision would be brought forward to the late autumn of 2015, but in fact this did not occur.

Our nuclear deterrent deters potential aggressors without a shot being fired. It is no coincidence that Syria and Russia have committed atrocities since the UK postponed the decision to renew Trident. As such, the UK is reduced to sanctions, which have no materiel effect to deter Russian aggression.

A constant at sea deterrence is the only viable deterrent, and this is only possible with four submarines to ensure one submarine is on constant patrol, and can launch an nuclear strike at any target in the world.

Furthermore, Trident must be retained permanently; it should not merely be used as a bargaining chip in negotiations to multilaterally reduce or abolish nuclear warheads across the world. An historic opportunity was missed at the 1986 Reykjavik Summit, when Reagan proposed abolishing all nuclear weapons, but Gorbachev opposed Reagan's deployment of SDI missile defence, to act as an insurance against clandestine development of nuclear missiles. During the Cold War, the doctrine of mutually assured destruction prevented either NATO or Warsaw Pact from first strike. Now, many rogue states have acquired or are developing nuclear weapons, and terrorist groups could potentially detonate a small "dirty bomb", a conventional bomb infused with radioactive material which could poison millions. These dictators and terrorists lack the rationality of a Kruschev or a Gorbachev, and would be prepared to use these weapons, if they detect a weakness amongst the free nations, especially the USA and the United Kingdom. Furthermore, internet technology leads to the instant dissemination of information on how to build such weapons; secrets that respect no national boundaries.

Only if the leaders of Russia, North Korea, and the IS insurgents became reasonable men and women, could even the possibility of nuclear disarmament be countenanced, and even then, only multilaterally. As such a utopia is but a far fetched fantasy, as there will always be threats, as IS replaced Al Queda, and the rogue states have replaced the Warsaw Pact. Therefore, the UK must establish and maintain a strong defence at all levels, including intelligence and reconnaissance, conventional ground, maritime, and aerial defence, and an independent nuclear deterrent. This defence system must be adaptable, and flexible, to meet new and emerging threats, from wherever in the globe these threats originate.

A full replacement for Trident must be announced without delay. Because of the delay, in 2026 one of the refurbished Vanguards will have been de-commissioned, while the first Successor submarine will enter service in 2028, leaving the UK with only three submarines (and therefore without a constant at sea presence) for 2 years. This is why the decision to renew must be taken now.

Renewal grants a historic opportunity for the UK to have a truly independent deterrent since 1962.

The UK has access to 58 Trident missiles supplied by the US, which are due for renewal in 2042. Some Trident missiles have been expended in test firing. The missiles are pooled, and missiles are selected at random to be placed either on US or UK submarines. The UK by definition, does not have a definitive say as to how many missiles are placed on the Vanguard submarines. Therefore, the UK does not have an independent nuclear deterrent, and those 58 missiles are not allocated exclusively to the UK.

The skills of the British aerospace industry should be utilised to build our own missiles now, to prevent the UK lacking sufficient missiles should the US decide to reduce nuclear missiles as part of arms reduction strategy.

Governments are tempted to reduce, if not the number of submarines or missiles, then the number of warheads as a token gesture of disarmament. This sends out completely the wrong message to aggressors such as Russia. The UK must retain the current number of missiles, and warheads, period.

Each submarine will have 8 missiles, each missile will have 5 warheads. There will be a total of 32 missiles, a total of 160 operational warheads; part of a total stockpile of 225.

Even the fuel supply for Trident missiles is in jeopardy. Since the cancellation of the US space shuttle in 2011, the cost of fuel for Trident has increased by around 80 per cent, rising from £6.3 million to £11.2 million from 2011 to 2012. In order to maintain an independent nuclear deterrent, the UK must also manufacture its own fuel for the missiles, and service and maintain the missiles within UK territory.

In order to prevent a 2 year gap in 4 submarine capability between 2026 and 2028 (a decade's notice of such a glaring deficiency in our armaments is a green light for aggressors such as Putin to extend their imperialist ambition), the first Successor submarine must be introduced into service in 2026, not 2028.

In the Cold War, the doctrine of mutually assured destruction prevented a first strike either by NATO or the countries of the Warsaw Pact.

Since the end of the Cold War, this doctrine is null and void; when Putin annexed Crimea and invaded Ukraine, there was barely a murmur of protest from the outside world.

In the uncertain post Cold War world, unstable regimes are led by leaders who lack the rationality of Kruschev. Today's despots (like Putin, and Kim Jong Il) are prepared to strike first, and are encouraged to do so when the leaders of the free world have reduced our defences to perilously low levels.

Our deterrent must be strengthened with a submarine based missile defence system, with a constant at sea presence, to destroy enemy missiles. Missile defence also enhances first strike capability, as it creates a shield impenetrable to retaliatory missiles.

President Obama's decision to scrap missile defence in Eastern Europe in 2009 (10 missiles in Poland, and a radar facility in Czechoslovakia) was a renaissance of detente with Russia, which has only served to fortify Putin to annexe Crimea, and invade Ukraine. The UK must contribute its own expertise and material to NATO missile defence system in Central Europe – although originally designed to intercept missiles from Iran, it will also intercept Russian missiles. NATO missile defence will protect against attacks from Russia and Iran.

Reverse the cuts in troop numbers (30,000 by 2020) to pre CSR levels. A military career will give many young people a career in the armed forces, with a wide range of skills, both academic and vocational, and provides civilian career prospects for young people from deprived backgrounds.

The UK needs 2 fully operational aircraft carriers (with aircraft) now to ensure our security on the high seas. HMS Queen Elizabeth should be launched now, not in 2017.

The HMS Prince of Wales is not scheduled to enter service until 2020; it would be unrealistic to introduce it immediately. In the interim, the UK should rent a USS Nimitz aircraft carrier and 82 aircraft. Half of these aircraft should be allocated to the HMS Queen Elizabeth. This is pending introduction of UK built fighters, and HMS Prince of Wales in 2020.

These measures will ensure a full complement of 2 carrier aircraft from 2015. 1 carrier is sent to deter Russian aggression, and another carrier can launch air strikes to deter IS in Iraq and Syria.

2 aircraft carrier capability is essential to ensure that a military operation can be launched anywhere in the world; if it were in place now, this could have deterred Putin's aggression in Ukraine, and (through the threat of airstrikes) IS. This increase in armaments will be facilitated through higher manpower by increasing troop numbers.

The UK must end the era of dependence upon the US for our own defences. The JSF couldn't even make the Farnborough air show in July, 2014. The UK must cancel the JSF contract, and award a contract to build 72 aircraft capable of Mach 2 by 2020, (with S/VTOL capability and with all weapons systems enclosed to enhance speed) to UK firms (as opposed to the 48 JSFs the government had ordered from the US). 36 fighters and 4 helicopters would each be allocated to the HMS Queen Elizabeth and MHS Prince of Wales.

These measures will mean that, in 2020, the UK will have an entirely independent complement of aircraft carriers and aircraft.

Many argue (sadly, even the UK Defence Journal) that a policy of the UK building its own combat aircraft is not feasible. I obviously vehemently disagree.

Importing aircraft from overseas is costlier in terms of the UK balance of payments, and in terms of the loss of potential jobs, and with it, tax revenues, and less expenditure on unemployment benefit.

In addition, importing aircraft also reduces the UK high tech skills base, and the crossover benefits into other sectors, such as developments in metallurgy; once cut to such a low level, it is very hard to restore.

The option of building aircraft in alliance with other countries at least gives the UK some capacity in terms of skills base and factories. The risk is if the other country pulls out, or the defence and economic priorities of that country change. The Eurofighter was over budget, and very late. The JSF (albeit a partially British design) is manufactured solely in the USA, and in any event is unable to attend an air show, let alone attack targets in war torn regions.

A policy of the UK designing and building its own aircraft is entirely feasible, provided the political willpower is there. The demand is present (due to the world situation). The manpower must be increased firstly by reducing tuition fees on engineering graduates (to recruit the designers we need), and encouraging our aerospace industry to increase apprentices. The indigenous apprentices and students must be encouraged to take up these roles.

Restoring our defence levels to those of 2010, through creating an independent defence capability, is essential, to deal with the severe threats the UK and our allies face. One such threat the Allies had thought had been destroyed forever has resurfaced with an aggressive tragedy since the spring of 2014.

THE THREATS FROM STATES: RUSSIAN EXPANSIONISM

As the Berlin Wall fell in Autumn, 1989, this heralded the liberation of states enslaved under the Soviet yoke since 1945. In 1991, Russia itself became the Commonwealth of Independent states, as Yeltsin took over from Gorbachev. The rapid transition from communism to capitalism yielded its own challenges.

While communism had provided security of a sort for the people, there were many losers under capitalism. This feeling of dispossession increased the appetite for extremist politicians, the first significant one being Zhirinovsky.

This dynamic has grown, and has resulted in Vladimir Putin aggressively pursuing an expansion of Russia's traditional imperialist ambitions.

By his own admission, Putin's goal is to reclaim all the satellite states that once constituted the Soviet Union.

In 2014, Putin annexed Crimea, after a referendum supported such a measure. It is clear that the "approval" for annexation was due to Russian intimidation of the Crimean people.

Later that spring, Putin invaded the Donbas, the Donetsk and Luhansk areas of Ukraine.

These two acts of Russian aggression are tragically similar to the annexation of Austria and the invasion of Czechoslovakia in 1938 respectively.

History tells us that when the UK resolve weakens, aggressors are strengthened.

Crimea is now under Russian yoke. With 30,000 – 40,000 Russian troops are on the Eastern border of Ukraine, that oppressed nation is set to follow suit. Russians have located 2.5 million Kalashnikov rifles.

The despicable shooting down of MH 17 (in all probability perpetrated by pro – Russian separatists) proves that the aggressors are still obtaining arms.

The concerned voter may well question the importance of intervening to assist Crimea and Ukraine. Why is this in the British national interest, when neither Crimea nor Ukraine is in NATO, and the UK is thus not bound to intervene?

The answer is clear. If Russia succeeds in illegally seizing Ukrainian territory and annexing Crimea, then Russia is emboldened to invade neighbouring nations, who are NATO members. If this occurred, then the UK (as a NATO member) is legally bound to intervene under Article 5.

It is precisely because Ukraine and Crimea were not in NATO that Putin knew he could intervene without a military response from NATO. Had the free world leaders shown courage and foresight, then Ukraine and Crimea would have been shielded under the NATO umbrella, and Putin would have been deterred from his aggression.

In September, 2015, Russia's intentions were made brutally clear when Russia launched airstrikes in Syria, not against IS targets as they claimed, but against rebel fighters. A withdrawal in March 2016 has been followed by a threat to re-enter Syria; after all, Russia has left forces and armaments in Syris for precisely such a purpose.

A disturbing historical parallel was when Churchill's call in 1938 for a Soviet-Franco-British pact to defend Czechoslovakia should Germany invade was rejected by Chamberlain. A similar lack of courage concerning Ukraine and Crimea was displayed by the leaders of the USA, UK and other leaders in Europe.

A further factor was that, in 1994, under the Budapest Memorandum on Security Assurances, Ukraine agreed to give up its nuclear arsenal in exchange for Russian assurances to maintain Ukraine's territorial integrity. Ukraine renounced its nuclear arsenal in 1996.

Another factor was when Obama withdrew NATO missile defence from Poland in 2009, the first act of his detente with Russia. This created an imbalance in NATO Russia military strength.

This in turn caused Ukraine to seek an association with the EU, which Putin used as an excuse to invade the Donbas, using pro Russian separatists as his army, who in April 2014, occupied government buildings in Donetsk, Luhansk, and Kharkiv, seeking independence, which they proclaimed in May 2014, after dubious referenda. Putin was able to perpetrate this imperialist strategy as Ukraine did not have a nuclear arsenal, combined with the fact that Ukraine was not a NATO member, and the missile defence system had been withdrawn.

A ceasefire was signed on 5th September 2014 in Minsk.

At this time, this prevented Ukraine from fighting a seemingly unwinnable war against Russia (when in August, Russian incursion with heavy weapons put paid to any chance of a Ukrainian victory) and Russia was left with swathes of Donetsk and Luhansk as bulwarks to be used to turn Ukraine into a Russian state; while their status is uncertain, it is certain that the Russian occupation is immoral.

On 20th September, Ukraine's president Poroshenko granted special status to Donetsk and Luhansk.

This consists of the following measures:-

i)   Autonomy for three years – i.e., until 2017
ii) Guarantees Russian language rights
iii) Guarantees self governance.
iv) Allows the regions to establish deeper ties with Russia.
v)   Amnesty to pro – Russian rebel fighters.

Kiev regards the areas currently under pro Russian rebel control (around one third of the w regions) as special status. However, the pro Russian rebels lay claim to the entirety of Donestk and Luhansk.

This is the so called "frozen conflict" doctrine; to wit, placing the ogre of Russian imperialism into deep storage, only to be thawed out, activated and let loose on the rampage at the whim of President Putin.

It is unlikely that the pro Russian rebels will stop with the territory they have seized in Donetsk and Luhansk.

Step by step, Putin has increased Russian involvement, and the West has accepted each small step on the road to an eventual Russian domination of Eastern Ukraine and Crimea. If this continues, Putin will soon control all of the former Soviet satellite states, who have been free of tyranny for barely a quarter of a century.

Fortunately, on 26th October, 2014, the Ukrainian people re-elected pro Western parties to their parliament. Although voter turnout was down in Ukrainian held areas in Donetsk and Luhansk, many brave voters defied the pressure of military rebels, and voted nonetheless.

Neither Crimea nor the Russian separatist held areas voted on 26th October, but Donbas held elections on 2nd November, including Slovianks and Mariupol, former rebel strongholds now under Ukrainian control.

Sham elections held in Donetsk and Luhansk prompted Russian backed separatists to declare sovereign governments on the back of these sham elections, thus imperilling the UN ceasefire in September. These are used as cover for Russian aid.

State funding and pensions have been cut off by Ukraine.

Promised higher wages have never materialised, and poor public services abound.

Igor Plotnitsky (head of the Luhansk People's Republic) and a signatory to the Minsk agreement said that "sooner or later, we will become a part of the Russian Federation." Schools in Luhansk now have Russian textbooks.

(Economist 11th October 2014)

THE RENEWED RUSSIAN BUILD UP

Russia sent in tanks, lorries, and artillery during the build up to the sham elections on 2nd November, 2014. On 12th November, Philip Breedlove saw Russian materiel entering Ukraine.

In August 2015, the Ukrainian Parliament voted to grant concessions to territories held by Russian – backed rebels. While Ukraine pledged special status to the Donbas region as part of the Minsk ceasefire, and under the Belarus ceasefire of February 2015, Moscow is doing little to maintain its side of the bargain. The bill to give concessions to the Russian rebels obtained 265 votes, short of the 300 votes needed to secure 2/3 support of the parliament. Poroshenko and his allies voted against the bill. Such a bill is a reward for Russian aggression, and will only encourage Russia to invade other areas of Ukraine.

Putin's tactic is to escalate a conflict, then agree to halt aggression in exchange for concessions by the West: this strategy is also known as appeasement.

Ukraine's UN ambassador has predicted a Russian invasion of Ukraine.

Putin's aim is economic collapse of Ukraine, followed by a division of Ukraine between the West and Russia.

I wrote twice to the Foreign Secretary (William Hague in May 2014, and then Philip Hammond in October, 2014), urging a build up of defences, to curb Russian aggression, and to demand the full restoration of territorial integrity to Ukraine and Crimea through internationally monitored referenda.

On 25th November, 2014, I received a letter of response from the Foreign & Commonwealth Office. It was immensely defeatist in tone. (All letters regarding defence can be perused in Appendices III & IV at the end of this book).

Firstly, the FCO ruled out a military response. History proves that ruling out a military response invites aggression. I had never advocated a first strike; I proposed sending an aircraft carrier (with a full complement of combat aircraft) along with allies, within striking distance of Russia as a signal that the UK and allies are serious about curbing Russian aggression. This would be in concert with fresh referenda to determine the destiny of Ukraine and Crimea.

Secondly, the FCO advised that NATO is not seeking to expand. It is the prerogative of putative member to states to apply to join NATO, and Ukraine's parliament voted overwhelmingly to join NATO in the late autumn of 2014. This also raises the question that many have asked:-

What is the rationale for the UK to intervene to protect a non NATO nation such as Ukraine?

The answer is clear. If Russia succeeds in illegally seizing Ukrainian territory and annexing Crimea, then Russia is emboldened to invade neighbouring nations, who are NATO members, and beyond. If this occurred, then the UK (as a NATO member) is legally bound to intervene under Article 5. In September, 2015, Russia's intentions were brazenly revealed when they launched air strikes in Syria, not against IS or Assad supporters, but to the rebel fighters. A withdrawal has been swiftly followed by an announcement of re-engagement in the Syrian conflict.

Thirdly, the FCO advised that NATO Russia Founding Act prohibits NATO members to permanently station substantial combat forces. The NRFA has already been violated by Russia, and the UK and Nato allies can hardly stand idly by while Russia extends its forces. This, combined with the UKs defence cuts, is why such a paltry number of combat aircraft have been sent to the Baltic states.

I was also told that the UK and allies must abide by the Minks agreement. But, like the NRFA, this had been rendered null and void by continued Russian aggression.

Czech general Pavel, (next Chairman of the NATO military committee) stated that the West would not be ready for military action by Putin. He said that "Russia could seize the Baltic countries in two days. NATO wouldn't be able to react to the situation in that time." (Express 29th May 2015)

Locating 100 soldiers of our NATO allies in the Baltics is a brave move. But far bolder measures are needed. The Baltic states will be defended under Article 5 of NATO, as they are NATO members. Ukraine and Crimea are not NATO members. The special status granted to the regions Donetsk and Luhansk in Ukraine makes it very hard for Ukraine to become a NATO member, and thus be granted security.

The only answer to the tragedy in Ukraine and Crimea is to embark upon a programme of undiluted resistance, through the holding of free and fair referenda to allow the people of Russia and Ukraine to determine their destiny, reinforced by the presence of a UK aircraft carrier with a full complement of aircraft (in concert with similar flotillae launched by Allies), a nuclear submarine which can target nuclear missiles at Russia within moments, not to declare war, but to establish a military presence within striking distance of Russia to prevent future atrocities.

The overriding aim must be a sovereign and free Ukraine and Crimea. Ukraine and Crimea must be free to determine their destinies, and whether they wish to join the EU. However, Ukraine and Crimea can be only be free from the Russian yoke by joining NATO.

ISLAMIC STATE AND RUSSIA'S BETRAYAL

The Islamic State of Iraq and the Levant (ISIL) forces, have led many Kurds into being stuck on a mountainside. IS has brutally murdered British citizens.

The French and Americans have taken the lead in supplying arms. The UK must do so immediately. The UK must supply offensive weapons, in addition to the defensive weapons (body armour and counter explosive equipment) currently proposed.

The UK is a prime target of Islamic fundamentalists; therefore UK action to defeat IS is vital to our national security.

From the outset, the UK was absolutely right to fly reconnaissance missions, and to provide humanitarian aid. But that humanitarian aid can only be assured of safe passage if the Kurds are protected by Allied military force.

Ultimate victory against IS can only be assured by fighting IS wherever they reside.

In October, 2014, the government capitulated to "public opinion" and the fear that Parliament would veto action against Syria (as had occurred in 2013) by proposing air strikes against IS targets only in Iraq, and not Syria.

Limiting air strikes to Iraq merely contributed to insurgence of IS into Syria, where they were fortified by the fact that the UK were not launching airstrikes.

With France and the USA seized the initiative, the UK was excluded from a leading role in combating the insurgency. With the UK fully involved, we now have a far greater say over the selection of targets air strikes.

The government's pre-emptive capitulation was not only based upon fear of public opinion; this has been shifting for some months in favour of action against IS. Their capitulation shielded a far more disturbing truth; that the UK lacks sufficient air, naval and manpower to implement air strikes against IS targets in Iraq AND Syria.

Finally, in December 2015, prompted in part to the IS terrorist attacks in Paris in November, Parliament voted decisively to sanction air strikes against IS targets in Syria as well as Iraq. Sadly, as so often with this government, this decision was delayed. The Russians had launched air strikes in Syria three months before the UK. An earlier decision by the UK to defend Free Syrian Army by attacking IS targets would have sent a signal to Russia not to bomb the Free Syrian Army. The UK is only contributing 8 Tornadoes to the aerial bombing operations. The decision to extend the Tornado's mission against IS to 2017 is welcome, but leaves a glaring gap in our airpower in a campaign set to endure beyond 2017. This is why I have consistently argued for an aircraft carrier with a full complement of aircraft to participate in airstrikes against IS targets in Iraq and Syria.

The UK working in concert with Allies could devise joint measures to safeguard the UK against counter attacks, and against UK interests both overseas and in the UK.

The campaign to defeat the insurgents must involve humanitarian aid, arms for the Kurds, and surgical air strikes against IS compounds, in Iraq and Syria, paving the way for the people in those countries to fight IS, so avoiding the need for UK ground troops. Of course the UK must never rule out the possibility of committing ground troops as a last resort.

The recent IS insurgency in Iraq and Syria must not be reason to open diplomatic talks with extremists in Iran, nor Assad in Syria. A decade of diplomacy has only fortified Iran in its determination to acquire a nuclear arsenal. Iran sponsors Hamas in Palestine, and Hizbollah in Lebanon. I opposed the renewed detente with Iran (epitomised by reopening the Iranian embassy all the while Iran supports such extremists). Assad has killed thousands of his own people. The leaders of Iran and Syria cannot be trusted.

The UK's fight against IS must not mean a reliance on an adversary of IS, President Assad. The Assad regime has killed its own people. Assad must play no part in the transition from dictatorship to democracy in Syria.

Fortified by seizing territory in the Donbas in the Ukraine, and annexing Crimea (actions ominously comparable to those of Hitler in relation to Czechoslovakia and Austria in 1938) without a serious response from NATO, Putin's evil expansionist plans now extend to Syria.

Russia has also contributed to instability in the region; in combination with Assad and IS, Russia has contributed greatly to the refugee crisis, which has directly affected the UK. Therefore, it is in the UK national interest to act against aggressors causing instability in the region. Putin's Russia (a key ally of Assad) continually vetoes any action against Assad at the UN Security Council. For some months, Russian forces were being strengthened in preparation for some kind of intervention in Syria. At the time, no one could foretell upon whose side Putin would intervene.

In late September, 2015, Russia commenced airstrikes, ostensibly against IS, in an apparent attempt to extend the coalition against IS. But the true intentions of Putin were starkly revealed when Russia (who carry out approximately 20 sorties per day) in fact bombed targets linked with the Free Syrian Army, who pose more of a threat to Assad. Michael Kofman (a US based analyst at the Kennan Institute) advises that Russia's targets include storage facilities, ammunition dumps, production facilities, and command and control infrastructure linked to the Free Syrian Army. More recently, Russia has launched cruise missiles from the Caspian Sea. All this could have been prevented had the UK shown the resolve to launch airstrikes against IS in Syria in 2014, when it launched airstrikes against IS targets in Iraq. The Free Syrian Army is the bulwark of freedom, and the ultimate instrument to rid Syria both of IS and Assad. In addition, Russia is targeting tanks, armoured cars, and rocket artillery that the Free Syrian Army have captured from the Assad backed army. While Russia announced a "withdrawal" in March 2016 in the hope that it would lull the West into a false sense of security, it left sizeable forces and armaments in Syria, in readiness for a resumption of its campaign against the Free Syrian Army and other allied groups.

Russia's aim is none other than to destroy the only credible opposition to Assad (the Free Syrian Army and other rebel groups), and to present a stark choice to NATO countries; to rely on Russia to attack IS, or risk the wrath of Russia by attacking Assad and his forces. The UK and allies must be equally clear in our strategy; to spare no time in building a coalition with the rebels to defeat IS and Assad. We cannot trust Putin as an ally against IS. If the UK fails to resist Russian aggression, then Russia will be emboldened to invade NATO countries, resulting in the UK having to declare war (under Article of the NATO Treaty). Much of the overseas aid budget should be redirected to defence, as many problems at which aid is directed, such as the refugee crisis, can only be tackled by a military presence to deter and remove the aggressor.

Russia is using aerial bombardment of Free Syria Army targets to pave the way for Syrian government forces (in alliance with Iranian and Hezbollah forces) to extend their ground offensives, which will in turn strengthen IS to extend their ground offensives.

Russia has used cunning to avoid incursions into NATO members, which would under Article 5, trigger a retaliatory response from NATO against Russia. However, in early October, Russian fighter jets went into airspace of Turkey, a key NATO ally. Allied jets must continue their strikes against IS; any interception of allied jets by Russian jets must be responded to in kind.

It is no coincidence that Russian aggression occurred after NATO removed the missile defence system from Poland in 2009, and after the UK slashed defences to perilously low levels in 2010. Indeed, history proves that when the resolve of the free world weakens, then aggressors are strengthened.

IS also has Aleppo in Syria, Lebanon and Jordan within its sights. If we do not act soon, IS could establish a caliphate on the Turkish border. As Turkey is a NATO ally, any aggression against Turkey would require a full retaliatory response from NATO members, primarily the UK and USA. Accordingly, the UK should deploy one of its Trident nuclear submarines within striking distance of Russia and Iraq (and the location of the IS caliphate state), reinforced by a submarine missile defence system. This will ensure deterrence against aggression, prevent war, and help to secure an honourable peace.

IMMEDIATE UK ACTIONS TO CURB IS AND RUSSIAN AGGRESSION

STRENGTHENING CONVENTIONAL AND NUCLEAR DEFENCE

The UK is now engaged in air strikes against IS targets in Iraq and Syria. The strategy must be for air strikes against IS targets to pave the way for ground offensives by the Free Syrian Army (and other rebel groups) to combat IS on the ground. Training and weapons must be given to the Free Syrian Army, to enable them to defeat IS on the ground. The option of UK ground troops must not be ruled out, but it must be a last resort.

There must be an immediate Commons vote to renew Trident with a like for like replacement with 4 submarines to ensure continuous at sea deterrence.

The HMS Queen Elizabeth must be launched within weeks. UK should rent from the USA a USS Nimitz aircraft carrier with a full complement of 82 aircraft (sufficient for the two UK aircraft carriers). Half of the 82 aircraft should be placed on the HMS Queen Elizabeth immediately, to ensure a full complement of 2 aircraft carriers with immediate effect. The carriers and aircraft must be manned by UK personnel. This is pending the introduction of HMS Prince of Wales in 2020, and the UK building its own fleet of carrier based combat aircraft.

One carrier should be sent to the Baltic Seas as a military defensive presence to deter Russian aggression. The second carrier should be sent to the Mediterranean to launch air strikes to defeat the ISIL insurgency in Iraq and Syria. This must be done in concert with NATO allies.

Speed up recruitment of troops, by extending the age limit, and use reserves to man the combat fighters and aircraft carriers. The aim must be 30,000 troops (army, navy and air force) long term, restoring troop numbers to 2010 levels.

Relocate NATO missile defence in Poland.

An arms embargo must be enforced by NATO allies against Russia, enforced by as many free nations as possible, to prevent further atrocities such as the shooting down of MH 17.

There should be a similar EU NATO wide embargo upon Russian aid.

We must assist the Ukrainians to defend themselves by supplying arms.

Increased armaments are justified to ensure the UK has capability to carry out airstrikes against IS targets, and to ensure a defensive posture to deter Russian aggression. To finance the extra defence, the overseas aid budget should be cut. Overseas aid should be prioritised for lower income countries (stopping aid for middle income and higher income countries), focussing on water sanitation, vaccinations, humanitarian aid due to political and environmental crises. Aid should be given directly to the recipient countries, rather than the EU. While aid is necessary for the refugees, and assistance to Free Syrian rebels, ultimate victory over Russian aggression and IS is largely dependent upon military force.

COUNTER TERRORISM MEASURES

The recent terrorist attacks in Paris and Brussels against people expressing free speech must be utterly condemned.

Freedom of speech (which does not incite hatred) must be safeguarded as an essential human right.

To limit free speech in response to terrorism hands a propaganda victory to the terrorists, and encourages more terrorism.

Nick Clegg was wrong to veto the government's proposals to ban extremists lecturing at universities - this is clearly an example of incitement, and radicalising young people, rather than free speech. I would ban extremist from speaking at universities.

The Prevent strategy must be retained in UK schools – this cannot be railroaded by a vote of the teachers' unions.

Intervening to help the Kurds (and other groups oppressed by terrorist organisations) is vital as a moral cause, and to protect the security of the UK. The UK must be prepared for the repercussions, from outside and within the UK.

The government is quite right to arrest people displaying extremist literature, flags, and to remove on line material.

There should be a sensible compromise between Lib Dem opposition to any form of monitoring of electronic media, and the government's proposal to access all emails.

The most effective policy is to focus the resources of our security services targeting the electronic communication of groups and individuals likely to perpetrate and support terrorism.

Implement the Communications Data Bill 2012 – This will extend the range of data communications companies have to store for 12 months. This will include details of messages sent on social media, webmail, voice calls over the internet and gaming, in addition to emails and phone calls.

Officials would only be able to see the content of the messages with a warrant, and the suspect will be entitled to an appeal if the warrant powers are abused.

Enhance encryption of emails for individuals and companies.

Implement Counter-Terrorism and Security Bill 2014-15 to add to the Data Retention and Investigatory Powers Act to allow internet protocol (IP) address matching, to identify the individual or the device that was using a particular IP address at any given time.

Use modern digital technology to jam mobile phone and internet traffic that terrorists use to wage their campaigns. Control orders (which bans suspect from using mobiles or internet) should be reintroduced, and replace TPIMs.

To facilitate speedier convictions, it is essential to allow use of intercept evidence in court, to reduce the time a suspect is detained before trial.

The ECHR must be repealed, and replaced with a British Bill of Rights to enable the UK to deport foreign criminals and terrorists, with immediate effect.

Stronger immigration controls to prevent extremists from entering the UK in the first place. While the UK can control immigration from states associated with Islamic fundamentalism, it cannot control immigration (including possible Islamic fundamentalists) entering the UK from EU members. Transitional immigration controls to prevent extremist infiltration must be put into place immediately. This will control the situation until the question of EU membership is permanently settled in the EU referendum.

SANCTIONS

I supported the government's introduction of sanctions in 2014 as part of a multi pronged strategy. Continue with the targeted sanctions against Russian leaders, and their economic interests. In addition, ban visits from Russian leaders, and investment from Russian companies.

On 5th August, Russia blocked food imports from countries that have imposed sanctions on Russia (mainly state controlled banks), in response to Russia's aggression against the Ukraine.

The West has stopped exports to Russia (mainly technology for offshore oil exploration), Russia has blocked Western imports.

The West is heavily dependent upon Russian oil and gas. Russia has not cut off the gas as this would result in ruin for Russian energy firms and the government.

Russia imports 40% of its food, and so price rises are inevitable. To counter food inflation, Putin has considered price controls, shifting the cost of sanctions from consumers to businesses. This statism would deter investors.

Putin's expansionist ambitions are epitomised by the customs union he is building, to link Russia with Belarus and Kazakhstan. However, these two countries have been reticent about blocking American and European imports.

A Russia v West trade war would hurt EU exporters (such as German carmakers), but would also prove ruinous for Russia heavily dependent upon imports for food, consumer goods, and industrial equipment.

This doctrine of mutually assured destruction is now applied to trade relations, rather than the Cold War, and thus is a temporary brake upon escalation, both of trade and military conflict.

However, let this be no excuse for the West to delay investment in fracking and indigenous energy production to reduce energy dependence upon Russia, and to re-arm, so that the UK can prevent a military conflict, or be fully equipped should military conflict arise with Russia.

CURBING RUSSIAN AGGRESSION

In conjunction with the aforementioned measures, the UK must lead the world in curbing Russian aggression nearer to its source; the overriding aim must be a sovereign and free Ukraine and Crimea. Although neither country is in NATO, if these territories remain under Russian control, then Russia is fortified to incur into NATO territory; Russia has already been fortified by its seizing of Ukrainian territory, and annexation of Crimea. Ukraine and Crimea must be free to determine their destinies and whether they wish to join the EU.

Seek UN mandate to hold a legitimate referenda in Crimea, Donetsk and Luhansk, and send in impartial election/referendum monitors, so that people can decide whether they wish to remain in Ukraine or Crimea, or remain under the rule of pro Russian rebels. If UN cannot agree upon this, then an alliance of free nations must act to ensure free and fair elections/referenda in Crimea and the Ukraine.

The UK must extend NATO across the whole of Central and Eastern Europe, to include Crimea and Ukraine. This would deter Russian aggression, as an attack on a NATO member would require a full retaliatory response from NATO allies. Nations left outside the security of the NATO umbrella are vulnerable to Russian aggression.

The annexation of Crimea, and its subsequent referendum, can hardly be a clear democratic expression by the people of Crimea.

While Kiev regards one third of Donetsk and Luhansk as under pro Russian rebel and therefore as special status, pro - Russian rebels lay claim to the entirety of Donetsk and Luhansk.

The only way to resolve this is to hold free and fair referenda in the disputed regions.

The UK and NATO allies must extend NATO across the whole of Central and Eastern Europe, to include Crimea and Ukraine (by this time, referenda determining the status of Crimea, Donetsk and Luhansk will have taken place). This would deter Russian aggression, as an attack on a NATO member would require a full retaliatory response from NATO allies. Nations left outside the security of the NATO umbrella are vulnerable to Russian aggression.

Continue with the targeted sanctions against Russian leaders, and their economic interests. In addition, ban visits from Russian leaders, and investment from Russian companies.

Impose an arms embargo against Russia, enforced by as many free nations as possible, to prevent further atrocities such as the shooting down of MH 17.

It is welcome that the UK has committed military personnel to Ukraine; we must help the Ukrainians to defend themselves by supplying arms.

For these measures to secure the freedom of the oppressed people of these territories to be effective, they need to be reinforced by a strong military presence.

Many express concerns that NATO is not seeking to expand. However, it is the prerogative of putative member to states to apply to join NATO, and Ukraine's parliament voted overwhelmingly to join NATO in the late autumn of 2014.

The NATO Russia Founding Act prohibits NATO members to permanently station substantial combat forces near the Russian border. However, The NRFA has already been violated by Russia, and the UK and Nato allies can hardly stand idly by while Russia extends its forces.

In addition, the Minks ceasefire agreement, like the NRFA, has been rendered null and void by continued Russian aggression.

CRIMEA AND UKRAINE:- RESTORATION OF TERRITORIAL INTEGRITY, FREE ELECTIONS AND NATO MEMBERSHIP

The aforementioned deployment of forces is designed to reinforce the second part of this strategy, the restoration of territorial integrity to Crimea and the Donbas in the Ukraine. The annexation of Crimea, and its subsequent referendum, can hardly be a clear democratic expression by the people of Crimea.

While Kiev regards one third of Donetsk and Luhansk as under pro Russian rebel and therefore as special status, pro - Russian rebels lay claim to the entirety of Donetsk and Luhansk.

The only way to resolve this is to hold free and fair referenda in the disputed regions.

Seek UN mandate to hold a legitimate referenda in Crimea, Donetsk and Luhansk, and send in impartial election/referendum monitors. If UN cannot agree upon this, then an alliance of free nations must act to ensure free and fair elections/referenda in Crimea and the Ukraine. If Donetsk and Luhansk vote to remain in the Ukraine, then impartial election monitors should ensure that people who could not vote in the elections on 26th October can cast their votes free from any intimidation. The heroic bravery of the people who defied the pro Russian rebels to cast their votes in Donetsk and Luhansk proves that the Ukrainian people will not surrender their sovereignty by intimidation.

The UK and NATO allies must extend NATO across the whole of Central and Eastern Europe, to include Crimea and Ukraine (by this time, referenda determining the status of Crimea, Donetsk and Luhansk will have taken place). This would deter Russian aggression, as an attack on a NATO member would require a full retaliatory response from NATO allies. Nations left outside the security of the NATO umbrella are vulnerable to Russian aggression.

For these measures to secure the freedom of the oppressed people of these territories to be effective, they need to be reinforced by a strong military presence.

THE REFUGEE CRISIS

The UK must continue to work with countries neighbouring Syria to admit refugees, for the UK to continue to admit refugees directly from Syria, focussing on women and children, the sick, and orphans. There are refuges already embarked upon their journey to Europe, which UK action will help to stem. The UK must work with other involved nations to admit a manageable number of refugees in this situation. Co-ordinating the desire of many families willing to adopt with the numbers of refugees admitted will ensure a stable home for many children, and mitigate the strain on public services and infrastructure.

There is inevitably an immediate and urgent response to the crisis. Humanitarian aid is required, in addition to a political solution as detailed below. To stop the huge danger to the refugees themselves of the long journey from Syria to Europe (exacerbated by the deal to open up the passport free zone from the English Channel to the Syrian border safe havens must be established in the next safe country to Syria. This is fairer for the refugees, and reduces the influx to EU nations, exacerbated by Schengen. These safe havens will be set up by the UN, and will be enforced by no-fly zones.

For this to happen, the immigration and asylum system in the UK must be rebalanced. The controls on economic migration (all migrants not being able to claim benefits for the first 4 years) must be introduced immediately. This would create the capacity to admit refugees, without increasing strain on public services.

TRANSITION TO DEMOCRACY IN SYRIA

The UK must play a leading role in co-ordinating a transitional Syrian government, working with Free Syrian Army and rebel forces to draft a constitution, and restore order. Neither Assad, IS nor Russia should be involved in the governing of Syria. The renunciation of terrorism must be a pre-condition for any group to participate for inclusion in any transitional government.

CHAPTER 5

Democratic Capitalism – Wealth Creation for a purpose

THE ECONOMIC FRAMEWORK:- TAXES, INVESTMENT, DEFICIT, AND DEBTS

- Personal Taxation
- The July 2015 Budget – How to help the low paid

COMPETITION v STATE CONTROL

- Setting Business Free
- Deregulation
- Sunday Trading

ECONOMIC GROWTH IN ONE NATION – INFRASTRUCTURE and INVESTMENT ACROSS THE WHOLE UK

- One North to create One Nation
- Airport expansion
- UK Steel: A Strategy for Growth

SKILLS- PARITY OF ESTEEM FOR VOCATIONAL EDUCATION

FORGING GLOBAL FREE TRADE: THE EU v THE OPEN SEAS

INTRODUCTION

At home, we must have a clear strategy of wealth creation for a purpose; to create the wealth which creates jobs, to pay our way in the world, and most importantly, to support those unable to help themselves. We must create what Harold Macmillan called "A Middle Way" for the 21st century, between Corbynist economics, which increases taxation, prices and state control, deters investment, and perpetuates poverty, and the Casino economy created by the Conservatives, based upon speculative property finance, cancellation of infrastructure projects, and cheap labour.

One Nation economics means a new strategy to counter the two big battalions; the Leviathan state, and the private monopoly/oligarchy. For example, the oligarchy of energy supplies ratcheting up prices must be replaced not by state owned monopoly, but by breaking up the Big Six, and enabling more providers to enter the market. Competition is the life blood of economic progress; innovation abounds, and prices fall, without a penny of taxpayers' money.

Wealth creation is the only method to provide jobs for those who can work, and fund the care of those who cannot work. Punitive taxation and regulation, deficit financing, and price controls push entrepreneurs abroad, and with it, the revenue upon which a civilised society depends. Competition is the life blood of economic progress.

Tax cuts must be focused on the low paid and small businesses, and funded up front, not by borrowing, nor by increasing tax on wealthy individuals and businesses, but by cutting government expenditure. Of course, tax evasion must be tackled, through reform of taxation on large corporations.

Only through democratic capitalism (that is, through competition replacing monopoly, and the creation of wealth for the purpose of eliminating low pay and poverty), can capitalism itself command moral superiority over socialism, and command the support of the people, who determine the government of the day, and the economic destiny of the United Kingdom.

THE ECONOMIC FRAMEWORK – TAXES, INVESTMENT, DEFICITS AND DEBTS

At the election, I placed a strengthened deficit reduction programme at the heart of my economic strategy, to maintain low interest rates. I supported the Charter for Budget Responsibility, setting limits on government spending, and the October 2015 vote to aim for a surplus by 2020 – this allows for investment spending in a downturn.

The central plank of my fiscal policy is to cut government expenditure, and use the proceeds to reduce the deficit, reprioritise spending from Barnett Formula and overseas aid to defence and health, and to finance tax cuts, targeted at the low paid and small businesses.

Once a surplus has been achieved, overall current government expenditure should grow at 1% less than GDP, year on year, to ensure a budget surplus.

A key pledge is that all current government expenditure commitments and tax cuts must be funded from savings in government expenditure.

The Chancellor, by his own admission, failed to meet his own 2010 pledge to abolish the deficit by 2015; I believe the main reason was the ideological cutting of capital expenditure on infrastructure. Maintaining infrastructure investment may have slowed the pace of deficit reduction in the short term, but, due to the employment and revenue infrastructure creates, would have yielded a greater return upon the initial investment, and in all probability, abolished the deficit by 2015. In addition, it would have been non inflationary, as it keeps capital and jobs within the UK, benefitting businesses in the UK. The cutting of infrastructure investment is an ideological shibboleth of recent Conservative governments from which I dissociate myself.

I agree with the Chancellor in that deficit reduction is achieved mainly by cutting government expenditure, and cannot be borne by excessive tax rises, as this deters investment, and, ultimately revenue, (although tax evasion must be tackled). However, growth can and must be instilled into the system, and this does involve capital investment.

The deficit is still nearly £72.2 billion, and with a possible second economic crunch, traditional government borrowing (even for investment) can risk demolishing the buffer of sound finances to counter external economic shocks.

From 2008, the government authorised the Bank of England to print £375 billion to invest in the banks, under a scheme known as quantitative easing. In October, 2015, for the second time in 2015 (and the second time since 1960), the UK is in deflation.

Traditionally central banks raise the amount of lending and activity in the economy indirectly, by cutting interest rates, which is why a strengthened deficit reduction programme is essential.

With interest rates at a record low of 0.5%, they can go no lower, then a central bank's only alternative is to pump money into the economy directly. That is quantitative easing (QE).

The central bank does by purchasing assets - usually government bonds - using money it has simply created out of thin air.

The institutions selling those bonds (the commercial banks, insurance companies, or other financial businesses sell these bonds, and will have "new" money in their accounts (purchase by the central bank), which then boosts the money supply. This is particularly pertinent in only the second period of deflation in the UK since 1960.

The increased demand for the government bonds increases their value, making them more expensive to buy, and so they become a less attractive investment.

So the companies who sold the bonds can then use the proceeds to invest in other companies or lend to individuals, rather than buying any more of the bonds.

This means that banks, insurance companies, and other firms are more confident about lending to companies and individuals, which keeps the interest rate low or lower, this increasing consumption and boosting the economy.

QE was tried first by a central bank in Japan to get it out of a period of deflation following its asset bubble collapse in the 1990s.

QE was first tried in the UK in 2009, for the banks after the financial crisis.

While expanding the stock of money, QE is effectively printing money, as it is an expansion of the central bank's balance sheet and the monetary base.

QE for bank lending was correct, but I question the scale, and that some of the funds should have been allocated to infrastructure investment.

It is notable that QE for infrastructure has been adopted by the new Labour leader Jeremy Corbyn. He was castigated for proposing an idea which sounds eminently reasonable when advocated by members of the Bank of England monetary policy committee in response to the deflation of October, 2015.

QE for investment will create less inflationary pressure that QE for consumption, resulting in lower interest rate rises than would otherwise be the case.

I propose to allocate £30 billion of QE to infrastructure:

- £12 billion to social housing to build 200,000 social houses over 4 years (Shelter's proposal).
- £15 billion for One North, to integrate the transport networks five great cities of Sheffield, Newcastle, Leeds, Liverpool and Manchester. This will improve transport links across the United Kingdom.
- £3 billion for sustainable energy production to make the UK self sufficient in energy.

As of March, 2016, the deficit stood at £72.2 billion.

I amended my budget proposals, and incorporated many of the Conservative government proposals in the March 2015 budget.

No child benefit and child tax credit to the third child born from 2016. This would save £3.1 billion per annum, £12.4 billion over 4 years. This will raise an identical amount of revenue as the cutting of tax credit thresholds, and cutting disability benefit.

An additional £1.05 billion should be re-directed to deficit reduction from abolishing student grants and freezing working age benefits NOT allocated to raising the tax credit threshold.

These measures alone will reduce the net welfare bill by £13.45 billion over the Parliament, well in excess of the £12 billion cuts proposed by the Conservative government.

Revenue from RBS and Lloyds privatisations would equal £25.6 billion.

This already yields £39.05 billion by 2019-20, well above the £30 billion outlined in the Charter for Budget responsibility.

These measures alone will almost halve the deficit from £89.2 billion to £52.415 billion by 2020. This does not include revenue from economic growth, nor streamlining central government, by contacting out HR & IT systems.

These measures alone will more than halve the deficit from £72.2 billion to £32.97 billion by 2020. This does not include revenue from economic growth, nor streamlining central government.

PERSONAL TAXATION

I have always supported the raising of the income tax threshold, to encourage people to take lower paid jobs to get on the jobs ladder, infinitely better than remaining on benefits. While all taxpayers have rightly benefitted from this policy, another group of workers has been ignored. People earning as little as £8000 per year have to pay NI; in reality, NI is an extension of income tax. I pledged to raise the threshold from £8060 to £8933.60, so that low paid would benefit by £19 per week. I would keep the threshold for income tax at £11,600, and continue to raise the National Insurance threshold until it was equal with the income tax threshold. If the UK leaves the EU, then £1.76 billion of the savings made from the EU budget contribution would be spent to further raise NI primary threshold from £8933.60 to £9807.20 for 2016-17. The income tax threshold will remain at £11,600 (allowing for inflation) until the National Insurance threshold is raised to same level. From this point, income tax and National Insurance would be entirely integrated.

A strong deficit reduction programme, combined with the first deflation since 1960, grants the UK a historic opportunity for massive investment in transport (One North), social housing (200,000 units by 2020), and investment in energy. This would provide housing for all, stabilise the property market, spread economic growth across the UK, enhance transport links across the UK, and make the UK self sufficient in energy.

THE CONSERVATIVE BUDGETS – THE EFFECT ON LOW PAID AND DISABLED

The Conservative Party's pre – election pledge to cut a further £12 billion from the welfare budget to contribute towards cutting the deficit was unspecified, and caused much needless anxiety for millions of people in receipt of benefits.

Even the possibility of cutting disabled benefits was mentioned – this was a possibility, as the government had consistently ruled out cuts to child benefits and pension related benefits since 2010.

In the event, the government proposed in July that much of the £12 billion would be met by reducing the threshold at which people start to lose tax credits from £6420 to £3850, as of next year. This means the average low earner would have lost approximately £1300 on average; the living wage will not have compensated for the loss of tax credits for these workers, many of whom are part time.

The second assault was the proposal to reduce PIP payments, based upon attaching less weight to people who needed toileting and bathing aids, crucial for people's dignity, and ability to find work.

These were tragically ironic policies for a party that claimed to represent striving working people.

If an MP, I would never have voted for such policies. This was never in my election manifesto. To me, welfare must not be cut from those who are in a particular situation through no fault of their own; for example, the disabled, pensioners, and those receiving supplements to their wages. This therefore rules out cutting DLA, and reducing the tax credit thresholds.

In my manifesto, I categorically ruled out cuts to disabled, carers benefit and pensions. By limiting child benefit and child tax credit to the first 2 children born from 2016, £12 billion would have been saved, without having to reduce the tax credit thresholds.

Furthermore, the government never had a mandate to cut tax credits, nor cut disability benefits.

In response to the July, 2015 budget, I proposed reversing the tax credit cut.

In the event, during the Comprehensive spending Review on the 26th November, 2015, the Chancellor George Osborne abolished the entire package of tax credit cuts.

The Chancellor has as yet not proposed an alternative method of cutting £12 billion from the welfare budget.

As an alternative, child benefits and child tax credits should be stopped from the third child born after April 2016. By the time of publication, this would need to be postponed to April 2017. This is a fair policy, as people make a conscious decision to bring another child into the world, and will make families responsible with family planning. It does not apply retrospectively, so families currently with three children or more will not be penalised. The policy would be phased in to allow time for families to make a conscious decision. This policy would actually save £12 billion over the Parliament, more than the cutting of the tax credit thresholds.

Income tax payers who are net beneficiaries of tax credits will have these tax credits protected. For income tax payers who are not, the tax credit will be replaced by a tax cut in kind. Where possible (and without reducing people's income) we must stop a system where people's money is taken by the government, who then reissue people's own money back to them in the form of tax credits.

COMPETITION V STATE CONTROL

- SETTING BUSINESS FREE

Prior to the March 2016 budget, UK businesses had the 3rd highest business rates in the OECD. Rate cuts were intially considered so important by the Chancellor that he would only provide relief for 1 year, and any cuts are dependent upon the local authority, many of the lower income authorities cannot afford to cut rates, thus preventing many businesses locating to these areas, to create jobs, and provide revenue for essential services. At the last election, I pledged to cut rates UK wide, and to make permanent the relief for smaller businesses.

I proposed that rate relief should be made permanent for businesses premises with a rateable value of up to £12,000 from 2015 onwards, and extend the £1000 discount for shops, pubs, restaurants from 2016 onwards. This would cost £1.120 billion, and would be funded by part of the scrapped Barnett formula. In the March 2016 budget, George Osborne announced almost identical proposals.

The self employed already are denied sick pay and holiday. Half of self employed earn less than £12,000. All self employed above NI threshold had to pay £143 fee (the NIC Class 2 contribution). I proposed before the election to scrap this regressive tax, to encourage more people to become self employed; George Osborne had the foresight to adopt this policy in the March, 2015 budget.

Many small businesses (especially one man bands) are subject to 20% VAT. While VAT on new build homes is zero rated, it is levied at 20% on renovation of existing properties. This does nothing for sustainability, and actively encourages new build. By cutting the VAT on building renovation to 10%, this would encourage councils, private and social landlords to renovate existing properties, make it cheaper for homeowners to renovate their properties (thus boosting their resale value), and encourage decorators, and home improvement companies to boost their income.

The recent Google tax fiasco is an example of how the existing corporation tax system does not prevent tax evasion (the illegal evasion of taxes by individuals, corporations and trusts). This is different form tax avoidance, the legal use of tax laws to reduce one's tax burden.

In January, 2016, Google paid £130 million in tax owed since 2005. This payment only occurred after ad hoc deals. Google made £3.8 billion in sales in 2013, but only paid £20.4 million in corporation tax in 2013. This represents a corporation tax rate of 0.54%!

Corporation tax applies tax on profits (on all profits from the UK and abroad) which larger companies are able to shift overseas to lower or zero tax areas. Smaller companies are unable to do this, so have to pay the full amount of corporation tax under UK jurisdiction. A sales tax should replace corporation tax, so that the tax applies where the sale takes place, before the profits are hived off. (BBC News, 30th January, 2016).

The sales tax should be levied at no higher a rate than the corporation tax. It could indeed be lowered, with the effect of maintaining or increasing revenue, as the tax would apply at the point of sale. In the interim, a combination of corporation tax and sales tax could be applied, if in the beginning, a sales tax would not bring in sufficient revenue. Such a dual tax system must not be levied at a higher rate than current corporation tax, so that no business should be worse off than those currently paying their full amount of corporation tax.

DEREGULATION

60% of small firms report that complying with regulation costs more than £1000 per year, and compliance costs have increased since 2010, according to the Federation of Small Business. The policy of one regulation abolished for every new regulation introduced is not sufficient. There should be a net reduction in business regulation. EU air quality legislation will result in many coal fired power stations closing. I will allocate £3 billion of QE funds to energy independence, including carbon capture for coal. This will ensure businesses have a stable supply of energy, and encourage growth of businesses that supply these power stations – engineering companies, for example. The Common External tariff stops the UK from trading freely with the rest of the world, and increases cost of imported raw materials. I will campaign for UK to leave EU, and for the CET (and other EU red tape) to expire under "sunset clause." Please refer to "The Positive Case for Brexit" for the EU regulations which I would repeal. Paid parental leave should only apply to the first two births.

REDUCING STRIKES

Currently, some strikes occur with only ¼ of the support of those entitled to vote. This is fundamentally undemocratic.

Raising the threshold to 50% of all those entitled to vote before a strike could take place would encourage participation in the decision, and reduce the power of militant trade union leaders to call strikes that only a minority of the union membership has voted for. It will also reduce intimidation of those who do not want to strike.

The proposed restrictions on communication via social media about strikes are an infringement of civil liberties, and should not be introduced.

The child who cannot go to school, the parent who has to take time off work, the pensioner who goes without their care, they have had no say in whether their workers should strike. They have no trade union.

SUNDAY TRADING

While small shops are allowed to open all day, larger shops (with over 3000 square feet) can only trade for 6 hours, between 10:00 and 18:00, and must close on Easter Sunday and Christmas Day.

The West End Company (representing 600 businesses in London) suggest that at an extra 2 hours of Sunday trading could generate 3000 jobs, and £200 million a year in London alone. Such a scheme was trialled during the Olympic Games in 2012.

Indeed, there are more transactions on a Sunday than a Saturday. Extending Sunday trading would also enable shops to compete with online retailers, who are available 24/7. There are no restrictions on Sunday trading in Scotland, so England, Wales and Northern Ireland are put at an unfair disadvantage.

Even these modest government proposals (giving councils and mayors the power to extend Sunday trading) have been allowed to be railroaded by the SNP.

On 10th November, the SNP advised it would vote against the relaxation of the Sunday trading laws in England and Wales, even though such measures do not affect Scotland. Although the government had its own rebels opposed to extension of Sunday trading, had EVEL been in place, then the government's proposals would have been voted for. Once again, the government has allowed the SNP to railroad proposals which do not affect Scotland, without even having the courage to put these proposals to a vote.

The government must urgently introduce EVEL, so that the SNP cannot block legislation not affecting Scotland. Until then, the government must stop capitulating, as this will encourage the SNP in its anti – democratic manoeuvres.

The decision to extend Sunday trading should be devolved to the businesses, rather than many councils who are not sympathetic to businesses.

ECONOMIC GROWTH IN ONE NATION – INFRASTRUCTURE, INVESTMENT & SKILLS FOR THE WHOLE UK

For decades, growth in the UK has been focussed in London and the South East, and has been dependent upon speculative property finance. This has exacerbated the inequalities in growth and income in the different regions of the UK. It has contributed to the rise of the SNP in Scotland, and the rise of UKIP in the North and the Midlands.

While the UK is building more cars than at any time since 1972, manufacturing lags behind the rest of the economy in terms of growth.

Since 1966, manufacturing has been in decline. Entry into the EEC in 1973 made raw materials imported from outside the EEC very high due to tariffs, and the UK lost export markets in the Commonwealth. Poor industrial relations were partially resolved by high unemployment, caused in turn by 17% interest rates in the early 1980s, and 15% in the early 1990s, which made it very expensive to export, and for businesses to borrow to invest. More recently, this has been further exacerbated by the glut of cheap Chinese steel (a process known as dumping), which undercuts UK steel; very high energy costs; and the 3rd highest business rates in the OECD; and by the ideological subservience of successive

UK governments to the EU regulations forbidding state aid, despite other EU member states (such as Italy) pursuing state aid.

This creates a vicious circle, whereby UK businesses import cheaper steel from China, which reduces the demand for UK steel, which in turn weakens the UK's steel capacity, undermining the security of UK steel.

There are two strategies for the UK. Via EU protectionism, which increases the price of raw materials, and the loss of UK export markets, and forbids the UK even to cut taxes for firms to compete, or a new vision, with the UK trading freely with the rest of the world, but buttressed not by protectionism, but by an army of skilled workers, a competitive tax rate, and an industrial strategy that ensures that UK raw materials are used in UK manufacturing.

The phrase industrial strategy conjures up images of governments in the 1970s propping up lame ducks. Subsidies only serve to featherbed the inefficient, and nationalisation deters investment and innovation.

I propose an industrial strategy based upon investment in infrastructure, an indigenous energy policy to reduce costs, producing essential raw materials (such as steel) in the UK where possible, tax cuts, and awarding government contracts to UK firms (certainly for defence and energy).

THE BANKS

The lack of available credit at a manageable interest rate is a deterrent for new businesses. There should be an Investment Bank; not state owned, nor charging interest rates below MLR, but specifically earmarked for capital and human investment. This radical idea has been championed by the Chambers of Commerce.

A mistake made by the Labour Government during the financial crisis of 2007-08 was to bail out all the banks equally – the more responsible banks should have been more highly rewarded, and the irresponsible banks rewarded less (a universal bail out was inevitable to keep the economy functioning), to provide incentives, and encourage the more responsible banks to take over failing banks.

The Coalition's policy on banks was correct – to create a firewall between high risk investment banking and retail banking.

However, with regards to the banking levy, a more proportionate system should be introduced, to provide a framework of rewards and punishments, to promote responsible banking, and deter irresponsible behaviour.

A variable bank levy would provide such a framework. There would be a higher levy for irresponsible banks, and responsible banks would be rewarded with a lower levy.

Return the nationalised banks to their rightful owners (the customers and shareholders) at the first prudent opportunity.

ONE NORTH TO CREATE ONE NATION

Infrastructure (especially One north) to create the transport links essential to make the North an economic power house (this MUST include electrification of the Pennines).

The Northern powerhouse is merely a rhetorical instrument wielded by this Conservative government. The record of rebalancing the economy to encourage Northern growth is poor. In 2010, the Coalition made swingeing cuts to the capital investment budget – QE could have been used to invest in infrastructure. After winning the 2015 election, the Conservative government cancelled the electrification of the Pennines, an essential foundation of the Northern powerhouse.

One North is designed to link the 5 great cities of the North; Sheffield, Newcastle, Liverpool, Manchester and Leeds. It centres around integrating HS2 with the existing rail network.

The North has a population of 15 million, larger than London, and almost as large as the Netherlands, yet the economic performance is below that of London and the Netherlands. Motorways in the north need to be extended East West on M60/62, and north-south on M1/M6. But rail connectivity (125 mph intercity capacity) between the 5 major cities essential, as this will enable the North to capitalise upon lower barriers between trading with the South of England.

By providing the infrastructure to enhance connectivity, this will encourage business to invest in the North, and will thus be self financing.

Enhanced connectivity will enhance labour mobility, increase competitiveness via access to larger markets, reducing trading costs through the economies of scale of enhanced transport networks. The construction of One North will create an army of skilled workers, whose skills will be transferrable into the new enterprises created in the North.

Improved road links to ports must be an essential plank of One North. There must be a fast intercity rail network, including a trans Pennine route, and a faster link to Newcastle, and crucially, a faster link to Manchester airport.

The connected rail network must be linked to trams/buses, and park and ride, to prevent congestion in city centres as the economy expands.

There must be real time digital timetables to enhance journey planning.

A key plank of the trans Pennine route must be an east – west freight capacity, linking major port estuaries and north-south rail links.

One North envisages the following increases in capacity.

A 65% increase in freight train movements between the north and the south.

A 60% increase in freight train movements accessing these south-bound corridors from Manchester, Leeds and Sheffield and surrounding areas.

Enhanced connectivity obviously reduces journey times. A 20 minute reduction in the journey time between Manchester and Leeds would be worth £6.7 billion across the whole North of England, £2.7 billion of which would be captured for the city regions of Manchester and Leeds. Enhanced links to Middlesborough and Carlisle training centres will reduce the number of people not in education, employment nor training.

In the short term, the priority must be for trans Pennine as well as north-south rail strategies involving new high-speed lines and an ongoing priority to complete gaps in the strategic highway network and to address congestion.

Similarly, with road links, existing gaps must be plugged to lay the foundations for the road networks of One North. A section of managed motorway has been completed on the M62 between Leeds and Bradford and another is under construction on the M1 around Wakefield as is the A1 upgrade to motorway in North Yorkshire. Work on managed motorways is due to start in the next year on the M1 around Sheffield and on sections of the M60 and M62 around Manchester, along with work to upgrade part of the Newcastle Gateshead bypass, the A556 (M56 to M6) and access to the Port of Immingham.

The link between Sheffield and Manchester must be a combination of road and rail, for reasons of environmental sustainability.

Movement of freight to and from ports and airports is an essential part of One North.

While highways and rail are publicly funded, the ports and distribution centres are subject to the competition of market forces. The North of England has 14 million square metres of warehouses, concentrated on both sides of the Pennines, on the M62 corridor.

Freight accounts for 40% of traffic on the M62; the logical conclusion is that a larger proportion of freight must be carried by rail. This is more environmentally sustainable, and less prone to adverse weather conditions. Expanding rail terminals in Mersey and East coast ports is an essential short term measure to commence this process.

Northern ports account for 30% of all port unit load traffic.

Electrification of the northern hub lines will enhance connection between Liverpool and Doncaster.

Manchester airport handles 20 million passengers per year. The Airport Master Plan to 2030 acknowledges surface access to Manchester airport to enhance the economy of the North West, but these advantages must be extended to the whole North. By extending connectivity between Manchester airport and the whole of the North, this will obviate the need for a further change for entrepreneurs at another European airport. The M56 is near to capacity, due to the volume of road traffic accessing Manchester airport.

The lack of sufficient rail connectivity to Manchester airport is highlighted by the long journey by rail to Manchester Airport; nearly 3 hours for Newcastle and 2h 30 minutes for Hull (both with an interchange en route), 1h 20 minutes for Sheffield and 1h 05 minutes for Liverpool. This highlights the need for an enhanced rail connectivity (especially in an east-west direction), light rail connectivity and direct cross city services to the North's principal international gateway airport.

One North means increasing commuting capacity by the following:-

120 - 150% for Leeds and Manchester.
100 - 130% for Liverpool, Sheffield and Newcastle.

AIRPORT EXPANSION

Airport expansion near London is essential; we will not make the North richer by making London and the South poorer by denying airport expansion.

As London is the world's leading financial centre, building an airport in the centre of London will shorten travel times between the airport and the City, thus enhancing business. I would rule out expansion at Heathrow and Gatwick (due to extra pollution, and the upheaval caused on the M25 by having to build a tunnel), and opt for Boris Island. The original proposal was for a 4 runway airport here to actually replace Heathrow. My proposal is for a single runway airport, aimed at the business community. This would prevent congestion associated with holidaymakers travelling into central London to fly on holiday, and prevent extra CO_2 emissions associated with driving from the City to Heathrow on a return journey.

UK STEEL – A STRATEGY FOR GROWTH

For example, One North (the project to link the five great northern cities Liverpool, Manchester, Newcastle, Sheffield and Birmingham) will involve massive construction of rail and road links. My proposal to build a new generation of carrier based combat aircraft in the UK will also increase jobs in the UK, and utilise British steel. Steel will also form a large part of the construction of One North, so here is an example whereby the UK government can award the contract to UK steel firms.

Government and firms purchasing steel and other raw materials from within the UK makes sense in terms of our national security (avoiding the reliance on unstable regimes), but to establish a skills base in the UK to diversify into other areas of manufacturing. It also reduces the economic cost to the balance of payments if the steel were to be imported, and the environmental cost of shipping the steel into the UK.

This alone is not a sufficient argument for buying British.

The first priority in the UK industrial strategy is to make the suppliers of steel and other raw materials more competitive, so that it wins contracts for UK projects not through favouritism, but by being the most attractive supplier on offer.

In 2014, 12.1 million tonnes of UK steel was produced, and employed 18000 workers.

UK gas price was 59.02 p per therm in 2014, more than twice that of the United States. 18.5 Gj is used per tonne of steel produced.

In 2014, the UK demanded 10691.1 tonnes of steel for various purposes, and a total of 11.9 million tonnes of UK steel was produced. Yet only 4.2 million tonnes were supplied by UK mills, and 6.5 million tonnes were imported. Of this, 687,000 tonnes came from China, double the 303,000 tonnes of 2013, and 4.7 million tonnes from the EU, but China's steel price has dropped; global steel prices have halved in the last year. (BBC News, 20th October, 2015). UK steel has 37.7 % share of its own market. UK supply actually exceeded UK demand in 2014, putting potential downward pressure on UK prices. Were steel capacity increased to meet increased demand, then this would further reduce the price of UK steel.

In 2014, 4.2 million tonnes of UK steel was delivered within the UK, 7.6 million tonnes was exported, so 6.5 million tonnes of the steel delivered to UK was imported, and goods containing 21.5 million tonnes of UK steel were imported.

UK steel comprised 40% of the share of steel within the UK.

In 2014, UK balance of trade for steel was a surplus of £2.763 million. Exported £4.943 billion, imported £2.719 billion.

At Llanwern and Rotherham, Tata announced that 970 jobs would be lost. At Redcar, 2200 jobs were lost. The situation at Scunthorpe, Dalzell, and Clydebridge is yet to be confirmed.

On Monday, Caparo went into partial administration, with 1700 jobs at risk, and Tata confirmed it will cut 1200 jobs at Scunthorpe and Scotland.

So, 3170 jobs have already been lost, and a further 2900 were set to be lost. (BBC News, 20th October, 2015).

Business rates for steel are staggeringly high in the UK vis a vis our industrial competitors, sometimes as much as 5 times. One of Tata's steel plants in the Netherlands pays £3 million in business rates, compared to £15 million for the plant in Scunthorpe. (City AM 23rd October 2015)

There are 2 projects which could reopen the plants recently closed, prevent closure of threatened plants, and increase capacity, and enhance the skills base in the UK.

One North (the project to link the five great northern cities Liverpool, Manchester, Newcastle, Sheffield and Leeds) will involve massive construction of rail and road links. By building a new generation of carrier based combat aircraft in the UK, UK steel will be used. Here are 2 examples whereby the UK government can award the contract to UK steel firms.

Government and firms purchasing steel and other raw materials from within the UK makes sense in terms of our national security (avoiding the reliance on unstable regimes), but to establish a skills base in the UK to diversify into other areas of manufacturing. It also reduces the economic cost to the balance of payments if the steel were to be imported, and the environmental cost of shipping the steel into the UK.

This alone is not a sufficient argument for buying British.

The first priority is to make the suppliers of steel and other raw materials more competitive, so that it wins contracts for UK projects not through favouritism, but by being the most attractive supplier on offer.

- Cut the business rates for UK steel by 50%.
- Immediate relief from the carbon tax and regulations, which put UK steel at a competitive advantage. Immediately, the government should implement the energy intensive industries compensation package.

- Allocate £3 billion of QE to energy independence and clean technology, and apply carbon capture technology to the steel industry.

Investment is often made in non EU steel plants as the EU carbon regulations do not apply in such countries. Even the most efficient plants do not receive all the ETS (Emission Trading System) allocations because of the benchmark set for steel, and an arbitrary cap on industry. A cap on the indirect costs associated with electricity generation mean that Steel plants are also paying for 20% of the ETS costs associated with electricity they purchase. Increasing carbon leakage provisions beyond 2020 could increase the cost of producing 1 tonne of steel to £28.47 by 2030, as they may have to purchase ETS beyond free allocations; the free allocations should are based upon a historic baseline of carbon emission, rather than current activity.

(Making reform of the EU Emissions Trading System work for steel)

EU carbon emission systems are unfair to the UK, make no compensation for innovation, and ignore the largest emitters, such as China and the USA. As discussed in the chapter on EU regulation, I would repeal the Climate Change regulations.

The UK must take a lead, and introduce a variable tax, which increases tax for use of carbon, and cuts taxes for those firms who cut carbon and use new technology.

China is dumping steel on the UK market. What this means in practice is that China is selling its steel at an export price lower than its selling price in China. Where such a practice can be demonstrated to cause injury to the importing country (namely the UK), the importing country can impose anti dumping duties against the aggressor (in this case China) under Article VI of the GATT 1994. The anti dumping duty is determined by the dumping margin – that is the difference between the export price and domestic selling price in the exporting country. The appropriate duty is added to the export price, thus rendering a "fair trade" price. (www.meti.go.jp/english/report/data/gCT9905e.html)

This may appear to be confronting protectionism with protectionism, but anti dumping measures are essential to ensure minimum standards and a level playing field, to make free trade work. If the UK were to impose anti dumping measures against China (through the WTO), this would act as a deterrent to other countries considering dumping their produce on the world markets, and the imposition of anti dumping duties would prevent the decimation of the UK steel industry through cheap imports.

The Appellate body of the WTO ruled against China, thus upholding the February 2015 Panel's decision that China's anti dumping duties imposed on imports pf Japanese and European steel tubes were in breach of WTO rules.

The UK urgently needs to implement anti dumping measures on Chinese steel. As the UK is currently a member of the EU, we have to appeal to the EU Commissioner on Trade, a lengthy process requesting the agreement of 27 other nation states, many of which have vastly different economic interests to the UK. There is no guarantee that the EU would agree to the UK's anti dumping request.

Outside the EU, the UK could reactivate full membership of the WTO (with full speaking and voting rights), and work with the WTO to impose anti dumping duties against China within weeks. With planning and foresight, these measures (anti dumping duties, cutting rates, cutting energy costs, and implementing infrastructure projects that use steel) have every chance of keeping steel plants open and expanding them, re-opening closed plants, and unemployed steel workers to get their jobs back.

The EU is considering conferring upon China Market Economy Status, which makes it hard to impose anti dumping duties against China. The EU can unilaterally confer MES on China, and UK (as a member of the UK) is powerless to act. The UK should, therefore, use its status with its own seat at the WTO to deny China Market Economy status. A highly regulated economy such as China's, (with a heavily subsidised steel industry) by definition should not meet the criteria for Market Economy Status.

UK should use influence as a large trading nation to impose anti dumping measures against Chinese. Inside the EU, the UK is unable to do this.

In addition, under WTO rules, the UK can UK should use its vast trading power as leverage in the investment deals with the Chinese; for example, forego Chinese investment unless they stop dumping cheap steel illegally onto the world market.

SKILLS - PARITY OF ESTEEM FOR VOCATIONAL EDUCATION

To create the skilled workforce we need to lead in technological innovation, we must recruit the best talent from our own population.

The tuition fee is £9000 per year, for all university courses. This one size fits all policy prevents graduates taking degrees in engineering and science. nation that invented the steam engine, TV, and radar must encourage the cream of British talent to forge the technological revolution. Tuition fees for science and technology must be cut, and funded by raising fees on humanities courses, far less beneficial to the UK economy.

The very last thing companies of any size need is the government's apprenticeship levy, announced in the November, 2015, Spending Review, and coming into effect in April, 2017. The levy will be at a rate of 0.5% of an employer's pay bill. There will be a £15,000 allowance for employers which will mean that the levy will only apply to pay bills over £3 million. It is estimated that less than 2% of employers will pay the levy.

Currently, based on 2014/15 figures, the government's annual expenditure is £1.48 billion on apprenticeships. If the same level were maintained throughout this Parliament, then this would equal £7.4 billion over the Parliament. The government was originally to finance this by reducing the welfare cap from £23,000 to £20,000 (£26,000 to £23,000 in London). This would save £405 million per year [or £2,025,000,000 over 5 years] (BBC News, 8th July 2015), redirected to the government's apprenticeship scheme. Clearly, this was not sufficient, so the government introduced a levy which will raise £3 billion by 2020 (Daily Telegraph, 25/11/15), bringing the total government expenditure on all apprenticeships (16-18 and adult) to at least £4.48 billion by 2020.

The government has been short-sighted. While correct to reverse the planned cuts to tax credits (for which they have no mandate), they have not proposed alternatives to cut £12 billion from the welfare budget. While all of these savings are pledged to reduce the deficit, the reduction in savings makes it even more challenging to fund alternative resources to finance apprenticeships, without resorting to higher taxation, which is a false economy, as it imposes an extra burden on business. Indeed, the apprenticeship levy actually punishes businesses for recruiting apprentices.

With my budget proposals pledged to cut NI for the low paid (which will help apprentice and non apprentice alike), cutting business rates and VAT on building renovation, restoring defence, there is little room for boosting expenditure on apprenticeships without higher taxation, and further cuts elsewhere.

If the UK left the EU, it would save £7.9 billion per year on average, and £2 billion of this would be redirected to apprenticeships. This is less than the levy would raise, but the apprenticeships would be targeted at the strategic sectors of the economy in energy and technological production. Increasing troop numbers by 30,000 will enable young men and women to be trained in engineering, and other skills which can easily transferred to the civilian economy. In addition, many engineers will be trained to build the next generation of UK manufactured combat aircraft, in accordance with the defence policy.

The lack of available credit at a manageable interest rate is a deterrent for new businesses. There must be an Investment Bank; not state owned, or at cheaper interest rates than MLR, but specifically earmarked for capital and human investment. This is a radical idea championed by the Chambers of Commerce.

GLOBAL FREE TRADE

The industrial future of the UK depends upon forging new export markets with the growing economies of the world. This cannot happen as long as the UK remains a member of the EU.

It is a scandalous waste of peoples' talents that customers overseas demand essential goods and services, while nearly 1 million young people in UK are unemployed.

The EU proclaims the great myth that it is a bastion of Free Trade. The EU trades freely within its borders, but imposes tariffs against imports from outside the EU, which it uses to subsidise its food prices. "Fortress Europe" denies the UK the cheap food of world markets, and denies developing nations export markets for their goods. In retaliation, other nations impose tariffs against our exports, so we lose export markets. In short, Fortress Europe extinguishes enterprise and exacerbates poverty, at home and abroad.

My vision is not for the United Kingdom to retreat from Fortress Europe to hide behind the barricades of Fortress Britain. Outside the EU, the UK would have its own seat at the WTO, (currently we are one of 28 countries represented by a single EU Trade Commissioner) and be free to forge free trade areas with the growing economies of the world. Food imports would be substantially cheaper, helping the poor in the UK and overseas. In return, the UK would win new export markets for our goods, creating a virtuous circle. By utilising the UK's unique global trade connections, we could forge and lead a massive free trade area, which (combined with weaknesses in China's economy) could prevent China from becoming the world's most powerful economy and leading military superpower, and therefore restore the Atlantic alliance as the leading military and moral force in the world.

The developing nations would escape poverty by growing their export markets, thus rendering redundant much overseas aid, which has been used to subsidise poverty. Brexit could tackle poverty at home and abroad.

History tells us of the folly of protectionism. The protectionism of the 1930s turned the Depression into a Slump.

Outside the EU, the UK could forge free trade areas with the growth areas of the world, creating huge opportunities for our entrepreneurs to expand and export across the globe, creating sustainable economic growth, and new jobs.

Concerns abound about possible EU trade retaliation against the UK if we became independent.

The EU has a massive trade surplus with the rest of the EU (the EU sells us more than UK sells to the EU, the UK had a balance of payments deficit with the EU of £39 billion in 2013). In addition, the share of exports going to the EU has fallen from 54% to 46 % from 2007 to 2013. (IEA Brexit Prize: Plan to leave EU by 2020 by Daniel C. Pycock).

Economic self interest dictates that the EU would never dare impose tariffs on UK goods should we leave the EU, and would not dare to start a trade war with the UK.

If the UK withdrew from the EU without a free trade agreement, then the value of exports from 2019 -2023 would be £25.7 billion lower than if the UK secured a free trade deal with the EU. In the former scenario, exports would also be lower than the status quo (ie the UK remaining in an essential unreformed EU). By negotiating EFTA + (with an EU "passport" for financial services), export growth would be £10.3 billion over and above a straightforward EFTA agreement over 2019 – 2023. (Lea, R. Global Vision Perspective House of Commons Library Data, April 2008. Niebohr, J. "The Four Lies about Leaving the European Union", The Bruges Group, January 2013).

Daniel Hannan (Conservative MEP South East), stated that "the IMF...nations within the eurozone will grow at an average of 2.7% over the next five years [up to and including 2017] while the Commonwealth surges ahead at 7.3%." In fact, this was grossly over optimistic, as in fact the eurozone grew at 0.3% and 0.1% for the 2 consecutive quarters 2013. (Hannan, Daniel "Look at these graphs: any possible argument for remaining in the EU has been blown away." (Daily Telegraph 7th June 2012).

The EU has no agreements with the technological industry leaders, USA, Japan and Singapore. These are lucrative markets (both for the UK and those countries) which could be tapped into by forging free trade agreements (under WTO rules) by the UK having its own seat at the WTO.

The abolition of trade barriers between the USA and UK could increase UK GDP by £4 billion to £10 billion per annum. (IEA Brexit Prize: Plan to leave EU by 2020 by Daniel C. Pycock)

Instant exchange of money and services on line does not recognise the artificial barriers imposed by the EU customs union. The forging of free trade areas (enhanced by the UK having its own seat at the WTO) will remove this obstacle. After Brexit, it is vital that the UK does not embark upon protectionism through customs unions, as the prime reason for Brexit is leaving the most protectionist customs union, the EU.

Until the EU referendum, the UK should establish links with new trading partners.

CHAPTER 6

A home for everyone

- Increasing supply, reducing demand
- Tenant's rights
- Ending homelessness

HOUSING

The number of people claiming housing benefit has increased by 500,000 since 2010, when the Coalition came to power. Spending on Housing Benefit has risen by £650 million a year on average since 2009-10, and HB bill is expected to reach £25 billion by 2017. 5 million people now claim housing benefits. 1.8 million people are on waiting lists for social housing. Hundreds of thousands more are renting privately, and thus vulnerable to higher rents, and rent rises.

The HB cap is £500 per week for a family with children, and £350 for a single person. Many people on HB are renting private properties that are dearer than this, and this struggle to pay the difference. By prioritising social housing for new build and renovation, this will provide more homes at a cheaper rent, thus reducing the Housing Benefit bill.

A comprehensive housing strategy based on reducing demand by controlling immigration (both from inside the EU and outside); increasing supply through QE funds for construction/conversion/renovation of homes assisted by a cut in VAT on building repairs/conversions to 10%. This will increase the supply of affordable housing, preserve the Green Belt, and provide a boost to home improvements industry, and stabilise house prices, avoiding an unsustainable housing boom.

Affordable housing is a key social problem in Brighton pavilion, where I stood for Parliament in May, 2015.

SUPPLY AND DEMAND

Too often, the debate on housing supply is one sided; it focuses on the number of homes needed to be built in the future, and does not focus on the other side of the equation; reducing demand.

It is a fact that an increase in population growth (both due to immigration and/or growth from the indigenous population) contributes to the increased demand for housing. It is estimated that (even accounting for an annual average of 145,000 per year, then 27.8% of additional households up to and including 2012/22 would be attributable to net migration. The high migration scenario with net migration at 217,000 (highly likely for the forseeable future due to the refugee crisis, and Cameron's failure to secure even limits to EU migrants' benefits in the EU renegotiations) estimates that 68,000 (or 27.8% of the 245,000 new homes required each year). (ONS – quoted by Tom Harris [former Labour MP for Glasgow South] Daily Record, 18 Mar 16)

My proposed policy of zero net immigration (implemented almost immediately by EU migrants not being entitled to benefits until UK withdraws from EU, when we could control our borders) would therefore reduce the annual demand for housing (of all types) to 177,000.

Demand would be further reduced from the indigenous population by child benefit and child tax credit being limited to the first 2 children from 2016. It is very difficult to quantify the effects of this, as to how many children would not be born as a result, and how many families would use their own resources (rather than child benefit) to bring a third child into the world.

Reducing demand for housing must be achieved by reducing population growth, both through immigration control, and limiting child benefit and child tax credit to the first 2 children.

To further protect quality of life and the green belt, all efforts must be made to convert existing and empty buildings into home before new build is implemented.

Substantial investment is needed in social housing. Since 2008, the Bank of England pumped £375 billion into the banks through QE. Using a mere 1/30 of this would substantially tackle the housing shortage. The current economic climate presents a historic opportunity to embark upon a one off investment of QE; with two episodes of deflation in 2015 (the first time since 1960), and record low interest rates, quantitative easing would hardly usher in an inflationary boom. It would not prove inflationary, due to spare capacity in the economy. In addition, as every £1 spent on construction generates £2.09 of economic output, a higher return than finance and banking, to which the whole tranche of previous QE was allocated. This will not be detrimental to the balance of payments, as for every £1 spent on construction, 92p stays within the UK, thus ensuring that the vast majority of labour and raw materials emanates from the UK.

Returns are quicker than for major infrastructure projects, due to the shorter lead in times between investment and economic activity.

For every £1 spent by the public sector, 56p returns to the Treasury, of which 36p is direct savings in tax and benefits.

Use QE funds (£12 billion to build an extra 51,072 houses per year [or 204,288 over 4 years]). These funds will be prioritised for social housing, 65% social housing, and 35% low cost ownership. By prioritising on renovating/converting existing stock, even more homes could be supplied.

The £12 billion of investment will be channelled though The Homes and Communities Agency. The Dept for Environment will conduct an audit (in conjunction with the new unitary authorities [based upon City and Council lines]) to prioritise areas for new build, empty buildings to be converted. The new homes will be planned as part of communities, ensuring GP surgeries, schools and shops are nearby, and designed to enhance labour mobility.

The new unitary city/county councils will create the machinery to build social housing on a county/city wide basis. These merged councils will be able to pool their resources to enable extra borrowing for investment. Currently, councils could borrow an extra £2.8 billion, within the existing national cap. A system similar to carbon trading could be established, so that borrowing capacity could be traded from council not needing to build, to those councils where there are housing shortages.

Raising the borrowing cap to allow additional local authority investment would permit borrowing of £7bn over five years, building up to 12,000 extra homes per year creating a total of 60,000 additional new homes, as opposed to the current 4,000 per year (or 20,000 over 5 years). It would make sense for the council investment to concentrate on conversion of existing buildings into homes (the councils have far better knowledge of empty building that central government) and for the national QE investment programme to concentrate on new build.

Conversion of social and private housing will be boosted by cutting VAT on building repairs/conversions to 10%. This will also preserve the Green Belt.

These combined measures will increase supply, reduce demand, and stabilise rents and mortgages across the entire housing sector.

Extend Right to Buy for social housing, and ensure that the proceeds are re-invested in building/renovating social housing stock, thus creating a virtuous circle of housing stock replenishment.

Prioritise social housing for people born in the United Kingdom, regardless of ethnic origin.

Ensure sufficient single occupancy accommodation, to enable people to downsize, in conjunction with the "bedroom tax."

Provide a £300,000 limit to the Help to Buy Scheme, so that the scheme benefits those who genuinely cannot otherwise ascend the property ladder. Help to Buy would be phased out as the stock of housing increases, and prices are stabilised.

TENANTS' RIGHTS

Tenants' rights are best protected not through rent controls (which deter investment, reduce stock, and would lead to a pre freeze hike in rents) but by reducing demand and increasing supply to stabilise rents, set in a framework of minimum standards.

There must be stricter enforcement of minimum standards (for example, tackling damp and unsafe electric installations), and this must be a UK wide minimum standard, enforce through the department of Environment, rather than local councils.

Tenants of council and housing association properties must be given the right to buy their properties. Help to Buy and shared ownership schemes do not tackle the biggest single obstacle form preventing people who can otherwise afford the mortgage payments; the huge deposits needed.

The most effective way of tackling this is through rent to mortgage schemes. Once a tenant has been renting for 3 years (and been a good neighbour, and not committed any anti – social behaviour), they would be able to convert their rent into a mortgage payments.

The 3 year limit would deter excessive investment in buy to let, which in turn drives up rent, and reduces the stock of affordable rented property.

Obviously, government could not force private landlords to adopt this scheme, but government must negotiate with landlords and property agencies to enable private tenants to enjoy the dream of home ownership.

The overall cost of the property would be discounted, up to 20%. This would effectively guarantee a 100% mortgage – i.e. no deposit. The flip side of offering 100% mortgage would be to only offer mortgages to those with stable incomes, good credit history, and ensuring that no one can buy a property worth more than 6 times their annual income.

For an example, a 1 bedroom flat worth £175,000 overall would be £140,000 when the 20% discount is applied. This would ensure that a household earning £23,333 per year or above could purchase a mortgage. This would actually put single person earning a respectable (if below average salary of £26,500) and even a couple who both work, and receive an annual salary of £12000 each, in a position to purchase their own home.

If the single person applied for a 30 year mortgage, the rent would be £389 per month; add on the 4% APR = £15.56, this results in a monthly mortgage payments of £404.56.

Given that most 1 bedroom flats are in excess of £600 per month, if the tenant continued to pay £600 toward the mortgage, then they would be living rent free within 20 years.

The weakness with the Right to Buy policy of the 1980s was that initially, only 50% of the proceeds from council house sales could be reinvested in rebuilding/renovating stock; this was reduced to 20%, causing a massive shortage of affordable housing. Quite rightly, the conservative government has pledged that for every home sold, to build a new affordable home (at up to 80% market rate). However, this is flawed as the sale of a property that been discounted by to 60% (or 70% for a flat) can only be used to build a similar property at up to only 30% or 40% of market rent. Clearly, this is unsustainable. It also ignores how the discount is funded. By limiting the discount to 20%, this provides sufficient revenue to build a property at 80% market rent – once the discount has been applied. By being creative, the sale of a council property can be used to renovate 2 or 3 properties, which (combined with the cut in VAT to 10% then 5% on building renovations) will increase housing stock exponentially.

Excessively discounting a property only distorts the market, to create an unsustainable property boom. The much smaller discount of 20% is possible due to the aforementioned investment in social housing to increase supply, and reducing demand by controlling immigration.

There will always be people who prefer the security of renting through the council or a housing association, and there will always be properties that will never be considered suitable for purchase. These tenants must be given the opportunity to manage their property and estate. Council tenants should be able to club together to form Housing Action Trusts. This would consist of the budget for that estate; the tenants could set up a social enterprise, and manage the budget themselves. They would have the power to choose different maintenance companies.

ENDING HOMELESSNESS

Homelessness is a scar on the conscience of the nation. Unemployment, family breakdown and drug addiction fuel a vicious circle of destitution. Hostels and charities provide short term support; they simply do not have the resources to solve homelessness.

£600 million will be invested in a national plan to provide interim accommodation for the homeless, where they will receive medical treatment, treatment to combat drug and alcohol addiction, chronic illnesses associated with homelessness, education, and skills. This will prepare people for the workplace, and the dignity to live in a place called home. The expertise provided by charities such as Shelters, Salvation Army will be used, and organisations will be allocated funding based upon results.

The £600 million will be funded by reducing lifetime allowance for tax free pension savings from £1.25 million to £1 million.

CHAPTER 7

A Green and Pleasant Land

- Energy Independence for the UK
- Protecting the countryside

ENERGY INDEPENDENCE FOR THE UK

The UK must become self sufficiency in energy, essential to our national security. It is a wanton act of negligence to place the UK at risk of ransom by relying on Russian gas.

Of electricity generated in 2014, gas accounted for 30.2 per cent (an increase of 3.6% from 2013) due to lower wholesale gas prices between June and August and to help meet the shortfall in generation caused by nuclear outages in the second half of the year, and coal accounted for 29.1 per cent of electricity generated (a drop of 7.4% from 2013).

Due to plant closures and conversions, only 6.4% of UK electricity was generated by coal mined in the UK. This will fall as coal fired power stations have closed, jeopardising the future of the mines that produce that coal. Nuclear's generation fell by 0.6% from 2013, to 19.0% due to outages in the second half of the year. Renewables accounted for 19.2% in 2014, a record.

Energy output fell by 1.5% from 2013 to 2014.

On a seasonally and temperature adjusted basis final energy consumption in 2014 was 1.2 per cent lower than in 2013. So there was a slight excess of demand.

Low carbon electricity's share of generation increased from 34.6 per cent in 2013 to 38.3 per cent in 2014, due to higher renewables generation. This will inevitably fall from 2015, due to the government's short sighted decision to cut renewables grants.

Total production of primary fuels fell by 6.3% in 2013 compared to 2012. The sharp fall in 2013 in coal output was due to mine closures while the falls in both oil and gas production were due to a number of maintenance issues and longer term decline. Primary oil (crude oil and NGLs) accounted for 39% of total production, natural gas 32%, primary electricity (consisting of nuclear, wind and natural flow hydro) 16%, coal 7% (11.54 million tonnes), while bioenergy and waste accounted for the remaining 6%.

UK mines produced 11.54 million tonnes of coal in 2014; total demand was 48.14 million tonnes. Total imported coal was 40.65 million tonnes, so the vast majority was imported. 4.05 million tonnes of UK coal was exported. 7.49 million tonnes of UK produced coal were used for UK power stations, blast furnaces, and final users, just 15.6% of the total was from UK coal.

UK Coal states that Kellingley could have continued to serve nearby power stations for decades and possibly for longer.

Kellingley Colliery alone produced 900 tonnes of coal every hour, or 7,884,000 tonnes of coal per year. Just by not exporting UK produced coal, 24% of coal demand would be met by UK produced coal.

To prevent further dependence upon imported coal to fire these power stations, the 2 deep coal mines threatened with closure by October, 2015 at the latest (Kellingley Colliery in Yorkshire, and Thoresby Colliery in Nottinghamshire), should remain open. This will save 1300 jobs, plus up to 700 at the 6 remaining surface coal mines. In addition, this would safeguard several hundred jobs associated with these mines.

Carbon capture technology will be fitted to all of these coal mines.

Due to EU air quality legislation, 4 coal fired power stations have now closed, along with 2 deep coal mines are scheduled to close by the end of 2015.

To ensure self sufficiency (and national security) the UK must keep open our coal fired power stations, and the coal mines that supply them, by harnessing carbon capture, in addition to nuclear, and renewables.

As an immediate step to secure energy security, carbon capture technology should be fitted to all coal fired power stations, including those ones earmarked for closure, and coal mines. The coal fired power stations and the mines that produce their coal must be re-opened.

Carbon capture technology has the potential to create 100,000 jobs in the UK by 2030, contributing £6.5 billion to the UK's economy. QE investment is essential if the UK is to take the lead, as potentially, the carbon capture industry could be as big as the North Sea oil industry, taking a significant share of a £5 trillion global CCS business by 2050. (Carbon Capture & Storage Association)

These are measures essential to an expansion of coal mining. As the supply of UK coal increases, so the price will fall, and it will become competitive vis a vis imported coal.

GAS

In 2014, total gas demand was 775.3 million tonnes. The UK exported 477.2 million tonnes of gas in 2014, exported 128.1 million tonnes.

Of the 425.2 TWh of gas produced by UK in 2014, 128.1 TWh was exported, leaving 297.3 TWh of UK produced gas used to meet demand, which totalled 775.3 TWh. This accounts for 32.9% of UK production; in other words, 67.1% of gas demand was met by imported gas.

The annual gas consumption is 2.6 Tcf; 1.75 Tcf is imported. Shale gas in the UK is estimated at 26 Tcf. Therefore, using the 2014 figures as a baseline, fracking would plug the energy gap for 15 years.

Output in the North Sea fell by 38% 2011 – 2014. (Guardian 04 Jun 14).

By 2025, UK will be importing 70% of the gas we consume.

The Bowland basin sits on top of 1300 trillion cubic feet of natural gas. Just extracting 1/10 of this will boost supply to meet existing demand for gas by at least another 25 years. Use fracking in the North West, North East, South and South East, and ensure there are sufficient gas fired power stations to take advantage of this supply, to contribute to self sufficiency.

Labour's price freeze would cause higher prices, as firms raise their prices before the freeze, and put bills up again after the freeze. This would hurt the very people Labour claims to represent. There are now 20 suppliers for electricity and gas in the UK, including the Big 6. The market share of the Big 6 has declined from 99.8% in 2009, to 92.4% now. This is still far too high. Ofgem referred the energy industry to the Competition and Markets Authority, whose investigation will conclude in December, 2015. One of their recommendations may be to break up the Big Six. I will propose that Ofgem restricts the Big Six market share to 49%, so that the new smaller suppliers have a combined market share of 51%. This will be implemented simultaneously with investment in energy independence, which will bring down costs. These measures will promote competition and reduce prices, without government intervention or subsidy. The winter fuel allowance will be abolished for pensioners who are higher rate taxpayers, and redistributed to pensioners on low and average incomes.

Allocate £3 billion of QE funds to individuals, research establishments, and businesses to produce the best ideas for sustainable, carbon neutral energy production. Some of the funds will be used to develop carbon capture, and apply it to new and existing power stations in the UK. In addition, carbon sequestration is essential, to actually remove existing carbon dioxide from the atmosphere. A further measure to reduce carbon dioxide will be afforestation, using part of the deficiency payments scheme to encourage farmers to plant trees in a programme of diversification. The QE investment programme will include investment in clean coal burning (prevent closure of the deep coal mines) and fracking; hydroelectric, solar, tidal, bio-fuel and geothermal energy production.

Tax incentives for car and aviation companies to develop clean fuel. Rather than punish individuals and businesses with green taxes, they should be rewarded with incentives. Raise tax on damaging fuels, to finance tax cuts for cleaner fuels.

The energy industry contributed 3.3% to the UK economy in 2013, employed 169,000 people (200,000 if those included in continental shelf production are included) this amounts to 6.2% of industrial employment. 18.1% of total investment. Only 2.3% of business investment was earmarked for energy production in 2012.

PROTECTING THE COUNTRYSIDE

The UK outside the EU will cease its application of the Common Agricultural Policy, and introduce a deficiency payment scheme. Much of this funding must be geared to sustainable agricultural production methods.

With regards to housing, the Green Belt must be preserved. Demand will be reduced by strict immigration control once the UK controls its borders, and restrictions on working age benefit in the interim. Priority must be given to renovating empty building to increase housing stock.

A programme of afforestation will protect and enhance wildlife, and contribute to reducing CO_2 emissions.

CHAPTER 8

Wellbeing for all

- Health and social care – Integration
- Poverty – An escape route vs A trap
- Education

HEALTH & SOCIAL CARE - INTEGRATION

The NHS was founded in 1948, to provide healthcare based upon need, and not the ability to pay. I have always believed in this principle (it was enshrined in my manifesto), but as the founder of the NHS (Aneurin Bevan) said, the religion of socialism, is the language of priorities. In essence, finite resources (and the need to eliminate the budget deficit) must be prioritised to those in greatest clinical need.

When I announced my candidacy in September, 2014, I pledged to boost NHS/social care spending by £2.5 billion per annum. My plan was financed by scrapping the Barnett formula (but giving Scotland equivalent tax raising powers), and redistributing that money to the rest of the UK. This would be invested in integrated social care budgets, focussing on preventative care, rehab, and physiotherapy. Labour's plan involved soaking the occupants of "mansions", many of whom were asset rich, but cash poor. This would lead to people moving to smaller properties, and a Labour government would never raise the necessary £2.5 billion. The Conservatives and Lib Dems pledged an extra £8 billion per annum by 2020, based upon the "proceeds of growth." This is a dangerous pledge, as it does not take into account external shocks, such as a eurozone crisis, or a slowdown in trade amongst the

Asian Tigers. Furthermore, integration of health and social care would lead to enhanced outcomes for the same amount of money, so that my "modest" £2.5 billion would yield positive results.

During the election (and indeed, before and since), countless people opposed the involvement of private companies in the provision of services and treatment in the NHS; it is regarded as privatisation. Expanding capacity by the use of private firms is NOT privatisation. Many such people prefer to put socialist dogma before patient care.

As mentioned in the chapter on the general election, many constituents emailed me with the following message:-

"Last week, the head of the British Medical Association warned that after the election patients could be charged for basic NHS services."

The petition asked if I was committed to keeping the NHS free at the point of use?

I advised that I believe that the NHS must remain free at the point of use for medical treatment. Many politicians call for charges for missed medical appointments; I wholeheartedly oppose this. Many people working long hours, or young parents, may unintentionally miss an appointment, and should not be penalised for this.

However, the squeeze on public expenditure grants an unprecedented opportunity for alternative funding streams for the NHS.

For patients seeking purely cosmetic treatment, I believe that the NHS should NOT provide this; patients should purchase this privately. Obviously, this would not include plastic surgery after an accident or a fire.

Every weekend, the brave staff on A&E wards face the aggressive and violent behaviour of binge drinkers. When many basic services are being cut, it is unacceptable that people who blatantly cause their own ill health in such a way should be treated ahead of patients with genuine illnesses, and at public expense. I advocated at the election (and I still do) charging binge drinkers (or if underage, their guardians) for treatment on A&E. This will have one of two effects, or a combination of the two. Those being treated will have to pay, and the revenue will pay for extra staff/treatment, or the threat of charges will act as a deterrent, so that extra resources and staff are not expended on treating binge drinkers. Either way, this will free up NHS staff and resources, and act as a deterrent. This reform is long overdue, and should be supported by all who believe in the NHS.

For too long, centralised targets have distorted clinical priorities. Too much time is spent ticking boxes than caring for patients. All central targets must be abolished, including the target to see patients in A&E within 4 hours. Government must trust the healthcare professionals to care for their patients. The CQC inspection regime will be toughened, and hospitals allocated funding based on whether or not outcomes have been met.

The savings made due to abolishing distorting targets, and contracting out HR and IT systems, must be diverted into frontline healthcare, including providing the staff and equipment to enable patient care at weekends and overnight, to ensure a 24 hour, 7 days per week NHS.

Labour puts socialist dogma before patient care, by preventing private companies from providing health care. Having a variety of private, voluntary and public agencies provides competition, and drives up standards, while still providing healthcare free at the point of use, and this must continue.

Labour's proposed 5% cap on profits for private firms deters new agencies from providing care for the NHS. Instead of such a cap, I would ensure that any voluntary or private agency commissioned by the NHS would pay all its staff the living wage, and abolish zero hours contracts.

The philosophy must be to enable NHS patients to use private healthcare, not the other way around. Therefore, NHS capacity must be expanded through private and voluntary providers (and private and voluntary hospitals), to complement in house services, free at the point of use. In order to be commissioned, these providers must pay their staff the living wage and zero hours contracts must be the exception and not the rule. There must be a cap on the cost of recruiting agency staff. This would be far more effective than a profit cap, which would simply deter investment. Patients should not be allowed to purchase NHS facilities privately; treatment must be given based upon clinical priority, not on ability to pay. Patients wanting private medicine must purchase from private hospitals and doctors; this frees up NHS capacity, and they still pay towards the NHS through taxation.

NHS patients could use a voucher to purchase NHS treatment, or to opt for medical insurance.

Patients could opt for a tax rebate or grant equal to the average annual per capita cost of NHS treatment, financed from the current cost of NHS treatment, purchase treatment or an operation at a private or NHS hospital of their choice. Alternatively, the patient could purchase medical insurance. All of these options will remain free at the point of use. Health Vouchers will take pressure off the NHS, prevent misallocation of finite resources by ensuring money follows the patient, and encourage the NHS to become more responsive through competition. Unlike the Patients Passports, access to private capacity and private insurance will be free at the point of use, based on clinical need, not the ability to pay.

The restrictive GP catchment areas should be abolished, so that patients can choose the GP of their choice (not the GP choosing their patients) even if outside their local area. State health insurance will prevent this restrictive and callous practice, as GPs will have an incentive to take on patients, not turn them away.

Hospitals will remain in NHS ownership if local communities wish them to be so. A private/voluntary hospital should be established in each Trust area, which will be able to take over failing NHS hospitals. NHS hospitals would be free to convert to private/voluntary status. In this instance, pay and pensions would be protected; this is a just reward for dedicated NHS staff, and incentives are needed to ensure recruitment.

Introduce performance related pay or GPs, nurses and ancillary staffs who "go the extra mile."

TTIP must be opposed. With TTIP, under the investor state dispute mechanism, US corporations can challenge national health policy decisions for loss of profit in reversing privatisation. The European Commission refused to accept a citizen's petition about TTIP. While I favour the best provider (whether public, private or voluntary) being an

NHS approved provider, I do not believe the UK should surrender our sovereignty over how these decisions are made – namely in Parliament. For example, my pledge that for a provider to become NHS approved it must abolish zero hours contracts, and pay its staff the living wage, could result in the UK government (in reality, the taxpayer) being sued.

The number of nurses GPs and staff for whom English is not first language presents a real challenge and potential danger to patient safety. In conjunction with strict immigration control, the indigenous population must be encouraged to work in the health profession, and rigorous training in English will be introduced.

The NHS must be a National Health Service, and only UK nationals (except students on VISAS and asylum seekers) should receive treatment free at the point of use. The NHS recoups just £50 million for treating EU visitors (nothing for the cost of GP care) yet pays out £750 million to EU nations who claim back the costs of treating Britons. So the cost of health tourism is £700 million per year.

As an immediate measure (and no retrospective action will be taken) the NHS will reclaim the cost of claiming back the cost of treating EU citizens from EU nations. Any foreign national (including those from the EU) will be required to purchase health insurance BEFORE visiting the UK, just as Britons are required to purchase health insurance before they go abroad. Students on VISAS and asylum seekers will still receive NHS treatment, free at the point of use.

INTEGRATING HEALTH & SOCIAL CARE

Integrating social care within the NHS will deliver better outcomes for patients, by preventing hospital admission, and speeding up hospital discharge.

Currently, the NHS is funded centrally, while social services are funded locally. The central government grant allocated to social services is not being spent on vulnerable people, but instead on keeping open libraries and swimming pools, for fear of adverse publicity if such facilities are closed.

Health and social care budgets will be integrated, so that patients are not denied the care they need while NHS and local authorities protect their own budgets. GPs, nurses, and social workers will access a single budget pooled between the city or county council and NHS Authority. Each Health & Social Care Trust will be City or Council wide, so that they serve the same population as local councils. It is vital that with integration, that the propensity to create several teams which duplicate work, and prevent patients getting treatment when and where they need it, is prevented.

For example, Proactive care teams only contain 1 professional of each discipline, while the Prevention teams also contain a similar number. The remit if the 2 teams is almost identical, and yet work is often passed from one team to the other, causing a delay. Nurses, physios, and OTs are also dispersed across different teams. Each Health & Social Care Trust must pool its resources; the nurses, OTs, physios and social workers and all professionals must be governed by a single manager, who then decides whether the community nurse should visit for a preventative visit, or whether the social worker of the admission avoidance team should be involved to provide urgent intervention.

The share of council tax allocated to social services will be earmarked, in a similar way to the contribution to the county police.

Central government grant for social services will be earmarked for social care, to be used as part of the integrated budget. IT systems must be integrated. The Department for Health & Social Care (with a Commissioner) will facilitate these changes.

An additional £2.5 billion (saved from scrapping the Barnet formula) will be invested in social care & health priority fund, including preventative drugs for dementia, and social care to prevent hospital admission. Legalise cannabis for medical use.

Abolish targets, establish outcomes, based upon prevention of hospital admission, keeping people in their own homes, prevention of disease, and effective management of chronic diseases. The achievement of outcomes, and the subsequent allocation of funding, will be monitored by the CQC.

Currently, the DWP assess for benefit entitlements such as Attendance Allowance, and a separate council finance team assesses the contribution that the patient has to pay from their benefit. Often this leads to delay, and people face arrears as their contribution is backdated. Patients in genuine need often cancel their care. In other words, the government gives with one hand, and takes the other.

DWP will assimilate financial assessors, so that only one departments assesses for benefits and assess contributions.

Contract out HR and IT systems in local councils, ensure one chief executive per local authority, and redirect savings to the front line.

It is not surprising that when homecarers are paid less than the minimum wage (as they don't get paid for travel time in between care calls), and work zero hours contracts, that there is a huge problem of recruitment and retention. The result is poor care for the patient. For a homecare agency to be approved by social services/NHS, the agency must pay its carers the living wage and abolish zero hours contracts. This would be UK wide, including Scotland. This would cost approximately £400 million, and would be paid for by cutting overseas aid.

Many home care workers are not paid for time between care calls, so they often earn less than the national minimum wage. Many care workers are on zero hours contracts, so cannot earn a decent weekly income. This results in a high turnover of carers, and a lack of consistency, causing neglect and inadequate care.

Care workers must be paid the living wage, end zero hours contracts, and make this an essential criterion for care agencies to be commissioned by NHS Healthcare Trusts. This will encourage British born people into care work, as it is important that carers can speak fluent English, and improve the quality and consistency of care.

POVERTY – AN ESCAPE ROUTE VS A TRAP

WELFARE AS A SAFETY NET. CAPITALISM: THE ANTIDOTE TO POVERTY

Welfare must be a means to an end, and not an end in itself.

The most effective antidote to poverty is employment, and this is achieved through wealth creation. I am passionate about creating a competitive and dynamic free market economy not only to create the jobs, but to generate the revenue to help those who cannot help themselves.

Welfare ought to be targeted to those in genuine need; universal welfare (apart from those people who actually need it) simply involves taxing people, and giving then back their own money in benefits they do not need. Where possible, people should be able to keep more of their own money, and therefore would not need to have their own money handed back to them in benefits. For example, tax credits should only be issued to workers who are net recipients of tax credits; that is to say, workers who are below the income tax threshold, and receive tax credits. For workers who are not net recipients, the tax credits should be stopped, and the worker given a tax cut in kind.

Therefore, a targeted welfare system by definition must be redistributive; in accordance with my vision of a dynamic and free market economy, wealth would be distributed through an ever increasing national cake, not redistribution through punitive taxation of existing wealth, which denies incentives, and dries up the stream of revenue essential to protect those who cannot protect themselves.

The welfare state as set up in 1909 and strengthened in 1948 was designed for a different demographic situation; to wit, when a majority of people needed supplementary benefits, and most people only had 10 or 20 years of retirement, whereas today, most of the working population earns a decent salary, and retirements can now last 30 or 40 years. In addition, a higher proportion of the population is of pensionable age.

A competitive and free market economy will generate some inequality; there will, and should be, differentials in pay levels between different professions, and within the same company to reflect different levels of experience and skills, and provide incentives.

The outcome of any programme to tackle poverty is measured not by the gap between the richest and the poorest; in communist countries, the gap was narrower, but the poorest 10% were much poorer than the poorest 10% in the UK. In a potential scenario, the gap between the richest and poorest could be wider than it is now, but the poorest 10% would all have some form of income to provide the basic dignities of life, and this would be provided for those unable to work. The critical test of any poverty programme is that the poorest 10% have the basic amenities of life concomitant with living in a civilised society.

The maxim "from each according to his ability, to each according to his needs", must govern any poverty programme. This aptly defines a system based upon people having no floor below which they can fall (but based on need, and not universality) and no ceiling that can limit their ambition (so a meritocracy).

Lady Thatcher was absolutely right when (on the day she was ousted as Prime Minister in November, 1990, and challenged by Simon Hughes about the gap between the richest 10% and the poorest 10%), she responded "he would rather that the poor were poorer, provided that the rich were less rich." Therefore, tax cuts across the board are essential to generate the wealth; tax cuts reward the successful employee and entrepreneur, and incentivise companies to expand and generate jobs and revenue for public services; tax cuts also provide a larger disposable income for the low paid, which in turn helps boost the economy.

A FAIRER TAX SYSTEM – LIFTING PEOPLE UP

In the 1909 People's Budget, Lloyd George introduced National Insurance. This was a contributory system, paid by workers to contribute towards pensions and unemployment insurance. Over the ensuing decades, NICs have not been earmarked for pensions or unemployment benefits, but have been included in the general coffers of government expenditure.

NICs are a further example of recycling money, whereby the government gives back to people their own money. At the last election, I proposed raising the NIC threshold for employees. This would be prioritised over and above raising the income tax threshold, until the NIC threshold equalled the income tax threshold, at which point, NICs would be integrated with income tax. This makes the system more redistributive.

The welfare system therefore should be redistributive, as with a contributory system merely recycles taxpayers' money, from and to taxpayers who neither want nor need the benefits.

I am a passionate tax cutter, but at the election and beyond, I advocated targeting tax cuts to the low paid and small businesses, to encourage small businesses to start and expand, and to encourage people to accept working in low paid jobs (as a start to their career) as they will have more disposable income.

I have always supported the raising of the income tax threshold, to encourage people to take lower paid jobs to get on the jobs ladder, infinitely better than remaining on benefits. While all taxpayers have rightly benefitted from this policy, another group of workers has been ignored. People earning as little as £8000 per year have to pay NI; in reality, an extension of income tax. I pledged to raise the threshold from £8060 to £8933.60, so that low paid would benefit by £19 per week. I would keep the threshold for income tax at £11,600, and continue to raise the National Insurance threshold until it was equal with the income tax threshold. If the UK leaves the EU, then £1.76 billion of the savings made from the EU budget contribution would be spent to further raise NI primary threshold from £8933.60 to £9807.20 for 2016-17. The income tax threshold will remain at £11,600 (allowing for inflation) until the National Insurance threshold is raised to same level. From this point, income tax and National Insurance would be entirely integrated.

However, tax cuts are one part of the armoury needed to defeat poverty. Tax cuts enable a higher disposable income, and actually increase revenues due to the fact they generate wealth. Many low paid workers are below the tax threshold, and even the NI threshold, so tax cuts do not directly benefit them.

The government proposed in July, 2015, that much of the £12 billion would be met by reducing the threshold at which people start to lose tax credits from £6420 to £3850, as of next year. This means the average low earner would have lost approximately £1300 on average; the living wage will not have compensated for the loss of tax credits for these workers, many of whom are part time.

Hence the need for tax credits for the low paid, which the Conservative government was going to reduce, but then decided to retain them. I am committed to maintaining tax credits for the low paid. Even in 2015, there have been some Conservative ministers who wanted to scrap the tax credits, and opposed the raising of income tax thresholds, to encourage the low paid to take higher paid jobs. This is immoral, and unrealistic. Many people are in low paid jobs for a number of reasons; young parents combining work with a parenting role; carers looking after relatives; people working part time due to health reasons. Many of these people will be in low paid jobs for many years; there will be future generations of workers in similar low paid jobs. Making work pay, and giving the lower paid a larger disposable income, are essential.

DEFINING POVERTY

In order to tackle poverty, and to measure the number of people who need welfare, the definition of poverty must be clarified.

The Child Poverty Act 2010 uses 4 measures:-

Relative income:- household income less than 60% of current median income.

Combined low income and material deprivation:- Children who experience material deprivation and live in households with incomes less than 70% of current median income

Absolute income:- Household income less than 60% of 2010/11 median income adjusted for prices

Persistent poverty:- Household income less than 60% of current median income for at least 3 out of the last 4 years.

Linking poverty to an arbitrary percentage of income is not an accurate way to measure poverty. What matters is disposable income, adjusted for reasonable definitions of expenditure on rent, food, and utilities. Many people on lower incomes are exempt from tax, sometimes NI, and are eligible for tax credits. When finance teams in adult social care carry out social care assessments, they measure income and expenditure, and allow a certain amount for rent, food, utilities etc, which defines the allowance for income to live safely, which in turn defines the contribution cost to the care. A similar method must be used for defining poverty; a minimum income.

THE END OF THE CONTRIBUTORY SYSTEM

FROM EACH ACCORDING TO HIS ABILITY, TO EACH ACCORDING TO HIS NEEDS.

The creation of National insurance in Lloyd George's people's budget of 1909 ushered in the first aspects of a welfare state. This was the ethos of a contributory system, whereby every citizen paid into the pot, and would draw the money in later years. This system made sense in an era of full employment, where almost everyone of working age worked, full time, and for the full length of their working career, often 16 – 60. However, people are reaching pension age who have been unemployed for a year or more; this number can only increase as the millions who were long term unemployed since the 1970s reach pensionable age. Many other people have been part time workers, looking after relatives, and parents. These people (who already have lower income and savings than the average) will receive a lower pension than their peers, and would have to apply for pension credit; often, this is not automatic.

Currently, the state pension is £115.95 per week. If the income is below £151.20 per week for a single pensioner (or £230.85 for a couple) for example for people who don't have private pensions, savings, or other benefits, then pensioners are entitled to pension credit.

The full state pension is dependent upon paying in a full amount of NI contributions over the working life. By definition, the UK demographic is moving away from a contributory system, to a redistributive system. The NI is another form of taxation. At the election, I campaigned for keeping the starting threshold for income tax as it is, and concentrate upon raising the NI threshold until it matches the income tax threshold. This will effectively merge the tax and NI system, and the pension system will be redistributive, not contributory, and funded through general taxation. I advocate a Citizens Pension; the full state pension should be awarded based upon number of working age years the person was resident in the UK. This deals with the immigration issue, which is a pension's time bomb waiting to explode. It also means that people will get their full state pension, and be eligible for pension credit if their income is below £151.20 – which it will invariably be. It will be fiscally neutral, as the increased expenditure required to pay the full state pension will be smaller for someone in receipt of £115.95 state pension than it would be for someone in receipt of say an 80% state pension.

Going forward, the retirement age for men and women should be raised in line with life expectancy.

The auto enrolment of workers into company pension schemes will provide an additional pension, based upon length of employment, and income, so this secondary pension will be contributory, and reward hard work.

To tackle pensioner poverty, the life chances of those going into work must be enhanced. The apprenticeship levy must be scrapped, to encourage apprenticeships, and to enhance career prospects (and therefore, increase pensions) and employment support allowance must be conditional upon an ESA recipient taking on an apprenticeship, or a training programme.

Having worked in adult social care for 13 years, there is unfairness and duplication in the system whereby DWP benefits assessors assess entitlements, and local authority finance officers assess contributions to packages of care people have to pay from their benefits.

Currently, the DWP assess for benefit entitlements such as Attendance Allowance, and a separate council finance team assesses the contribution that the patient has to pay from their benefit. Often this leads to delay, and people face arrears as their contribution is backdated. Patients in genuine need often cancel their care. In other words, the government gives with one hand, and takes the other.

The DWP will ensure that the same assessor assesses entitlements and contributions.

FAIRNESS IN THE BENEFIT SYSTEM

The Coalition introduced sudden cuts to welfare recipients before an investigation had been held. Many recipients have mental health impairments, and need assistance with contacting benefit agencies. A yellow card system must be introduced so that an investigation can take place to decide whether the claimant is eligible for benefits. A red card would follow if the benefit is clearly no longer required; obviously, fraud would be tackled through the courts with stiffer penalties. These measures would reduce the dependence upon food banks.

The folly of paying Housing benefits directly to the tenant has been proved; many recipients of Housing benefit have mental health concerns, and struggle with finances. It has led to the eviction of vulnerable people, and the landlord losing money. I pledged to pay HB directly to the landlord.

While the government's reversal of the proposed tax credit cuts was welcome (I campaigned for this), the Chancellor has as yet not proposed an alternative method of cutting £12 billion from the welfare budget, which protects disabled benefit and carers benefits.

Income tax payers who are net beneficiaries of tax credits will have these tax credits protected. For income tax payers who are not, the tax credit will be replaced by a tax cut in kind. Where possible (and without reducing people's income) we must stop a system where government takes people's money, and then gives people their own money back in the form of tax credits.

To cut the welfare bill, child benefits and child tax credits should be stopped from the third child born after April 2017 – at the time of publication, almost 1 year's notice. This is a fair policy, as people make a conscious decision to bring another child into the world, and will make families responsible with family planning. It does not apply retrospectively, so families currently with three children or more will not be penalised. The policy would be phased in to allow time for families to make a conscious decision. This policy would save £3.1 billion per annum, £12.4 billion over 4 years, and raise more than the cutting of the tax credit thresholds. In addition, child benefits should be in voucher form (for food, clothing, and heating), and this would be for all recipients of child benefit, to engender responsibility, and to ensure the money gets to the child. This will drastically reduce child poverty.

I agreed to reduce social housing rents by 1% a year 2016 – 2020. Saving £2.835 billion up to and including 2019-20.

No child benefit and child tax credit to the third child born from 2016.

An additional £1.05 billion will be re-directed to deficit reduction from abolishing student grants and freezing working age benefits NOT allocated to raising the tax credit threshold.

I've argued consistently that there must be clearly defined exemptions, for example, for those who need a bedroom for carers, and where special needs children cannot share a bedroom. I pointed out that there is money available for tenant who downsize, and this must be accompanied by building more single occupancy accommodation, to reduce the need for the bedroom tax in the first place.

These measures alone will reduce the net welfare bill by £16.235 billion over the Parliament, well in excess of the £12 billion cuts proposed by the Conservative government.

THE RESIDENCY TEST

As mentioned in the section about pensions, people will have to have been resident in the UK for the entirety of their working age to qualify for the full Citizen's pension.

If and when the UK leaves the EU, the UK will have full control over borders. Whether the UK remains in the EU or not, the residency test should also apply to in work benefits, and migrants from both the EU and outside will have to wait 4 years before claiming in work benefits.

The government's restriction on immigration by definition has to limit non EU migration, as the UK cannot control EU migration while we remain in the EU. This means that migrants enter the UK not based on talent, and what they can contribute, but simply because they are members of the EU. A policy of zero net immigration, with an annually amended cap based upon a points system, which assessed the demands for skills in the UK, should be the UK immigration policy post EU. Integral to this must be a drive to make work pay, though cutting NI for low paid, apprenticeships. This will be aided and abetted by preventing the downward spiral of wages caused by mass immigration. A policy of ultimate zero net migration actually increases the capacity of the UK to accept refugees fleeing atrocities and natural disasters. A UK migration policy will be firm, but fair and humanitarian.

THE FAMILY

The family is the bedrock of society. All politicians and civic leaders must understand that families come in all shapes and sizes. The majority of single parents are not single parents through choice, but through bereavement, economic factors, and other circumstances beyond their control.

As a priority, the allowance should be transferrable to all parents, married, civil partnership, or not in any legally defined relationship. This will encourage flexibility in the parenting role.

Responsibility is key to family planning. I have mentioned the reforms to child benefits which this will engender. By limiting child benefit to the first 2 children born from 2017, this will encourage parents to assume responsibility over how many children they decide to bring into the world, and represents a fundamental shift in philosophy, as taxpayers should not subsidise rearing children beyond a sustainable level. By controlling immigration, and providing incentives to responsible family planning, the UK population growth is sensibly managed. Subsidising the first 2 children is a sensible and balanced policy, to create sufficient working population to promote economic growth, especially as immigration will be tightly controlled.

Furthermore, the child benefit must be issued in voucher form, for food, clothing and heating. Too often, child benefit is used as additional family income. The voucher system will eliminate much of child poverty, as the money will be directed at the child.

In addition, parental leave should also be restricted to the first 2 children. Just as the taxpayer must not be expected to subsidise child rearing beyond a sustainable level, neither must the burden fall on businesses, and disproportionately on smaller businesses.

The government's expansion of child care is necessary, in light of the fact that both parents need to work to afford rent/mortgage, and an acceptable standard of living. However, and disturbingly from a Conservative government, the system is skewed against stay at home parents. It is obvious that children who have a parent at home are more emotionally stable, less likely to commit crime, perform better at school, and are more likely to obtain a well paid job. Part of the existing child care budget should be allocated to stay at home parents (this must be means tested) so that stay at home parents receive an income. Redirected from the existing budget, this would not add to existing government expenditure, enable parents to look after children without sacrificing one half of the family income, and free up jobs for those who really need them, especially many of our younger people. This measure will strengthen the family, reduce congestion, and reduce unemployment.

EDUCATION – MERITOCRACY AND DIVERSITY

In education, selection by intelligence is preferable to selection by mortgage. There are two competing visions for education that have been tried and failed abysmally over the last 50 years. First, the socialist system of comprehensive education. It is ironic that under socialism, only the wealthy can send their children to a good school by paying privately, while parents on average and lower incomes cannot afford to buy a house within the catchment area of good schools. Free schools empower parents to set up a school, but structural change is needed. Grammar schools should be allowed to expand, but new ones must be set up across the UK, to make social mobility a reality.

Secondly, the feudal system engendered by the privilege of private schools, which reduces social mobility, has never seriously been challenged by any government, Labour, Liberal or Conservative. Private schools were designed as charitable institutions.

Currently, if parents need to move their child from a failing school, they either have to move to expense residential areas, or purchase to private education. It is a situation of selection by mortgage. Encourage free schools, grammar schools, or academies in deprived areas, to encourage social mobility.

I propose a genuinely meritocratic system, based upon talent, not wealth. Abolition of private schools is not the answer.

Private schools must open up all of their places to scholarships, so that parents cannot buy education regardless of the educational aptitude of the child, to ensure meritocracy. Yes, this means effectively abolishing the purchasing of a school place based upon parental wealth. Essentially, there will be a voucher system which increases funding per pupil, across the UK. This will raise the funding per state pupil to the level for private pupils. Inevitably, the voucher will be larger for schools which excel. This system will be funded by the abolition of LEAs across England and Wales, and Northern Ireland.

Increase investment in early years education (in priority areas) by £1.12 billion in 2016/17; £1.39 billion, in 2017/18; £1.75 billion 2018-2019; £1.91 billion 2019 – 2020; £2.06 billion in 2020-2021.

£1.12 billion from scrapping Barnett Formula per year from 2016-17, and the savings from scrapping raising the inheritance tax threshold from 2017 will be redirected to investment in early years education, from 2017-18. The inheritance tax savings are a different figure in each year.

Allow pupils to study vocational courses from age 14.

The curriculum must be tailored to meet the needs of local businesses. Employers should be involved in vocational education, and the content of the curriculum.

Abolish all LEAs, and all schools to be direct grant schools. The share of council tax allocated to education will be earmarked, similar to the contribution to the local police. Contract out HR and IT systems, and reinvest the savings into front line education.

Ensure parents can send their children to the school of their choice by allowing the best performing schools to expand, and to take over failing schools.

Give pupils a second chance to attend grammar school, rather than one chance at age 11.

Tuition fees will be reduced for courses essential to the UK's economic future, such as medicine, engineering, chemistry, biology, computing and technology. This will be financed by raising tuition fees for arts and humanities degrees, in a way that is fiscally neutral.

CREATING SUFFICIENT SCHOOL PLACES

There must be central government co – ordination to allocate existing school places more fairly, as there are surplus places in some areas, and huge shortages in other areas. Schools should be allowed to expand beyond their catchment areas, to where the demand originates. The money must follow the pupil, not the school.

There are expected to be 8,022,000 pupils in England's schools – an increase from the 7,143,000 in the current academic year.

880,000 extra pupils are expected to need school places by 2023, 113,000 in London alone; this will push space and resources to the limit. (Daily Record, 16th march, 2016). The extra places are expected to cost £12 billion; the government has pledged £7.35 billion to school places by 2012, leaving a shortfall of £4.65 billion.

The school population increase is most acute in the inner cities, with the highest birth rate since the 1950s. By contrast, the school age population has fallen in some areas.

There has been a 6% increase in the number of women of child bearing age since 2003, in addition to more older women having babies.

One quarter of babies were born to women who were born outside the UK – first generation immigrants.

18% of primary schools do not have capacity for their pupils, causing either overcrowded class sizes, or makeshift accommodation to teach pupils.

Currently, local authorities are forbidden from building schools where there is shortage of places, when money is allocated to areas with surplus places.

The division between central funding (75%) and local funding (25%) prevents national co-ordination to ensure fair allocation of school places across the country.

The poorest local authorities have the highest shortage of school places, and have the lowest local revenue to fund school places.

The Dept of Education will immediately assess the need for school places across England, Wales and Northern Ireland, and allocate the existing number of places more fairly, granting surplus places to areas with a shortage of places. What must allow schools to expand not just within the catchment area, but to set up sites nearer to where the extra demand is coming from. This will ease congestion, and shorten travel times, and prevent schools from having high pupil to teacher ratios. Parents, teachers and others wanting to set up free schools can apply for a share of school places.

The Dept of Education will co-ordinate the supply of school places. However, demand for school places must also be controlled. ¼ of children born since 2003 were born to mothers who are first generation immigrants. Current levels of immigration generate an unsustainable demand for school places. The immediate plan to extend the time EU migrants must wait before claiming benefits from 3 months to 6 months, and to ban immigration from an EU country until the average wage in that country is 50% of the UK average wage will reduce mass immigration (and demand for school places) until a decision is made upon EU membership (and the ability of the UK to control all immigration) in 2015.

Indigenous population growth also needs to be controlled. Limiting child benefit to the first 2 children (apart from multiple births, i.e. triplets etc) will also reduce demand for school places, and encourage parental responsibility.

By reducing tuition fees on engineering, science and technology courses (by raising fees on humanities courses) the UK could lead a massive recruitment drive for the best engineers, and scientists from our own population.

CHAPTER 9

Justice for all

- A British Bill of Rights – Rights and Responsibilities
- Proportionate and minimum sentencing
- Civil Liberties and Security.
- Trial by jury
- Innocent until proven guilty.
- A British Bill of Rights – Rights and Responsibilities

A BRITISH BILL OF RIGHTS

At the time of writing, the Conservative government (freed from Lib Dem restraint) has pledged to withdraw from the ECHR, and draft its own Bill of Rights – although this has been postponed.

Opponents of withdrawal are denounced as opponents of human rights in principle. This is emphatically not the case. I propose a British Bill of rights, implemented by British Courts. Surely one of the most important human rights of all is to be tried by one's own fellow countryman in a court located, using laws decided, in their own country?

Human rights are the bedrock of a democratic nation.

The right to free speech, the right to vote, equality before the law, all of these are hard won civil liberties, won by the people over centuries. The UK has been in the vanguard of civil liberties: Cromwell and his levellers; the Great Reform Act; and the Suffragettes. Two world wars were fought to defend liberty itself.

Yet, over the last 20 years, these liberties have slowly, yet surely been, eroded. The right to trial by jury has been undermined by the Criminal Justice Act 2003. In the aftermath of 9/11 and 7/7, the government introduced detention without trial for up to 90 days.

The civil liberties of the victim have been undermined by early release, lenient sentencing, The Human Rights Act prevents foreign criminals from being deported, and are thus free to commit further crimes. It even allows for prisoners to vote. Those who break the law, should not make the law.

THE RIGHT TO FAMILY LIFE

The aspects of the Human Rights Act I support are Article 10, espousing freedom of speech and expression, and this has helped journalistic freedom, and diversity of opinions through digital channels.

However, Article 8 (the right to family life) has been abused.

Learco Chindamo, who killed Stephen Lawrence in 1995, in 2007, won an appeal against deportation in 2007. This was due to immigration rules that stipulated that, as an EU national who had lived in the UK for 19 years (even excluding his 10 years in jail) he was a natural resident, and could not be deported except on grounds of public security." Surely murder would constitute a huge threat to public security. Even without the EU immigration rules, Article 8 of the human rights act would have prevented his deportation, as he had lived in the UK since the age of 6. In 2014, he was released.

In short, the right to family life protect the rights of the criminal, at the expense of the rights of the victim.

In a British Bill of Rights, the right to family life would be conditional upon not committing serious crimes against the person.

FREEDOM OF SPEECH

Article 10 of the HRA gives everyone the right to freedom of expression, to hold opinions, and receive and impart information without state interference. Political, artistic and commercial expression. Obviously, the act contains provision to prevent free speech where this causes incitement or violence. That's why Theresa May was right to ban extremist preachers from universities.

There are two pieces of legislation that are so broadly defined that they can undermine legitimate expression. Sections 4A and 5 of the Public Order Act (1986) make it an offence for a person to use threatening words that could cause distress. This could cause a protestor to be prosecuted.

Section 127 of the communications act 2003 makes an offence to send "a grossly offensive, indecent, obscene or menacing" message. This can criminalise people who send jovial, albeit silly, messages. Section 127 was used to prosecute a young man who tweeted his frustration at not being able to see his girlfriend due to airport closure, anyone in such circumstances would have been frustrated, and vented it on social media.

Fortunately, the conviction was overturned.

In a British Bill of Rights, freedom of speech (apart from incitement) would be enshrined in law. Sections 4A and 5, and Section 127 will be amended to ensure a proportionate infringement on free speech which punishes harassment, violence or incitement.

TRIAL BY JURY

The right to trial by jury must be retained as a fundamental human and democratic right.

PRESUMPTION OF INNOCENCE

The concept of innocent until proven guilty is sacrosanct. Detention without trial should only be used in terror trials, and must be time limited, to well below 90 days.

People going to Syria without good reason should be detained, and intercept evidence used in court. This would actually speed up trials, and work towards a 14 day limit, and enhance UK security, while preserving liberty.

A BRITISH LEGAL AND CRIMINAL JUSTICE SYSTEM

- Withdraw from ECHR, and create a British Bill of Rights to enshrine:
- Retain trial by jury
- The right to be tried in the
- Retain the proud tradition of innocent until proven guilty.
- Freedom of speech and expression, without incitement.
- The right to freedom, forfeited if a crime is committed.
- The rights of the victim of crime to be sacrosanct.
- The right to vote, which will be forfeited if crime is committed.
- Retain the proud tradition of innocent until proven guilty.
- Deportation of foreign criminals and terrorists.

SHARIA LAW

In the UK, there should be one law for all, and laws determined by the British people through their Parliament. Therefore, Sharia law will not run alongside, or be incorporated into British law. Sharia Law is a system that relegates children born out of wedlock to second class citizenship.

When British people visit other countries, we quite rightly have to abide by that countries law, and that principle should apply when people visit the UK.

A FAIR EXTRADITION POLICY

The European Arrest Warrant means national judicial authority can issue a EAW to get a suspect extradited, and a mutual recognition of criminal justice systems across the EU.

This assumes a common standard of criminal justice across EU – this is patently not the case, as France has a system of guilty until proven innocent, the exact opposite of the UK. The logical conclusion is a single European criminal justice system. Extradition requests between

UK and nations outside EU are not subject to an arrest warrant, so it is not consistent across the world.

Scrap the EAW, and introduce a fairer extradition policy.

1). Suspect should be tried in the country where the alleged offence took place.
2). A person should not be sent to stand trial in a foreign court without a basic case being presented in a British court.
3). If the majority of whole crime has occurred in UK, then extradition should not occur if UK court decides it is not just to extradite.

PROPORTIONATE AND MINIMUM SENTENCING

Criminals will not be deterred, nor will prisons refrain from being overcrowded, unless proportionality is introduced into our sentencing.

10% of court cases are related to non payment of TV licences. The TV licence should be abolished, and the BBC funded by private and voluntary means. In the meantime, people who do not pay TV licences should never be given custodial sentences – community service is a far more proportionate response.

Custodial sentences are inconsistent, and do not reflect the severity of the crime perpetrated. Dangerous drivers who kill children are given shorter sentences than people who commit no crime against the person. This has two effects – it exposes the public to the danger of the criminal wandering free on the streets of the UK, and such sentences weaken the deterrent effect of sentencing, sending out the wrong message to potential criminals.

Many judges – not exposed to the reality of crime in their daily lives – issue far too lenient sentences.

While the judiciary should be and must remain independent of the state – for this reason, I rule out elected judges – it is the elected official (to wit, the Justice Secretary) who has the duty to decide the sentencing for each crime. I propose minimum sentencing. This would give a historic opportunity to restore proportionality to the sentencing system.

Sentencing must reflect the severity of the crime, not the availability of prison places. Prison must be retained for serious offenders.

Punishment must be proportionate – Crime against the person must carry the most severe penalties. Community service should be reserved for low level crime.

Lady Thatcher allowed a free vote on the death penalty (the restoration of which she personally favoured); throughout that period, Parliament never voted to restore it. Throughout Lady Thatcher's premiership, public opinion was to the right of Parliament on this issue. Earlier in 2015, public opinion for the first time was apparently against the restoration of the death penalty. The reasons are a more liberal population (due to the younger generation), and the fall in crime generally. However, incidents such as the brutal murder of Lee Rigby in 2013, and all too frequent murders of young children call for tougher sentences for murder. Opposition to capital punishment stems not only from its apparent brutality, but to the lack of redress if a person is wrongfully sentenced. Advances in DNA technology, and forensic science generally, actually reduce the possibility of wrongful conviction. The presence of the capital punishment would in fact ensure a thorough investigation to ensure conviction of the actual criminal responsible. I propose the reintroduction of a free vote on capital punishment in each Parliament (it must be a free vote, and not part of a government's programme due to the issues of conscience).

End early release.

POLICING

The Police have borne the bulk of the cuts since 2010. Currently, police levels are at the minimum level needed to ensure security in the UK.

The focus must be on reforming the police structure, to ensure faster crime prevention enhanced communication across forces, and with other agencies such as social services, and emergency services, such as ambulances and fire services.

England and Wales currently have 43 forces, with forces ranging from 600 to 32,000 (the London Met). In addition, police forces use different IT systems.

The police forces should be merged into following seven authorities, who will use the same IT systems:-

The Met (London); South East; South West; Wales; Midlands; North East; North West

In addition, the Police & Crime Commissioners only secured an average vote of 15% at the first elections in November, 2012; this is not a mandate from the people. When finances are so stretched, I propose that IPPCs should be abolished when their terms end in 2016. The elections are scheduled to cost £50 million, and the administration costs £14 million over a 4 year term. This £64 million should be reinvested into front line policing.

The role of policing must be limited to crime prevention. For example, welfare visits should be carried out by social workers and health visitors.

The police should be armed to deal with gun crime and terrorism.

A Budget for Growth - March 2016

By Nick Yeomans

Independent Parliamentary Candidate, Brighton Pavilion.

16th March 2016

ECONOMIC FRAMEWORK

THE ECONOMIC FRAMEWORK

- Strengthen the deficit reduction programme, to maintain low interest rates. I support the Charter for Budget Responsibility, setting limits on government spending. Over the medium term, overall government spending should grow at 1% less than GDP, year on year, to ensure a budget surplus.
- All current public spending commitments and tax cuts must be funded from savings in government expenditure
- Deficit reduction, with all spending commitments and tax cuts fully funded, enables the government to borrow to invest in infrastructure; use QE to invest in housing, transport (to link great cities across the UK) and energy independence.
- Wealth creation is the key to creating opportunities, and eradicating poverty. There will be no new taxes on individuals or businesses. Labour claims to help small businesses by taxing larger corporations, which will destroy incentives for enterprise across the economy. Tax cuts aimed at the low paid and small

businesses will encourage expansion, and encourage more people into work.

CUTTING THE DEFICIT

- The deficit currently stands at £72.2 billion.
- To reduce the deficit, the following measures must be implemented:-
- Limit child benefit and child tax credit to the first 2 children (or first multiple birth for a family) from 2016. This would save £3.1 billion per annum, £12.4 billion over 4 years, while protecting tax credits, and disability benefits.
- An additional £1.05 billion would be saved from abolishing student grants and freezing working age benefits NOT allocated to raising the tax credit threshold.
- These measures will reduce the net welfare bill by £13.45 billion over the Parliament.
- Sell the remaining 10% government shares on Lloyds, and 73% of government shares in RBS. This would raise £2 billion and £23.6 billion respectively. While RBS shares have taken a hit due to litigation issues, announcement of privatisation will engender confidence, and boost the share price. This will raise a minimum total of £25.6 billion, more once confidence is restores to RBS.
- This already yields £39.05 billion by 2019-20, well above the £30 billion outlined in the Charter for Budget responsibility.
- Savings from efficiencies in central government departmental expenditure, by contracting out IT and HR systems will be directed into reducing the budget deficit.
- These measures alone will more than halve the deficit from £72.2 billion to £32.97 billion by 2020. This does not include revenue from economic growth, nor streamlining central government.

DEFENCE

With the rise of IS, aided and abetted by Russian aggression, restoring our defences (air, naval and ground troops) must assume the highest priority.

- Cut the overseas aid budget by just over half. £6 billion. Allocate £4,451,400,000 of the overseas aid budget will be redirected to defence, prioritised as follows:-
- £860 million per year to reverse the cuts in troops (RUSI Spending Review – 2010)

Cost of replacing trident without delay is £1.2 billion (Economist, 19-10-10). The cost of a submarine missile defence system is £2 billion. ((http://fantasyfleet.blogspot.co.uk/2010/09/anti-ballistic-missile-system-for-uk.html)

- Annual cost of renting USS Nimitz aircraft carrier = £141,400,000 (Wiki answers).
- Cancel JSF and build out own aircraft carrier based aircraft.

Cost of each Trident missile is £17 million. (Trident missile fact file – 23rd Sept 2009). To build 32 Trident type missiles would cost = £544 million. £290 million of this will be saved as the UK will not participate in the upgrading of US missiles in the 2020s. (Trident nuclear Weapons Submarines in the United Kingdom and the USA – BASIC (British American Security Information Council November, 2013). £250 million net cost of building 32 Trident type missiles.

TAX

Tax cuts must be prioritised for low earners in order to enhance incentives to work, reduce poverty, and increase demand in the economy. Raising the employee National Insurance threshold is a priority. NI has become income tax by another name.

I support the raising of standard income tax threshold to £10,800 April 2016, and £11,000 in April 2017, and raising higher income tax threshold to £43,000 in April 2016, and £45,000 in April 2017. These tax thresholds will then remain at these rates until the NI threshold has been raised to match the income tax threshold, effectively integrating NI and tax.

While people earning as little as £8060 per year (2/3 of the money a full time worker earns on the minimum wage) do not pay income tax, they pay 12% in NI.

- Raise the NI employee primary threshold from £8060 to £8933.60. Raising the NI threshold should be the priority over raising the personal income tax allowance for the next few years, until the starting levels for NI and tax are the same. Cost of £2,016,480,000. (1).
- Cut VAT to 10% on building repairs, to increase housing supply by converting existing stock. Cost = £560 million. (2).

EDUCATION:- PRIORITIES FOR SOCIAL MOBILITY

- Set benefits cap to £20,000, saving £1.175 billion up to and including 2019-20.
- Increase investment in early years education (in priority areas) by £1.12 billion in 2016/17; £1.39 billion, in 2017/18; £1.75 billion 2018-2019; £1.91 billion 2019 – 2020; £2.06 billion in 2020-2021.
- Abolishing local education authorities, and using the savings to equalise funding per pupil between state and private schools. All private school places to be awarded on merit, not ability to pay.
- Central government co-ordination to re-allocate surplus school places to areas of shortage. Control immigration through Brexit, to reduce demand.

HEALTH AND SOCIAL CARE

- Invest an additional £2.5 billion (saved from scrapping the Barnett formula – in return Scotland will be given tax raising powers) in social care & health priority fund in England and Wales, including preventative drugs for dementia, and social care to prevent hospital admission. £1.25 billion to health, £1.25 billion to social care.

- Fully integrate health and social care. Create a single budget pooled between the city or county council and NHS Authority, to fund health and social care.

- Pay home care workers (for NHS Healthcare Trust approved care the living wage. This is estimated to cost £316,901,250 per year.

This is based upon the £600,000 earmarked by Islington Council to pay their 800 homeworkers the living wage. (Guardian, 29/01/14). This costs £750 per worker. There are approximately 422,535 home care workers in the United Kingdom (England, Wales and Scotland). (UKHCA [UK Homecare Association Ltd] Summary Paper – An overview of the UK domiciliary care sector, February, 2013). 422,535 x 750 = £316,901,250. This is a higher estimate, as Islington pays London living wage of £8.80 per hour (as opposed to the UK figure of £7.65).

HOUSING & HOMELESSNESS

- A policy of zero net immigration (implemented almost immediately by EU migrants not being entitled to benefits until UK withdraws from EU, when we could control our borders) would reduce the annual demand for housing (of all types) to 130,000.

- Reducing demand for housing must be achieved by reducing population growth, both through immigration control, and limiting child benefit and child tax credit to the first 2 children.

- To further protect quality of life and the green belt, all efforts must be made to convert existing and empty buildings into home before new build is implemented.
- Substantial investment is needed in social housing. Since 2008, the Bank of England pumped £375 billion into the banks through QE. Using a mere 1/30 of this would substantially tackle the housing shortage. The current economic climate presents a historic opportunity to embark upon a one off investment of QE; with two episodes of deflation in 2015 (the first time since 1960), and record low interest rates, quantitative easing would hardly usher in an inflationary boom. It would not be inflationary, due to spare capacity in the economy. In addition, as every £1 spent on construction generates £2.09 of economic output, a higher return than finance and banking, to which the whole tranche of previous QE was allocated. This will not be detrimental to the balance of payments, as for every £1 spent on construction, 92p stays within the UK, so ensures that the vast majority of labour and raw materials emanates from the UK.
- Returns are quicker than for major infrastructure projects, due to the shorter lead in times between investment and economic activity.
- For every £1 spent by the public sector, 56p returns to the Treasury, of which 36p is direct savings in tax and benefits.
- Use QE funds (£12 billion in 2015 to build an extra 51,072 houses per year [or 204,288 over 4 years]). These funds will be prioritised for social housing, 65% social housing, and 35% low cost ownership. By prioritising on renovating/converting existing stock, even more homes could be supplied.
- The £12 billion of investment will be channelled though The Homes and Communities Agency. The new homes will be planned as part of communities, ensuring GP surgeries, schools and shops are nearby, and designed to enhance labour mobility.
- The new unitary city/county councils will create the machinery to build social housing on a county/city wide basis. These

merged councils will be able to pool their resources to enable extra borrowing for investment. Currently, councils could borrow an extra £2.8 billion, within the existing national cap. A system similar to carbon trading could be established, so that borrowing capacity could be traded from council not needing to build, to those councils where there are housing shortages.

- Raising the borrowing cap to allow additional local authority investment would permit borrowing of £7bn over five years, building up to 12,000 extra homes per year creating a total of 60,000 additional new homes, as opposed to the current 4,000 per year (or 20,000 over 5 years). It would make sense for the council investment to concentrate on conversion of existing buildings into homes (the councils have far better knowledge of empty building that central government) and for the national QE investment programme to concentrate on new build.

- Conversion of social and private housing will be boosted by cutting VAT on building repairs/conversions to 10%. This will also preserve the Green Belt.

- These combined measures will increase supply, reduce demand, and stabilise rents and mortgages across the entire housing sector.

- Extend Right to Buy for social housing, and ensure that the proceeds are re-invested in building/renovating social housing stock, thus creating a virtuous circle of housing stock replenishment.

- Prioritise social housing for people born in the United Kingdom, regardless of ethnic origin.

- Ensure sufficient single occupancy accommodation, to enable people to downsize, in conjunction with the "bedroom tax."

- Provide a £300,000 limit to the Help to Buy Scheme, so that the scheme benefits those who genuinely cannot otherwise ascend the property ladder. Help to Buy would be phased out as the stock of housing increases, and prices are stabilised.

Homelessness is a scar on the conscience of the nation. Unemployment, family breakdown and drug addiction fuel a vicious circle of destitution. Hostels and charities provide short term support; they simply do not have the resources to solve homelessness.

£600 million will be invested in a national plan to provide interim accommodation for the homeless, where they will receive medical treatment, treatment to combat drug and alcohol addiction, chronic illnesses associated with homelessness, education, and skills. This will prepare people for the workplace, and the dignity to live in a place called home. The expertise provided by charities such as Shelters, Salvation Army will be used, and organisations will be allocated funding based upon results.

ENERGY

- UK mines produced 11.54 million tonnes of coal in 2014; total demand was 48.14 million tonnes. Total imported coal was 40.65 million tonnes, so the vast majority was imported. 4.05 million tonnes of UK coal was exported. 7.49 million tonnes of UK produced coal were used for UK power stations, blast furnaces, and final users, just 15.6% of the total was from UK coal.

- Due to EU air quality legislation, 4 coal fired power stations are scheduled to close by 2016, and 2 deep coal mines have already been closed.

- UK Coal states that Kellingley can continue to serve nearby power stations for decades and possibly for longer.

- Kellingley Colliery alone produces 900 tonnes of coal every hour, or 7,884,000 tonnes of coal per year. Just by not exporting UK produced coal, 24% of coal demand would be met by UK produced coal.

- To prevent further dependence upon imported coal to fire these power stations, the 2 deep coal mines closed in October, 2015 at the Kellingley Colliery in Yorkshire, and Thoresby Colliery in Nottinghamshire, must be re-opened. This will create 1300 jobs, plus up to 700 at the 6 remaining surface coal mines. In addition, this would safeguard several hundred jobs associated with these mines.

- Carbon capture technology will be fitted to all of these coal mines.

- To ensure self sufficiency (and national security) the UK must keep open our coal fired power stations, and the coal mines that supply them, by harnessing carbon capture, in addition to nuclear, and renewables.

- As an immediate step to secure energy security, carbon capture technology should be fitted to all coal fired power stations, including those ones earmarked for closure, and re-opened coal mines.

- Carbon capture technology has the potential to create 100,000 jobs in the UK by 2030, contributing £6.5 billion to the UK's economy. QE investment is essential if the UK is to take the lead, as potentially, the carbon capture industry could be as big as the North Sea oil industry, taking a significant share of a £5 trillion global CCS business by 2050. (Carbon Capture & Storage Association)

- 67.1% of gas demand was met by imported gas.

- The annual gas consumption is 2.6 Tcf; 1.75 Tcf is imported. Shale gas in the UK is estimated at 26 Tcf. Therefore, using the 2014 figures as a baseline, fracking would plug the energy gap for 15 years.

- Allocate £3 billion of QE funds to individuals, research establishments, and businesses to produce the best ideas for sustainable, carbon neutral energy production. Some of the funds will be used to develop carbon capture, and apply it to new and existing power stations in the UK. This will include investment in clean coal burning (prevent closure of the deep coal mines) and fracking; hydroelectric, solar, tidal, bio-fuel and geothermal energy production.

HOW THESE PROPOSALS WILL BE PAID FOR

TOTAL COMMITMENTS:- £14,668,901,250

- Scrapping the raising of the inheritance tax threshold from £325,000 (£650,000 for a couple), to £500,000 (£1 million for a couple). Total revenue = £270 million 2017/18; £630 million 2018-2019; £790 million 2019 – 2020; £940 million 2020-2021. (HM Revenue & Customs: Policy paper: Inheritance tax: main resident nil – rate band and the existing nil rate band – Updated 9th December 2015).

NB £1.12 billion from scrapping Barnett Formula per year from 2016-17, and the savings from scrapping raising the inheritance tax threshold from 2017 will be redirected to investment in early years education, from 2017-18. The inheritance tax savings are a different figure in each year.

Cut the overseas aid budget by just over half. £6 billion

Scrapping Barnett formula = £4.5 billion.

- Freeze working age benefits Replace maintenance grants with loans (less money for deficit reduction) £3.108 billion per year.

The £600 million homelessness project will be funded by reducing lifetime allowance for tax free pension savings from £1.25 million to £1 million.

Savings by privatising the BBC, so that the £604 million pledged to TV licences for over 75s would not be needed. Pensioners would still pay nothing, as the all TV will be funded commercially.

Cost of TV licences for over 75s (£591 million in 2012/13, and £604 million in 2013/14) is relatively small. Source: DWP Benefit Expenditure Tables (Budget 2013) In House of Commons Library, Pensioner Benefits, SN 6354. Updated 18th July, 2013.

TOTAL SAVINGS: £14,812,000,000

This leaves a £143,098,750,000 surplus, to allow for margins of error.

FURTHER NOTES ON NI CUTS AND VAT CUT TO 10%

(1)   Table 1.6 shows that a £2 per week/£104 per year increase in the primary threshold would cost £240 million, suggesting the costs of raising the primary threshold to £10,000 and £12,500 may be around £5 billion and around £11 billion respectively.

http://www.hmrc.gov.uk/statistics/expenditures/table1-6.pdf

(Daily Hansard - Written Answers
22 Oct 2013: Column 73W
Written Answers to Questions
Tuesday 22 October 2013)

(2)   A reduction in the rate of VAT to 10% on building repairs would give a base VAT receipt loss of £560m to HM Treasury in 2010. This would boost renovation of existing properties, boost associated trades (decorators, plumbers, furniture, home improvements), reduce tax evasion, and increase housing supply while preserving the Green Belt. (The Opportunities and Costs of Cutting VAT: The effects of selected reductions in the rate of VAT on the labour element of housing repair, maintenance and improvement – [A Report for the Cut the VAT coalition].)

FURTHER SAVINGS IN GOVERNMENT EXPENDITURE

The following savings are difficult to quantify, but the savings will be redirected into a combination of cutting taxes for the low paid and small businesses, and investing in health and social care, and deficit reduction.

SAVINGS REDIRECTED TO DEFICIT REDUCTION

Child benefit payable only to the first two children from 2016 (unless triplets or higher multiple births).

Reduce the size of central government by scrapping Department of Culture; merge other departments, having only 10 Cabinet ranking departments.

Contract out Human resources and IT support across central government.

SAVINGS REDIRECTED TO FRONT LINE HEALTH AND SOCIAL CARE

Contract out Human resources and IT support across local government.

Cap senior council servants and council chief executive pay at £100,000. One chief executive per council.

INFRASTRUCTURE

QE for investment will create less inflationary pressure that QE for consumption, resulting in lower interest rate rises than would otherwise be the case.

Allocate £30 billion of QE to infrastructure: £12 billion to social housing;

£15 billion for One North, to integrate the transport networks five great cities of Sheffield, Newcastle, Leeds, Liverpool and Manchester. This will improve transport links across the United Kingdom.

£3 billion for sustainable energy production to make the UK self sufficient in energy.

A STRATEGY FOR UK STEEL

One North (the project to link the five great northern cities Liverpool, Manchester, Newcastle, Sheffield and Leeds) will involve massive construction of rail and road links. By building a new generation of carrier based combat aircraft in the UK, UK steel must be used. Here are 2 examples whereby the UK government can award the contract to UK steel firms.

Government and firms purchasing steel and other raw materials from within the UK makes sense in terms of our national security (avoiding the reliance on unstable regimes), but also to establish a skills base in the UK to diversify into other areas of manufacturing. It also reduces the economic cost to the balance of payments if the steel were to be imported, and the environmental cost of shipping the steel into the UK.

This alone is not a sufficient argument for buying British.

make the suppliers of steel and other raw materials more competitive, so that contracts for UK projects not through favouritism, but by being the most attractive supplier on offer.

- Cut the business rates for UK steel by 50%.
- There must be immediate relief from carbon taxes and regulations, which put UK steel at a competitive disadvantage. Immediately, the government should implement the energy intensive industries compensation package.
- Part of the QE funds for energy independence and clean technology should be applied to the steel industry.
- Investment is often made in non EU steel plants due as the EU carbon regulations do not apply there. Even the most efficient plants do not receive all the ETS (Emission Trading System) allocations because of the benchmark set for steel, and an arbitrary cap on industry. A cap on the indirect costs associated with electricity generation mean that Steel plants are also paying for 20% of the ETS costs associated with electricity they purchase. Increasing carbon leakage provisions beyond 2020 could increase the cost of producing 1 tonne of steel to £28.47 by 2030, as they may have to purchase ETS beyond free allocations; the free allocations should are based upon a historic baseline of carbon emission, rather than current activity.
- (Making reform of the EU Emissions Trading System work for steel)

- EU carbon emission systems are unfair to the UK, make no compensation for innovation, and ignore the largest emitters, such as China and the USA.
- The UK must take a lead, and introduce a variable tax, which increases tax for use of carbon, and cuts taxes for those firms who cut carbon and use new technology.
- UK should use our influence as a large trading nation to impose anti dumping measures against Chinese. UK should use this as leverage in the investment deals with the Chinese; for example, forego Chinese investment unless they stop dumping cheap steel illegally onto the world market.

GLOBAL FREE TRADE

It is a scandalous waste of peoples' talents that customers overseas demand essential goods and services, while nearly 1 million young people in UK are unemployed.

The EU proclaims the great myth that it is a bastion of Free Trade. The EU trades freely within its borders, but imposes tariffs against imports from outside the EU, which it uses to subsidise its high food prices. "Fortress Europe" denies the UK the cheap food of world markets, and denies developing nations export markets for their goods. In retaliation, other nations impose tariffs against our exports. In short, Fortress Europe extinguishes enterprise and exacerbates poverty, at home and abroad.

History proves the folly of protectionism. The protectionism of the 1930s turned the Depression into a Slump.

While the eurozone is in melt down, the emerging economies forge ahead; some nations are growing by 6% per year, while the eurozone is declining by 1% per year.

Outside the EU, the UK could forge free trade areas with the growth areas of the world, creating huge opportunities for our entrepreneurs to expand and export across the globe, creating sustainable economic growth, and new jobs.

Concerns abound about possible EU trade retaliation against the UK if we became independent. The EU sells far more goods and services to the UK, than we sell to the EU. Economic self interest dictates that the EU would never dare impose tariffs on UK goods once we leave the EU, and would dare not start a trade war with the UK. Until the EU referendum, the UK can establish links with new trading partners.

A Budget for Brexit

Bring forward the EU referendum to October, 2015. A sunset clause should be set on the next transfer of money to EU Budget in November, so that the benefits can accrue to the UK within months, not years.

UK is due to pay a net contribution of £7.4 billion in 2014-15. Average annual net contribution from 2014-15 through to 2017-2018 is £7.9 billion. This figure should be used as the annual "Independence Dividend."

TOTAL SAVINGS:- £9.567 billion

(Annual average net contribution to EU budget 2015/16 – 2020/21 - OBR).

Redirect this money for the following annual ongoing commitments:

Reduce VAT on building repairs from 10% to 5%. £2.14 billion

Expenditure on cancer, dementia drugs, and preventative social care - £3.667 billion

Tax incentives to firms who recruit apprentices (i.e.reverse the apprenticeship levy- £2 billion)

Raise NI primary threshold from £8933.60 to £9807.20 for 2016-17 - £1.76 billion.

Any remaining funds from the Independence Dividend, or extra revenue, will be used to cut the budget deficit.

TOTAL COMMITMENTS:- £9.567 billion.

Correspondence Between Mr Yeomans & FCO Re: Russia and Ukraine

4th May 2014 and 21st July 2014

SECURING FREEDOM IN UKRAINE

By Nick Yeomans

4th May, 2014

By his own admission, Putin's goal is to reclaim all the satellite states that once constituted the Soviet Union.

History tells us that when the UK resolve weakens, aggressors are strengthened.

Crimea is now under Russian yoke. With 30,000 – 40,000 Russian troops are on the Eastern border of Ukraine, that oppressed nation is set to follow suit. Russians have located 2.5 million Kalashnikov rifles.

Locating 100 soldiers in our NATO allies in the Baltics is a brave move. But far bolder measures are needed. The Baltics are safe, as they are NATO members. Ukraine and Crimea are not NATO members.

Ukraine must be free to determine her destiny, and whether she wishes to join the EU. However, Ukraine can be free from Russian yoke and the EU joining NATO. The UK must extend NATO across the whole of Central and Eastern Europe. This would deter Putin, as an attack on a NATO member would require a full retaliatory response from NATO allies. Nations left outside the security of the NATO umbrella are vulnerable to Russian invasion.

An arms embargo against Russia, enforced by as many free nations as possible.

Help the Ukrainians to defend themselves by supplying arms.

Deploy submarine nuclear deterrent within striking distance of Russia, reinforced by a submarine missile defence system. UK and NATO allies to deploy aircraft, artillery based on aircraft carriers within striking distance of Russia to enforce a no fly zone. These measures will act as a signal to Russia.

If UN cannot agree this, then an alliance of free nations must send election/referendum monitors to Ukraine and Crimea.

Accelerate fracking by granting more permits, to reduce UK dependence upon Russia, and to enable the UK to take action to defence Ukraine and Crimea.

STRENGTHENING UK DEFENCES – PROPOSALS FOR SECURITY

Overseas aid budget is £10,765 million (2013/14). The aid budget should be cut in half. This will not affect front line aid, and charities would be encouraged to fund more aid, without the bureaucracy. ½ of aid budget = £5,382,500,000.

(Department for International Development Annual Report and Resource Accounts 2010-11 and Business Plan 2011-15: Government Response to the Committee's Fourteenth Report of Session 2010-12 - International Development Committee).

£4.260 billion of the overseas aid budget should be redirected to defence, especially aircraft carrier presence and enhanced nuclear offensive and defensive systems, which provide deterrence against aggression.

A like for like replacement is essential. Land based and airborne deterrents are vulnerable to attack. The submarine based cruise missiles would be dearer than the 5.6% of the budget that Trident costs to run over its lifetime, with insufficient range.

4 submarines are required; 3 on constant alert, able to launch a strike against a target anywhere in the world, with 1 submarine as a back-up. (Economist, 23rd June, 2012).

Cost of replacing trident without delay is £1.2 billion (Economist, 19-10-10)

Use existing satellites to perform maritime reconnaissance.

Allocate £860 million per year to reverse the cuts in troops – to complement the reserve training programme. (RUSI Spending Review – 2010)

HMS Queen Elizabeth and HMS Prince of Wales are due enter service in 2017 and 2020 respectively. Bring forward the schedule for operations by 1 year: date for crew moving aboard from May 2016 to May 2015, beginning sea trials in October, 2015, and handing over to Royal Navy in early 2016, with JSF operations starting in 2017. This is vital to ensure a military operation can be launched anywhere in the world. This can be achieved through the increase in manpower.

Hargreaves, Richard (December 2013). "Asset management". *Navy News*. p. 8.

House of Commons Hansard Debates for 10 May 2012, UK Parliament, 10 May 2012

The UK needs 2 fully operational aircraft carriers now to ensure our security on the high seas. HMS Queen Elizabeth and HMS Prince of Wales are due enter service in 2017 and 2020 respectively. Bring forward the introduction of HMS Queen Elizabeth to early 2016. In May 2015, rent Nimitz aircraft carrier and 82 aircraft (including the 41 aircraft for HMS Queen Elizabeth) from USA pending introduction of JSF in 2018, and HMS Prince of Wales in 2020. This will ensure a full complement of carrier aircraft from 2015, and 2 carrier capability from 2016. This is vital to ensure a military operation can be launched anywhere in the world. This will be facilitated through the increase in manpower.

Annual rent of £200 million, £1 billion over the 5 years until HMS Prince of Wales is ready.

Merge the forces into a Marine Corps, to integrate command, and increase efficiency.

Missile defence system. The threat of massive retaliation is not a little deterrent to Iran or North Korea, who would be prepared to sacrifice millions of their people in a war. However, these countries can only build 5-10 missiles which are unlikely to penetrate a shield with a 90% intercept success rate, this acts as a deterrent, and provides the UK with a formidable first strike capability. Ship and missile system. Cost £2billion. (http://fantasyfleet.blogspot.co.uk/2010/09/anti-ballistic-missile-system-for-uk.html)

RESPONSE FROM FCO 21 July 2014

Dear Mr Yeomans,

Thank you for your email of 5 May to the Foreign Secretary about Ukraine. We are grateful for your observations on a possible solution to the crisis. I have been asked to reply, and apologise that the unprecedented volume of work on Ukraine since the crisis began has meant that we have not been able to respond to you as quickly as we would have liked. You may also like to direct some of your points to the MOD and Department for International Development.

Events in Ukraine have moved on since you wrote and it may be most helpful to set out our approach to the situation in Ukraine and our continuing efforts to help resolve it.

We believe that the situation in Ukraine represents, as the Foreign Secretary has said, the biggest crisis that Europe has faced this century.

We have been appalled by Russia's actions in Ukraine and condemn its illegal violation of the sovereignty and territorial integrity of Ukraine. We do not recognise the 16 March referendum in Crimea or its outcome as legal, legitimate or meaningful. We will not recognise attempts to undermine Ukraine or divide its territory, including in Crimea. Our shared history clearly illustrates that turning a blind eye when nations are trampled over can have far-reaching and sometimes catastrophic consequences.

The UK's objectives remain to support the independence and sovereignty of Ukraine, to avoid any further military escalation of the crisis, and to uphold international law.

The Prime Minister met President Putin on 6 June and reiterated that there is an opportunity for a successful, peaceful and stable Ukraine, but that the current situation needs to change. The Prime Minister said that Russia must properly recognise and work with President Poroshenko and there must be action to stop arms and people crossing the border.

G7 leaders issued a joint statement on 4 June condemning the Russian Federation's continuing violation of the sovereignty and territorial integrity of Ukraine and stating that Russia's illegal annexation of Crimea, and its actions to de-stabilise eastern Ukraine are unacceptable, violate international law, and must stop. The recent European Council welcomed President Poroshenko's peace plan and his willingness to extend the ceasefire to 30 June. The Council issued four specific steps that needed to be taken by 30 June:

- An agreement on a verification mechanism, monitored by the OSCE, for the cease-fire and for the effective control of the border;
- A return to the Ukrainian authorities of the three seized border checkpoints;
- The release of all hostages;
- Launch of substantial negotiations on the implementation of President Poroshenko's peace plan.

We regret that these four conditions were not met by 30 June. The onus is now on Russia to respond positively by pressing the separatists to respect a genuine ceasefire, release the remaining hostages and return occupied border posts to the Ukrainian authorities. President Putin's decision to ask the Federation Council to revoke its decision of 1 March which allows Russia to deploy troops into Ukraine is an important gesture. However, the European Council agreed that, if we do not see further concrete progress very soon, we remain willing to impose further sanctions on Russia.

We welcome the bold steps President Poroshenko has taken since his election under difficult circumstances on 25 May, including his peace plan. The strong turnout resulting in his victory underlined the determination of Ukraine's citizens to decide the future of their country. President Poroshenko's commitment to work with Ukrainian people in the East, normalising relations with Russia and setting a European future for Ukraine are welcome first steps. There is a pressing need for constitutional reform, improvements to Ukraine's political culture, an end to pervasive corruption and the construction of a stable political structure. We welcome the steps the Ukrainian authorities have been taking to implement the Geneva agreement to help de-escalation, including tabling an amnesty law, commitment to constitutional reforms aimed at decentralisation, guarantees on protection and special status for the Russian language and condemnation of incidents of anti-Semitism, xenophobia and intolerance. We will work with the Ukrainian government to support it to pursue constitutional and economic reform to strengthen Ukraine's democracy, prosperity, and the rights and aspirations of all people in all regions of Ukraine.

Since you wrote there has of course been the terrible incident of the apparent shooting down of flight MH17. The growing weight of evidence strongly suggests that the plane was shot down by a missile fired by pro-Russian separatists. There must be a swift, transparent and credible investigation into the incident and we support a Ukrainian-led investigation with specialist experts from other countries, in line with international aviation standards. This tragedy has brought into sharp focus the consequences of destabilisation in Eastern Ukraine. The G7 and EU had repeatedly called on President Putin to cease support for the separatists (including provision of weaponry) and to work with the rest of the world to find a peaceful resolution. Russia's failure to do so has contributed to this appalling tragedy.

The UK, together with the EU and the international community, will continue to use every diplomatic channel to help resolve the issues between Russia and Ukraine, and we will continue to call on the Russian leadership to take the steps required. Our national interest is for a territorially stable, democratic and prosperous Ukraine which can meet the legitimate needs of its people.

You may be interested to keep abreast of FCO updates on the situation in Ukraine at the following link: https://www.gov.uk/government/news/ukraine-latest-updates.

Yours sincerely,
Sandra Higginbottom
Assistant Desk Officer, Ukraine

Correspondence Between Mr Nick Yeomans and FCO Re: Russia and Ukraine 3rd August 2014 and 25th November, 2014

Email to Foreign Secretary 3rd August 2014

Dear Foreign Secretary,

I am a Conservative supporter, gravely concerned about the aggression of Russia.

Please find attached the response from Foreign Office (dated 21st July 2014), to my original e-mail and proposals, sent on 5th May, 2014 - please find this attached.

Please find attached an updated plan to secure freedom in Ukraine and Crimea, based upon measures that are fully costed, which would restore freedom to Ukraine and Crimea, and deter Russian aggression without a shot being fired.

I strongly believe that these proposals should be adopted at the NATO Summit on 4th to 5th September.

Yours sincerely,

Nick Yeomans

SECURING FREEDOM IN UKRAINE

By Nick Yeomans

Updated 3rd August, 2014

BACKGROUND TO SITUATION IN UKRAINE

By his own admission, Putin's goal is to reclaim all the satellite states that once constituted the Soviet Union.

History tells us that when the UK resolve weakens, aggressors are strengthened.

Crimea is now under Russian yoke. With 30,000 – 40,000 Russian troops are on the Eastern border of Ukraine, that oppressed nation is set to follow suit. Russians have located 2.5 million Kalashnikov rifles.

The despicable shooting down of MH 17 (most likely by pro – Russian separatists) proves that the aggressors are still obtaining arms.

Locating 100 soldiers in our NATO allies in the Baltics is a brave move. But far bolder measures are needed. The Baltics are safe, as they are NATO members. Ukraine and Crimea are not NATO members.

It is only by strengthening our defences that the recommendations of the European Council, (announced on 30th June, 2014) are likely to become realised.

These recommendations are:-

- An agreement on a verification mechanism, monitored by the OSCE, for the cease-fire and for the effective control of the border;
- A return to the Ukrainian authorities of the three seized border checkpoints;
- The release of all hostages;
- Launch of substantial negotiations on the implementation of President Poroshenko's peace plan.

THE AIMS OF NATO TO SECURE FREEDOM IN UKRAINE and CRIMEA

The overriding aim must be a sovereign and free Ukraine and Crimea. Ukraine and Crimea must be free to determine their destinies, and whether they wish to join the EU. However, Ukraine and Crimea can be free from the Russian yoke by joining NATO. The UK must extend NATO across the whole of Central and Eastern Europe, to include Crimea and Ukraine. This would deter Russian aggression, as an attack on a NATO member would require a full retaliatory response from NATO allies. Nations left outside the security of the NATO umbrella are vulnerable to Russian aggression.

Continue with the targeted sanctions against Russian leaders, and their economic interests. In addition, ban visits from Russian leaders, and investment from Russian companies.

An arms embargo against Russia, enforced by as many free nations as possible, to prevent further atrocities such as the shooting down of MH 17.

Help the Ukrainians to defend themselves by supplying arms.

UK to deploy (in conjunction with NATO allies) a submarine nuclear deterrent within striking distance of Russia, reinforced by a submarine missile defence system. Establish a NATO missile defence in Poland and Czechoslovakia.

UK to deploy (in conjunction with NATO allies) a fully operational aircraft carrier within striking distance of Russia to enforce a no fly zone. These measures will act as a deterrent to Russia, without the allies firing a shot.

Seek UN mandate to hold a legitimate referendum in Crimea, and send in election/referendum monitors to Ukraine and Crimea. If UN cannot agree upon this, then an alliance of free nations must act to ensure free and fair elections/referenda in Crimea and the Ukraine.

Accelerate fracking by granting more permits, to reduce UK dependence upon Russia, and to enable the UK to take action to defence Ukraine and Crimea.

STRENGTHENING UK DEFENCES – ENSURING SECURITY AND FREEDOM

The overseas aid budget is £10,765 million (2013/14).

The aid budget should be cut by just over half. This will not affect front line aid, and charities would be encouraged to fund more aid, without the bureaucracy. The proposed cut to aid budget should be £5,593,000,000.

£4,471.4 billion of the overseas aid budget should be redirected to defence (the rest is allocated to tax cuts) especially aircraft carrier presence and enhanced nuclear offensive and defensive systems, which provide deterrence against aggression.

THE NEED FOR A FULLY INDEPENDENT NUCLEAR DETERRENT

A like for like Trident replacement is essential. Land based and airborne deterrents are vulnerable to attack. The submarine based cruise missiles would be dearer than the 5.6% of the budget that Trident costs to run over its lifetime, with insufficient range.

4 submarines are required to enable sufficient back up for 1 submarine to be on constant alert, able to launch a strike against a target anywhere in the world.

Renewal presents a historic opportunity for the UK to have a truly independent deterrent since 1962. The UK has access to 58 Trident missiles supplied by the US. The UK does not have an independent nuclear deterrent, and those 58 missiles are not allocated exclusively to the UK. The UK cannot guarantee that the USA will always lease missiles to the UK; the UK must build its own fully independent, nuclear deterrent. The skills of the British aerospace industry should be utilised to build our own missiles now. Each submarine will have 8 missiles, each missile will have 5 warheads. There will be a total of 32 missiles, a total of 160 operational warheads; part of a total stockpile of 225. (Trident nuclear Weapons Submarines in the United Kingdom and the USA – BASIC (British American Security Information Council

November, 2013). This must be retained. Even the fuel supply for Trident missiles is in jeopardy; since the cancellation of the US space shuttle in 2011, the cost of fuel for Trident has increased by around 80 per cent, rising from £6.3 million to £11.2 million from 2011 to 2012. (Daily Telegraph 15 Jul 14). UK must also manufacture its own fuel for the missiles, and service and maintain the missiles within UK territory.

Our deterrent must be strengthened with a submarine based missile defence system, with a constant at sea presence, to destroy enemy missiles. Missile defence also enhances first strike capability, as it creates a shield impenetrable to retaliatory missiles.

The decision to scrap missile defence in Eastern Europe in 2009 (10 missiles in Poland, and a radar facility in Czechoslovakia) as part of detente with Russia, has only served to fortify Putin to annexe Crimea, and invade Ukraine. The UK must contribute its own expertise and material to NATO missile defence system in Central Europe – although originally designed to intercept missiles from Iran, it will also intercept Russian missiles. NATO missile defence will protect against attacks from Russia and Iran.

Use existing satellites to perform maritime reconnaissance.

Merge the forces into a Marine Corps, to integrate command, and increase efficiency.

Reverse the cuts in troops – to complement the reserve training programme.

THE NEED FOR 2 AIRCRAFT CARRIERS

HMS Queen Elizabeth and HMS Prince of Wales are due to enter service in 2017 and 2020 respectively.

The UK needs 2 fully operational aircraft carriers now to ensure our security on the high seas. Bring forward the introduction of HMS Queen Elizabeth from 2017 to now. UK should rent a USS Nimitz aircraft carrier and 82 aircraft (half of those aircraft [41], would be allocated to the HMS Queen Elizabeth) from USA. This is pending introduction of UK built fighters, and HMS Prince of Wales in 2020. This will ensure a full complement of 2 carrier aircraft with immediate effect. 1 carrier should be sent to deter Russian aggression, and another carrier can launch air strikes to deter the Sunni insurgency in Iraq.

This is vital to ensure a military operation can be launched anywhere in the world; if the UK had 2 fully operational aircraft carriers now, this could have deterred Putin's aggression in Ukraine, and (through the threat of airstrikes) the Sunni insurgency in Iraq. This increase in aircraft and aircraft carriers will be facilitated through higher manpower by increasing troop numbers.

The UK must not depend upon the USA for our own defences. The JSF has experienced severe technological problems, which prevented it from making the Farnborough air show in July, 2014. The UK must cancel the JSF contract, and award a contract to build 72 aircraft capable of Mach 2, (with S/VTOL capability and with all weapons systems enclosed to enhance speed) to UK firms (as opposed to the 48 JSFs the government had ordered from the US). 36 fighters and 4 helicopters would each be allocated to the HMS Queen Elizabeth and MHS Prince of Wales. In 2020, the UK will have an entirely independent complement of aircraft carriers and aircraft.

HOW THESE PROPOSALS WOULD BE FINANCED

Cut the overseas aid budget by just over half. £6 billion.

£4,451,400,000 of the overseas aid budget will be redirected to defence, prioritised as follows:-

£860 million per year to reverse the cuts in troops (RUSI Spending Review – 2010)

Cost of replacing trident without delay is £1.2 billion (Economist, 19-10-10). The cost of a submarine missile defence system is £2 billion. ((http://fantasyfleet.blogspot.co.uk/2010/09/anti-ballistic-missile-system-for-uk.html)

Annual cost of renting USS Nimitz aircraft carrier = £141,400,000 (Wiki answers).

Cost of each Trident missile is £17 million. (Trident missile fact file – 23rd Sept 2009). To build 32 Trident type missiles would cost = £544 million. £290 million of this will be saved as the UK will not participate in the upgrading of US missiles in the 2020s. (Trident nuclear Weapons Submarines in the United Kingdom and the USA – BASIC (British American Security Information Council November, 2013). £250 million net cost of building 32 Trident type missiles.

Eastern Europe & Central Asia Directorate, King Charles Street, London, SW1A 2AH

25th November 2014
Nick Yeomans
Prospective Independent Parliamentary Candidate
Brighton Pavilion,
Flat 1,
St. Anne's Court,
Howard Place,
Brighton BN1 3UP
Dear Mr Yeomans,

Thank you for your email of 22 October to the Foreign Secretary about Russia/Ukraine and ISIL. Your letter has been passed to the Eastern Europe and Central Asia Directorate for reply.

The British Government welcomes the ceasefire agreement reached between Ukraine and Russia in Minsk on 5 September. We now need to see this being implemented fully. We are concerned by continued breaches of the ceasefire and reiterate the importance of all parties implementing a ceasefire without delay and further loss of life. We urge all parties to act to de-escalate tensions and engage constructively with the Government of Ukraine.

The international community has a clear role to play by exerting the greatest possible pressure upon Russia to withdraw its troops from Ukrainian soil, cease its support for the separatists, and enable the restoration of security along the Ukraine-Russia border under effective and credible international monitoring.

The Foreign Secretary has been clear that there cannot be a military solution to the conflict in Ukraine. There has to be a political solution. NATO acts by consensus, including under Article 5, it cannot become involved in any conflict unless all Allies agree to do so.

You raise the expansion of NATO. Under NATO's Open Door policy, membership is open to all those who seek it but all applicants must fulfil the criteria. NATO is not seeking to expand.

The NATO Russia Founding Act (NRFA), amongst other things, commits NATO not to permanently station substantial combat forces in former Warsaw Pact countries. We continue to support the NRFA and press Russia to return to the international norms of behaviour on which it is based.

The sanctions imposed by the EU in September will further increase the economic cost to Russia for its behaviour. The decision to impose additional sanctions followed months of destabilisation of Ukraine by Russia, and months of political and diplomatic efforts to restore peace and stability.

The 26 October parliamentary elections were a clear demonstration of Ukraine's commitment to democracy. The UK helped to make these elections free, fair and transparent by providing 71 independent observers to the OSCE's election observation mission.

The Ukrainian electorate have made their choice. Hard work now lies ahead. The election of a new parliament offers a new opportunity to press ahead with the political, economic and governance reforms that are vital to delivering the stability, democracy and prosperity that the people of Ukraine deserve. The UK, together with our international partners, will continue to support the Government of Ukraine in delivering this reform.

You express concerns about the self-styled Islamic State of Iraq and the Levant (ISIL). The UK Government is horrified by the barbaric acts of ISIL against the people of Iraq, including the Sunnis, Shias, Kurds, Christians, Yazidis and other minorities, and the humanitarian crisis they have brought about. As the Prime Minister said recently in Parliament, if they are left unchecked we risk a terrorist caliphate on the shores of the Mediterranean, and bordering a NATO member state, with a declared and proven intention to attack our country and our people.

We have to confront and defeat ISIL through a comprehensive and sustained counter-terrorism strategy. This starts at home, where we are focussing our efforts on preventing attacks and pursuing those who are planning them. It is now a criminal offence to be a member of ISIL in the UK. We are also working to combat radicalisation of Muslims and monitoring individuals who pose a significant risk. We are introducing new powers to seize passports to stop suspects travelling, remove British nationality from dual nationals of concern and temporarily prevent some British nationals from re-entering to the UK.

We are working closely with our international allies to engage the widest possible coalition of countries in the region, including Iraq's regional neighbours, to deal with the threat from ISIL. On 26 September, in response to an appeal from the Iraqi government, Parliament voted to join these allies in air strikes against ISIL in Iraq. We are supporting the Kurdish regional government, who are holding the front line against ISIL, through the supply of weapons and other military equipment.

The UK has also been at the forefront of efforts to rally wider international support against ISIL, including at the NATO conference in September and through the United Nations (UN). Under our Presidency in August, the UN Security Council (UNSC) adopted Resolution 2170 to restrict ISIL's financial, trade and recruitment networks, as well as sanctioning individuals. Resolution 2178 built on this by strengthening the international response to threats posed by foreign terrorist fighters. We also supported the UN Human Rights Council Resolution mandating the UN to investigate urgently and report on ISIL abuses.

The UK continues to support humanitarian efforts by providing £23 million to help the 1.8 million displaced Iraqis, many of whom have been victims of ISIL's abuses and persecution. This is providing clean water, sanitation, essential medicines, and funding for NGOs and charities to directly support these displaced individuals, some of which is specifically targeted to protect women and children.

Recent events in and around the town of Kobane in northern Syria are a cause for particular concern. The UK is not involved in military action in Syria, but other members of the US-led coalition have undertaken airstrikes to protect Kobane. We support their efforts, and UK officials have been in touch with those representing Kurdish groups inside Kobane to understand the situation on the ground. In response to the numbers of displaced Syrians from Kobane our humanitarian support has been concentrated on the people entering Suruc on the Turkish border. DFID has to date provided 8,300 mattresses and are also considering proposals to fund 500 tents and winter kits, including warm blankets.

Foreign & Commonwealth Office

Printed in the United States
By Bookmasters